THE OXFORD ART BOOK

HERBERT PRESS
Bloomsbury Publishing Plc
50 Bedford Square, London, WC1B 3DP, UK
29 Earlsfort Terrace, Dublin 2, Ireland

BLOOMSBURY, HERBERT PRESS and the Herbert Press logo are trademarks of Bloomsbury Publishing Plc

First published in England in 2018 by UIT Cambridge Ltd.
This edition published 2024

A CIP catalogue record for this book is available from the British Library
Library of Congress Cataloguing-in-Publication data has been applied for

ISBN: 978-1-90686-084-4 (hardback) ISBN: 978-1-90686-086-8 (ePub) ISBN: 978-1-90686-085-1 (pdf)

3 5 7 9 10 8 6 4 2

Printed and bound in India by Replika Press Pvt. Ltd.

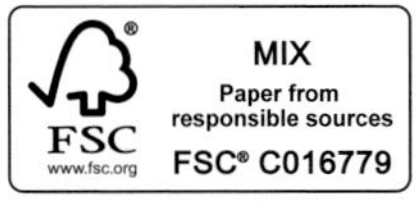

To find out more about our authors and books visit www.bloomsbury.com and sign up for our newsletters

THE OXFORD ART BOOK

The City Through the Eyes of its Artists

EDITED BY

EMMA BENNETT

HERBERT PRESS

LONDON • OXFORD • NEW YORK • NEW DELHI • SYDNEY

Acknowledgements

The Oxford Art Book has been made possible by the enthusiasm of not only the contributing artists, but also the artists of Oxfordshire as a whole. To them I am eternally grateful. You are a talented bunch.

An illustrious panel of local art and city experts helped in the selection of the images for publication and I am indebted to them for their help. They are:

- Tiffany Black (*Artist and Senior Lecturer in Fine Art, Oxford Brookes University*)
- Rosie Jacobs (*Co-Founder of Independent Oxford and Owner of A Rosie Life*)
- Esther Lafferty (*Festival Director of Oxfordshire Artweeks*)
- Andrew McLellan *(Head of Education, Pitt Rivers Museum*)
- Julia Sadler (*Managing Editor, GTI Publishing*)
- Lucy Stopford (*Chair, Oxford Art Society*)

I thank Niall Mansfield, Sheila Stickley and Ada Coghen at UIT/Green Books for their enthusiasm and support for The Art Book Series.

For my Oxfordshire host family – thank you to Julia Sadler and Adrian Sadler, and thank you to Annabelle King, Megan Sadler and Carys Sadler for looking at images.

Thank you to my brother Andrew and Dad, Peter Birch, for singing in the church choir in days gone by, which meant childhood visits to Keble College Chapel, where I fell in love with the city of Oxford. To Betty and Norman Adams, thanks; you inspired creativity from an early age.

To my Mom (Toni), Len and Val, Craig, Molly and William Bennett for boundless enthusiasm and encouragement, I give thanks. For help with all general things book-like (and coffee and cake) thank you to Lynn Fraser, Alison Schuldt, Jen Hurst, Naomi Triggol and all those who helped along the way.

CONTENTS

FOREWORD

I grew up in Oxford, making regular visits to Cambridge to see my father, so I am thrilled that the excellent *Cambridge Art Book* now has its rightful companion, for these are cities with so much in common and – to those with an interest in their beauty and charm – so many finely nuanced differences. In a comparison of the delightful and varied images collected in these two books, I can continue my joyful (and endless) quest to pin down the cool elegance of Cambridge versus the worldly charm of Oxford.

It is being said that we should all turn off our smart phones and wean ourselves from the seductive pinging of incoming messages, but how to break away? This book is a very good place to seek an answer, for *The Oxford Art Book* is all about the value, the pleasure and the fun of just looking. Don't take a picture on your phone at each landmark but, instead, stand still, look around (or up or down or out!) and feast your eyes.

Spend a pure and quiet minute or two noticing and relishing the details of the sunlight on the Radcliffe Camera and Tom Tower from across St Aldates – with buses and bicycles whizzing by. Or take a look at the remote Emperors in front of the Sheldonian Theatre and the blossom-strewn streets of North Oxford. Admire St Barnabas Church dreaming the afternoon away across Port Meadow or Magdalen Bridge seen as you deftly wield the pole from a punt on the Cherwell, and you will have stood for a moment in the shoes of an artist. You will bring a sharpened eye to the wonderful collection of images in this book. Best of all, you will remember these outstandingly lovely places far better than you would if you had taken a snap and dashed on.

For as you will immediately realise when you open this pleasing book, Oxford is one of the world's most wonderful places, right up there with Paris, Venice and Istanbul (as well as Cambridge!) and the eye and the heart can never tire of its beauties.

Emma Bridgewater

Designer and Founder of Emma Bridgewater

INTRODUCTION

Oxford, a city known and loved across the world, is celebrated here by 65 artists who find creativity in its every spire and doorway.

Oxford is a city that inspires: travellers from across the world who marvel at its cobbled streets and architecture; students huddled over great novels in the Bodleian Library; locals who picnic on its river banks and canoe its canals in the summer then hunker down in its cosy pubs in winter. Oxford has a great historical past as well as a modern independent present.

It is all of these things and more that have inspired generations of artists to show Oxford through their eyes. Hidden doorways, bustling streets, punts on the river, the wonder and awe of the Pitt Rivers Museum and the calm of the glasshouses of the Botanical Gardens; it is all here within these pages. Using a huge range of different art techniques, *The Oxford Art Book* bristles with vibrancy, charm and wit.

The map in the book encourages you to walk around the city and see how the artists have interpreted the buildings and the sites that inspired them.

Following the huge success of *The Cambridge Art Book*, it is an honour to bring together another unique collection of artists and images, this time for Oxford, a city close to my heart. To find out more about the artists in the book, the 'Artists' Credits' section will give you some useful links to their websites.

The book represents just some of the talented artists working in Oxfordshire. There are many others and I encourage you to use local art networks, galleries and exhibitions to discover them.

Emma Bennett
Artist and Editor

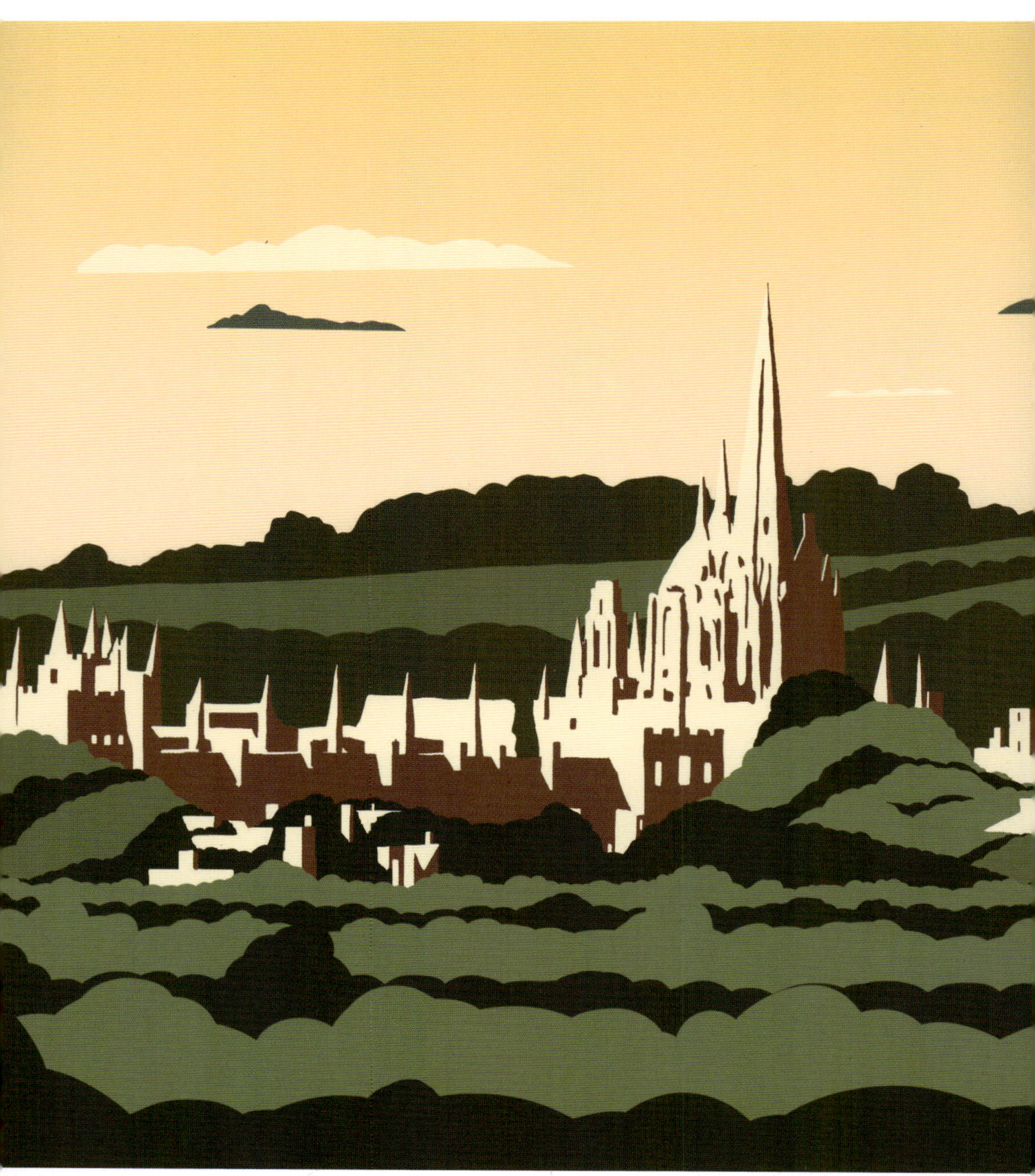

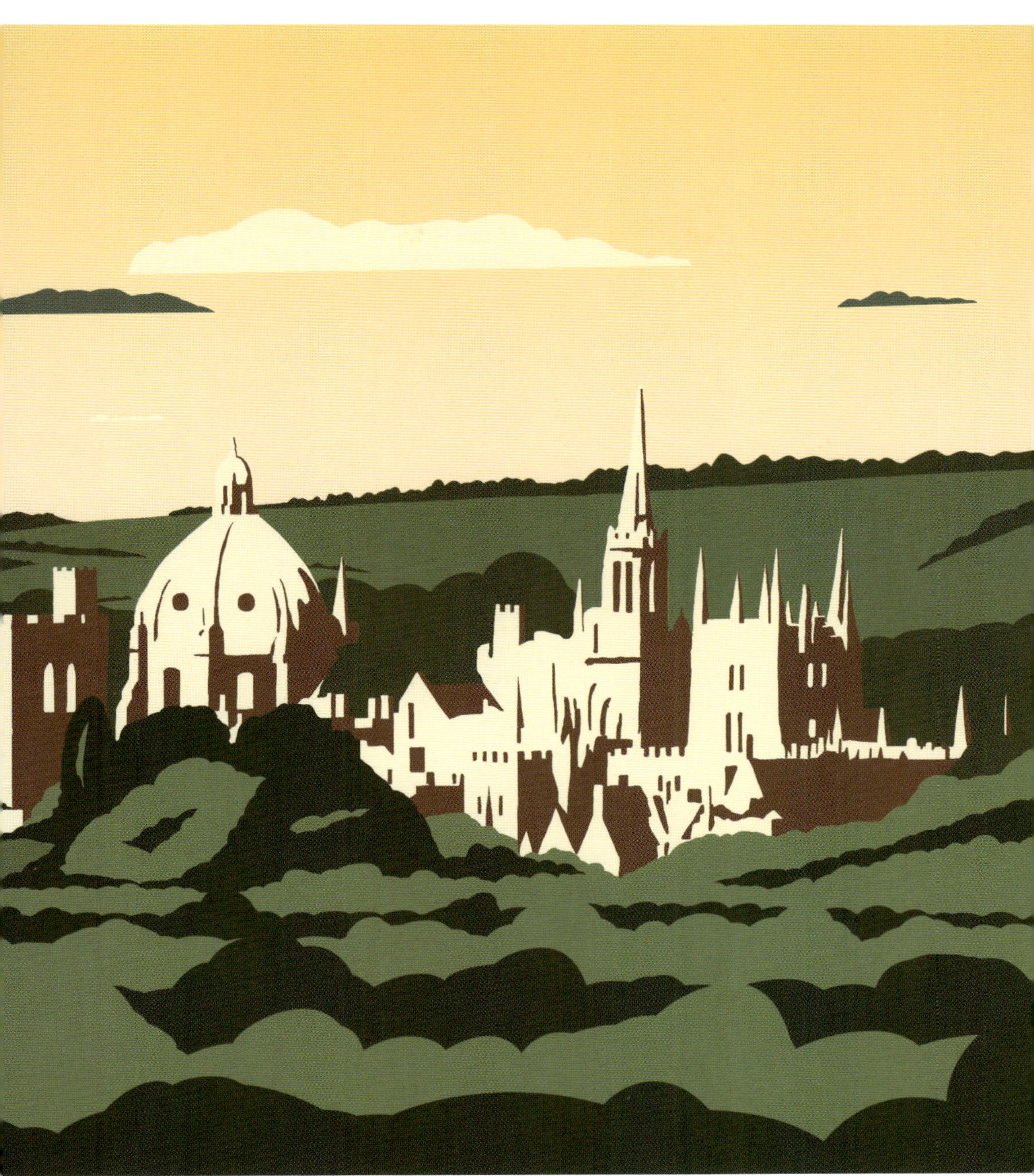

Oxford, Richard O'Neill

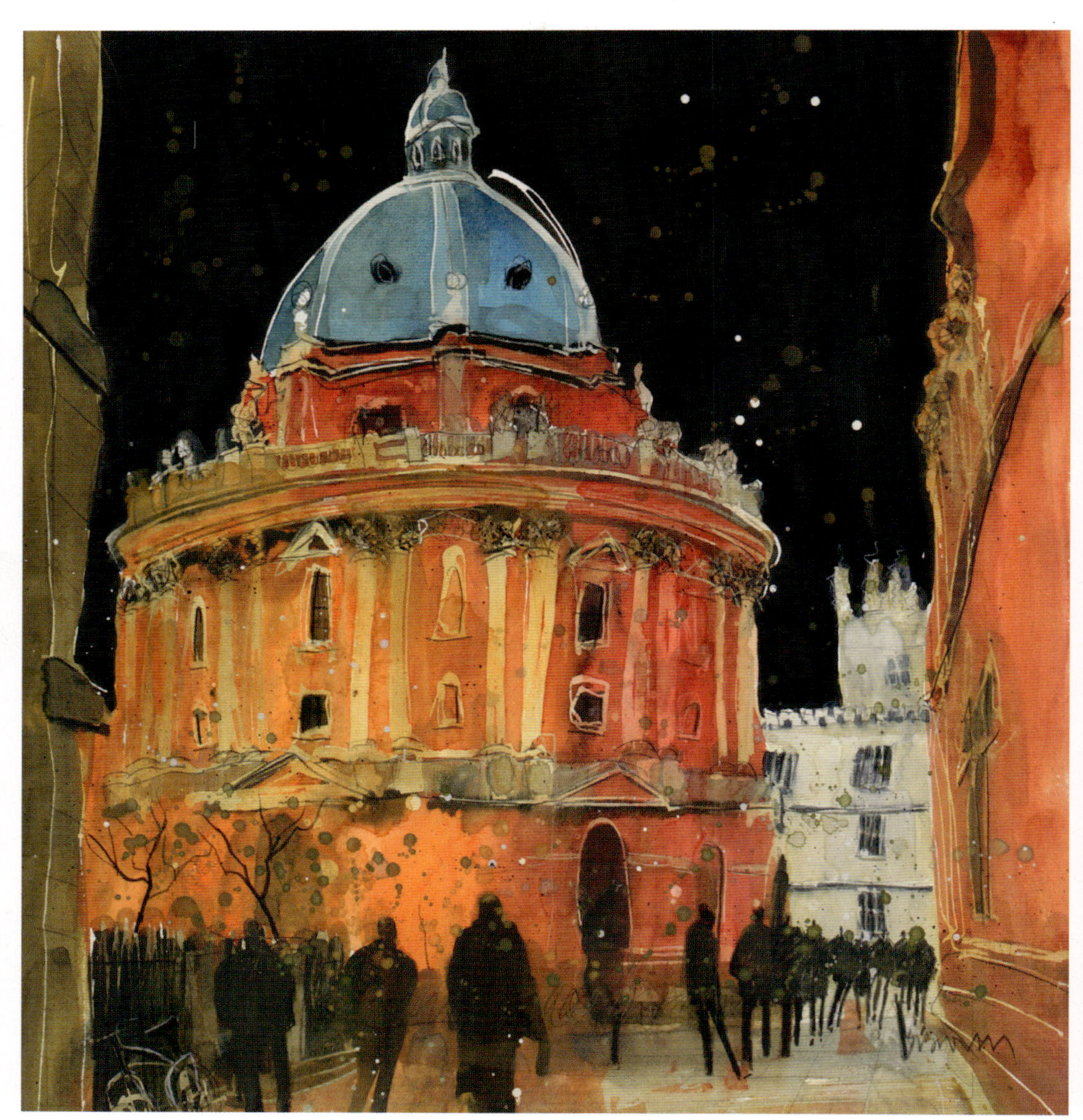

The Radcliffe Camera, Susan Brown

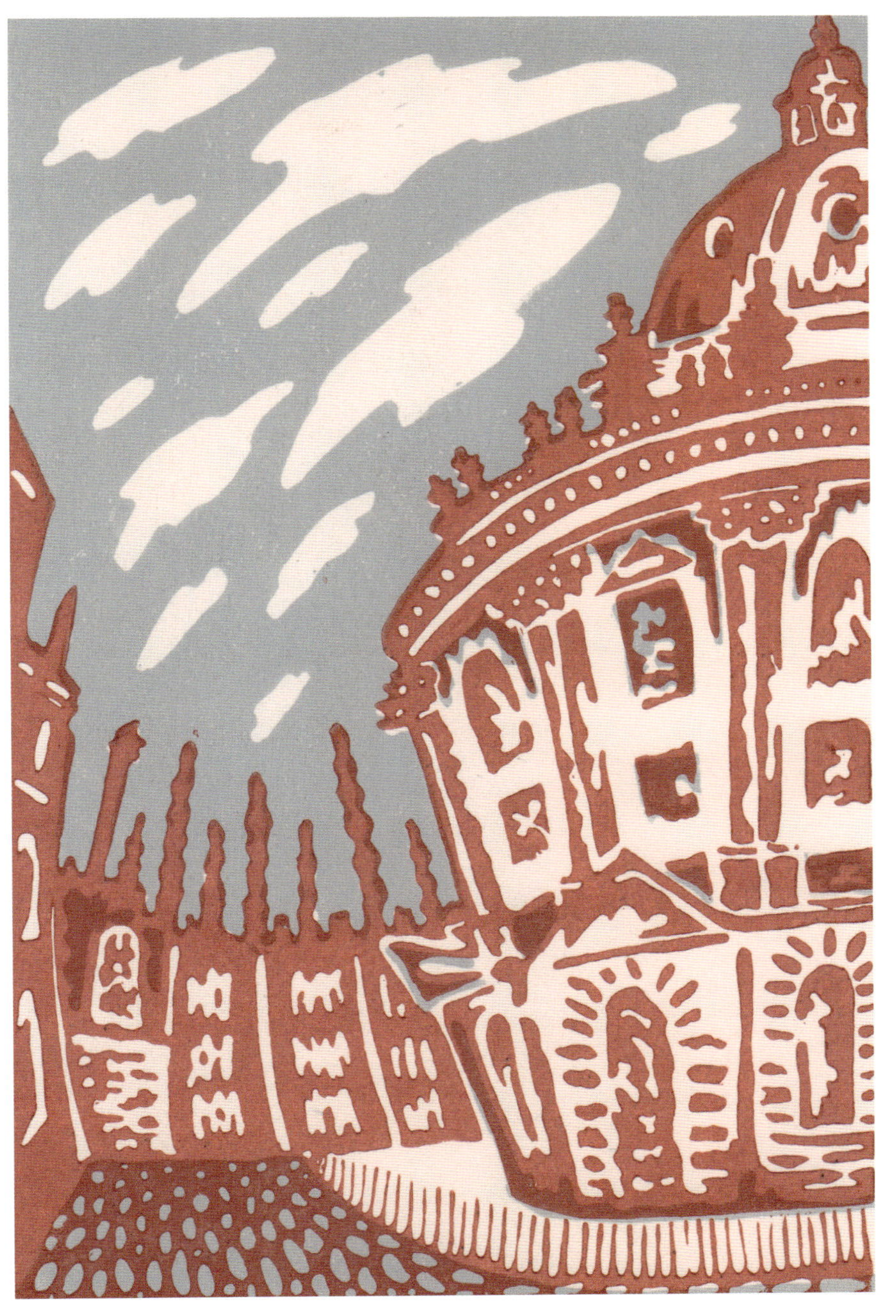

Radcliffe Square, Jan Ritchie

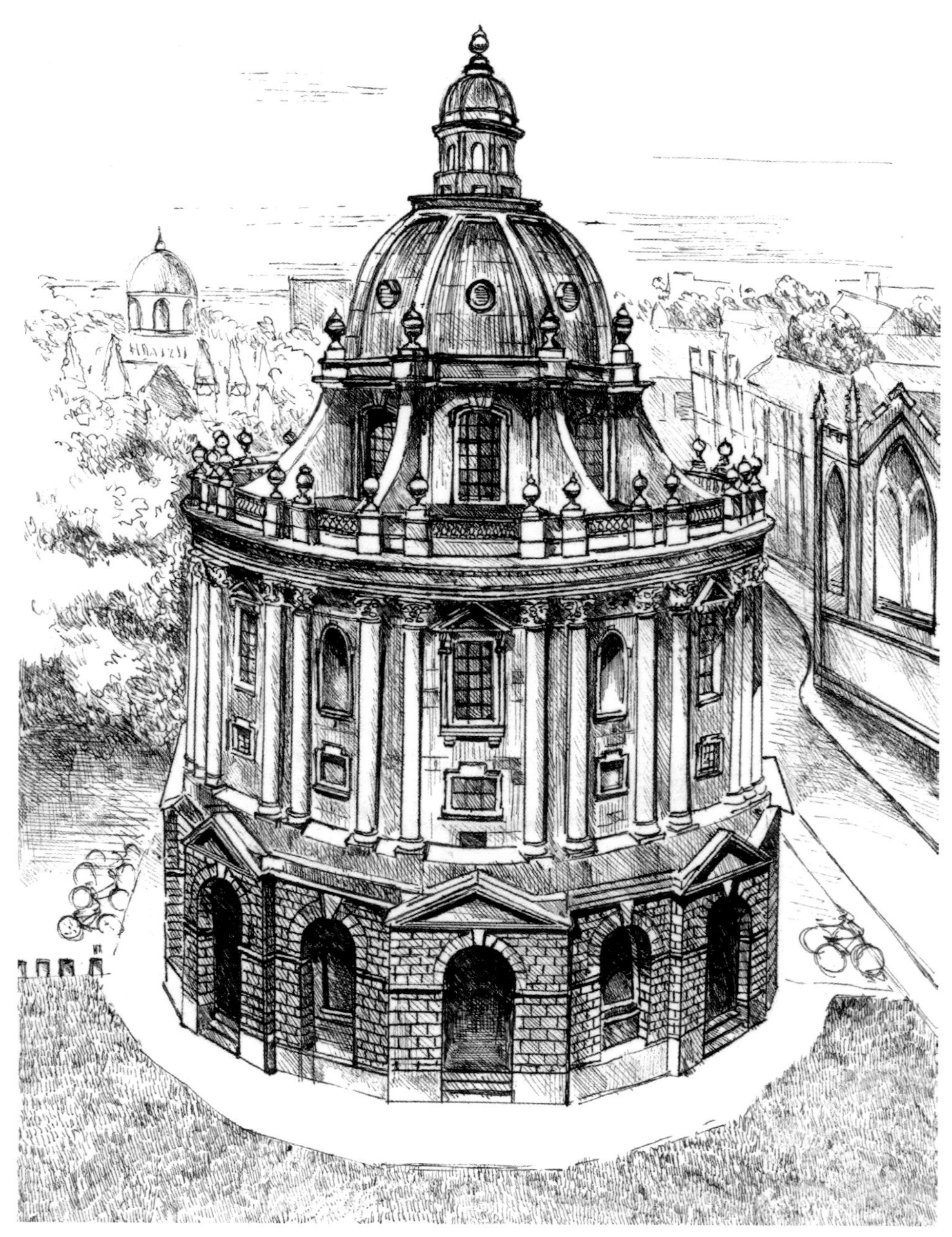

The Radcliffe Camera, Jane Peart

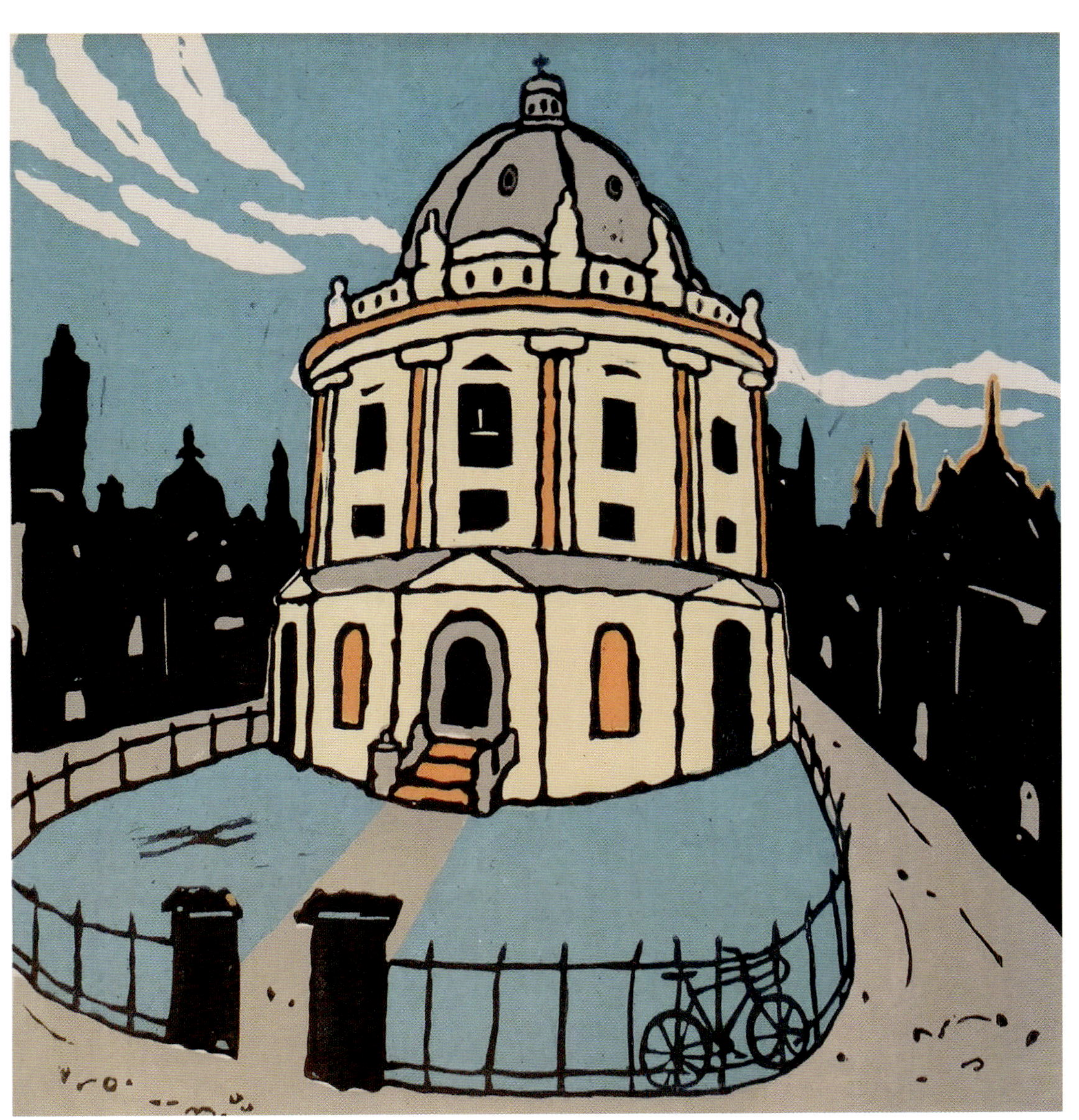

The Radcliffe Camera, Simon East

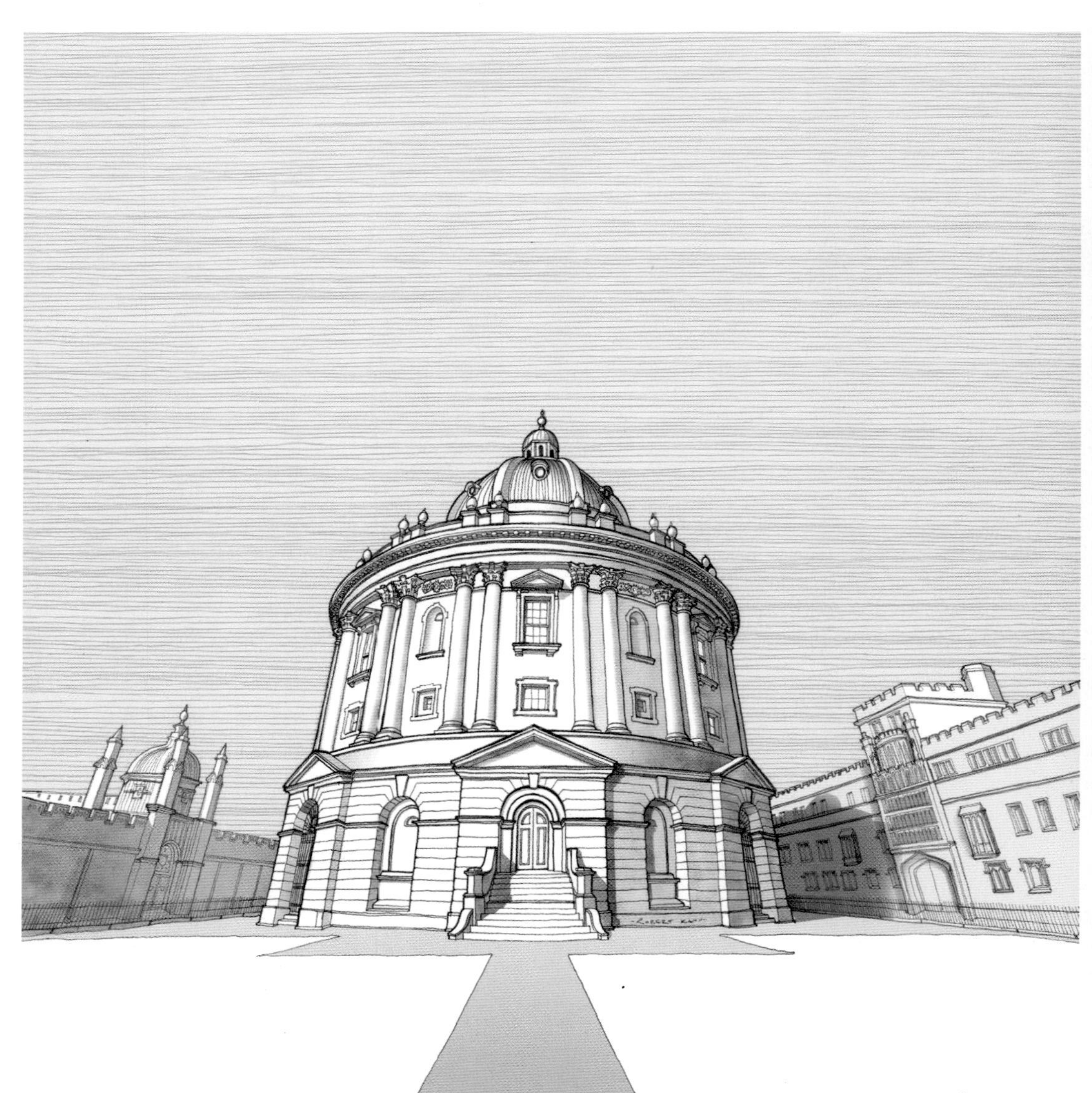

'Golden Skies', Robert Kann

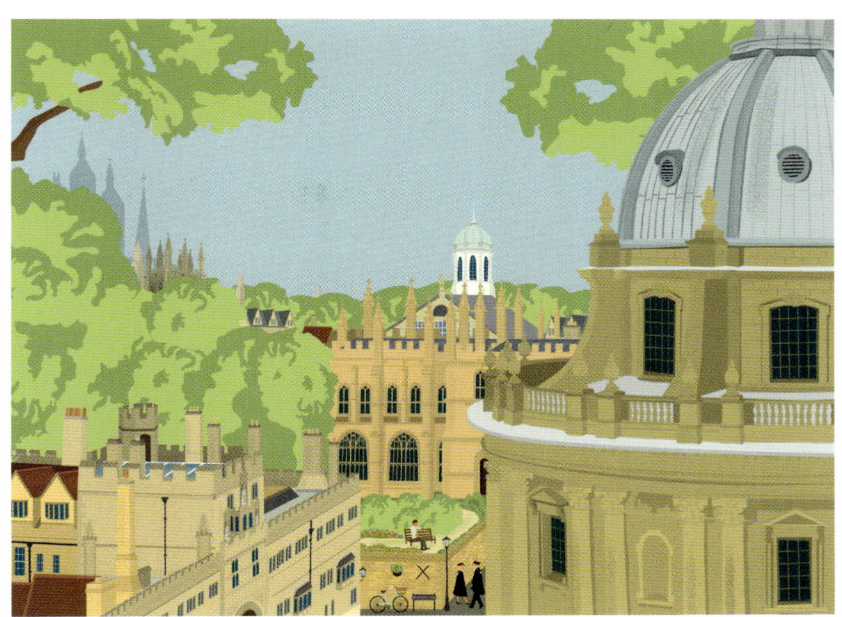

Oxford And Her Dreaming Spires, Clare Phillips

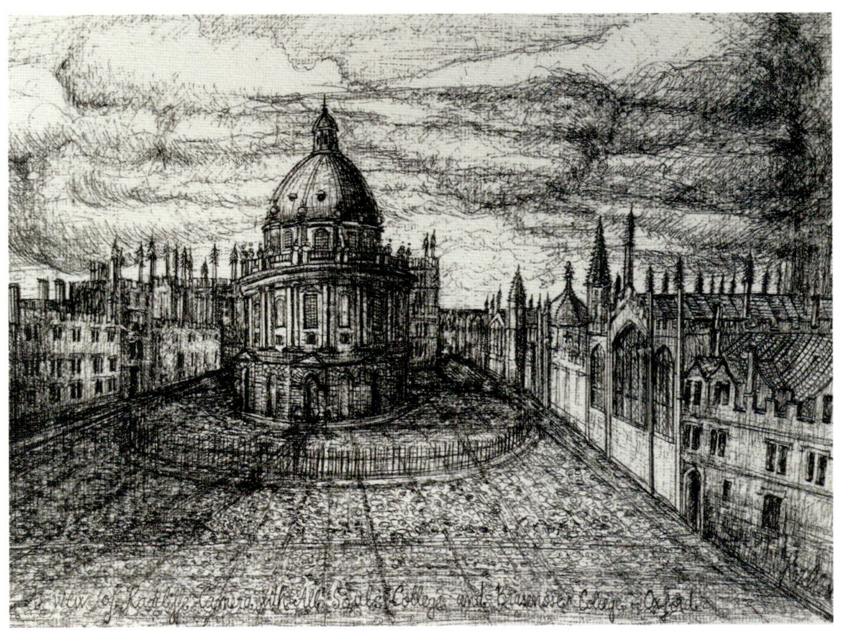

A view of Radcliffe Square, Orsi Kozel

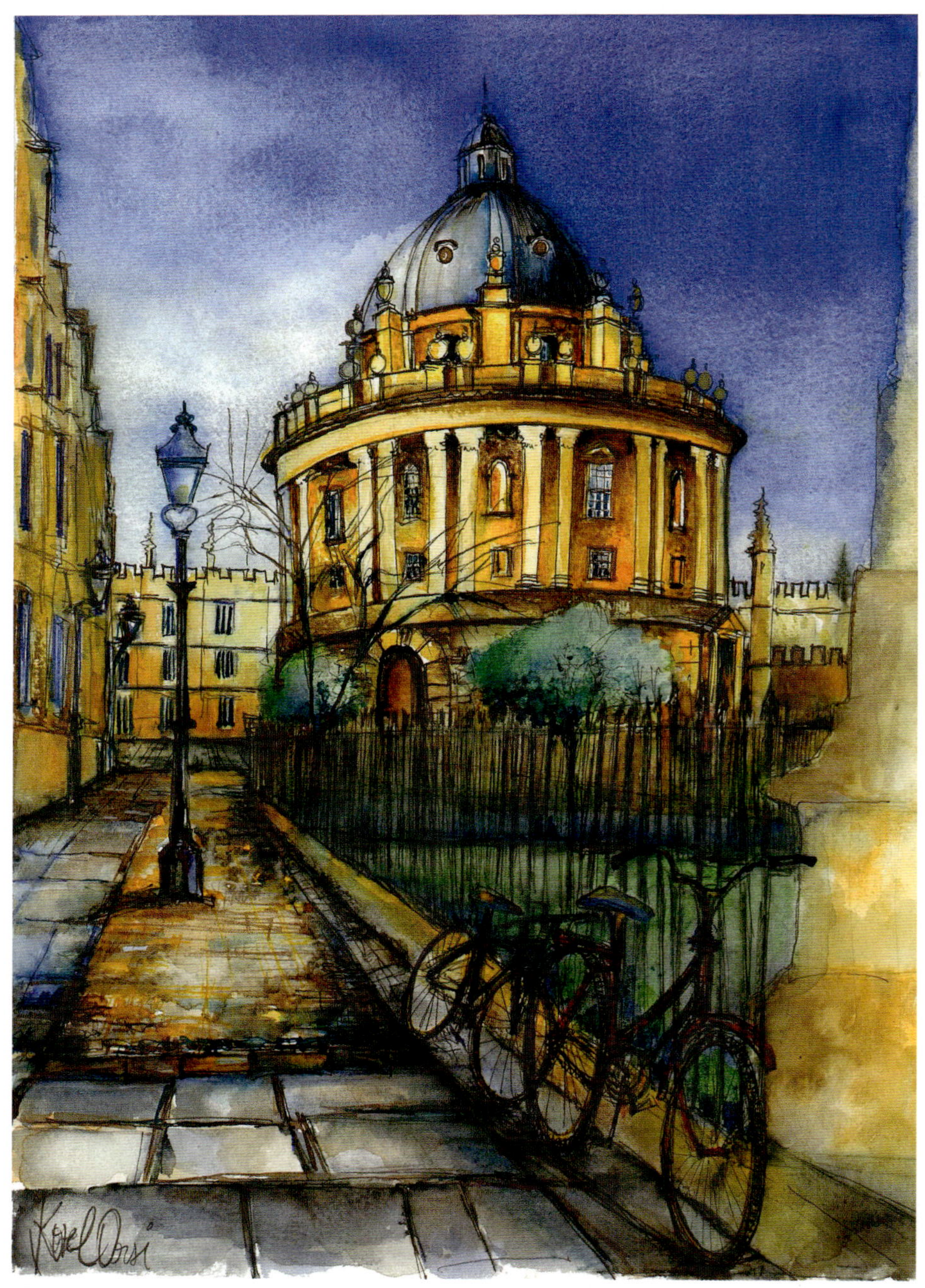

The Radcliffe Camera, Orsi Kozel

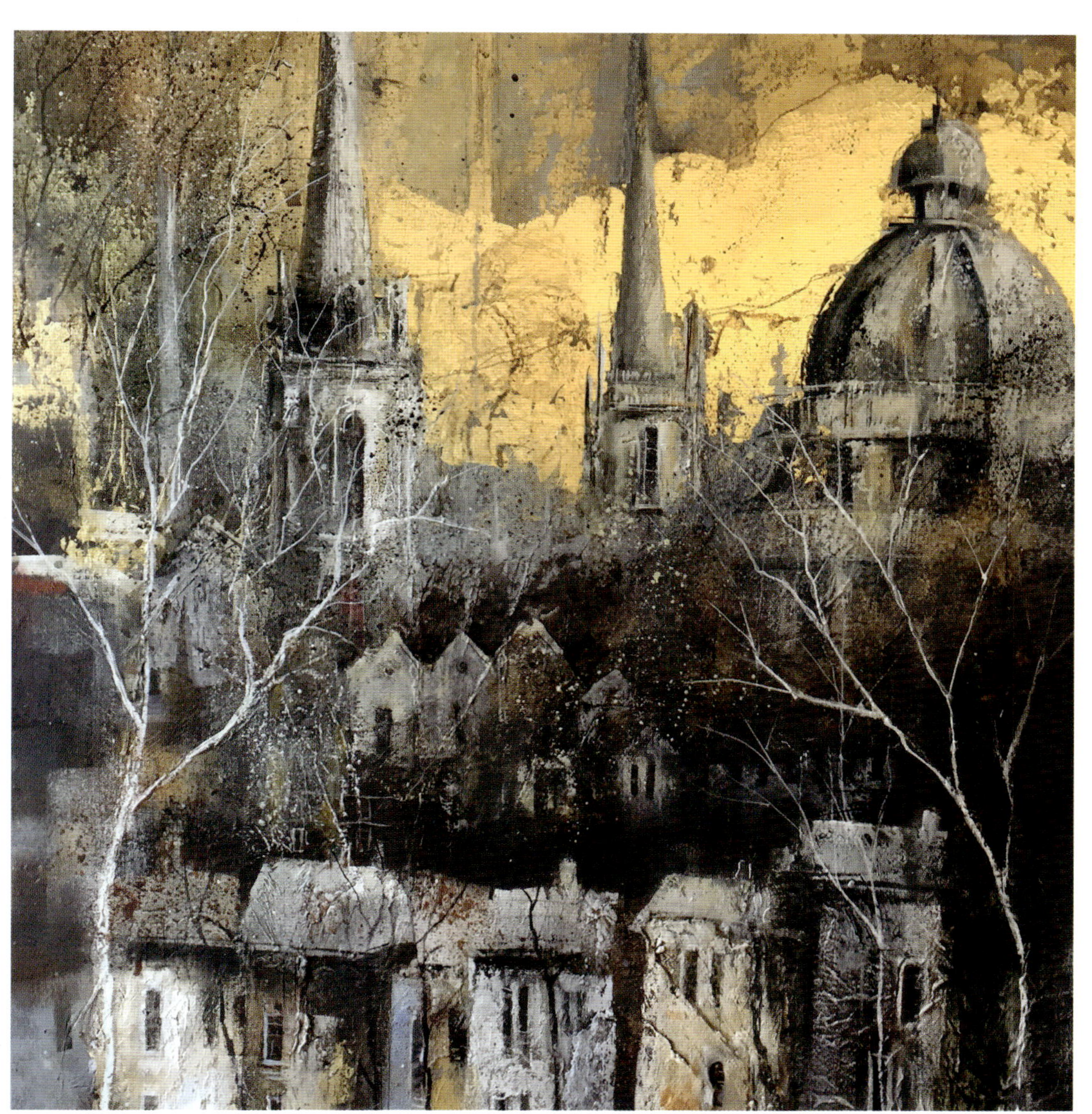

View from South Park, Bee Bartlett

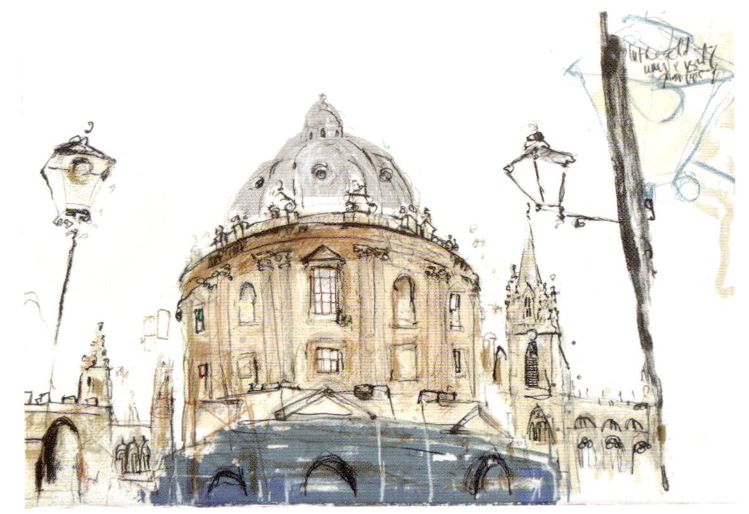

The Radcliffe Camera, Kelly Stewart

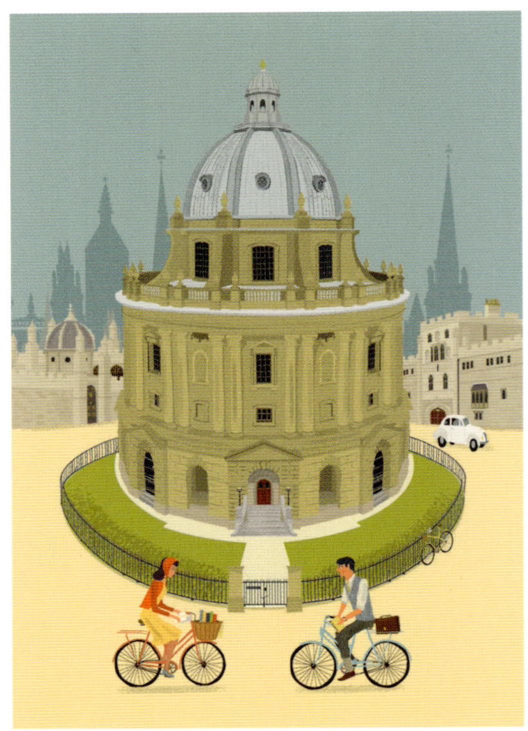

The Radcliffe Camera, Clare Phillips

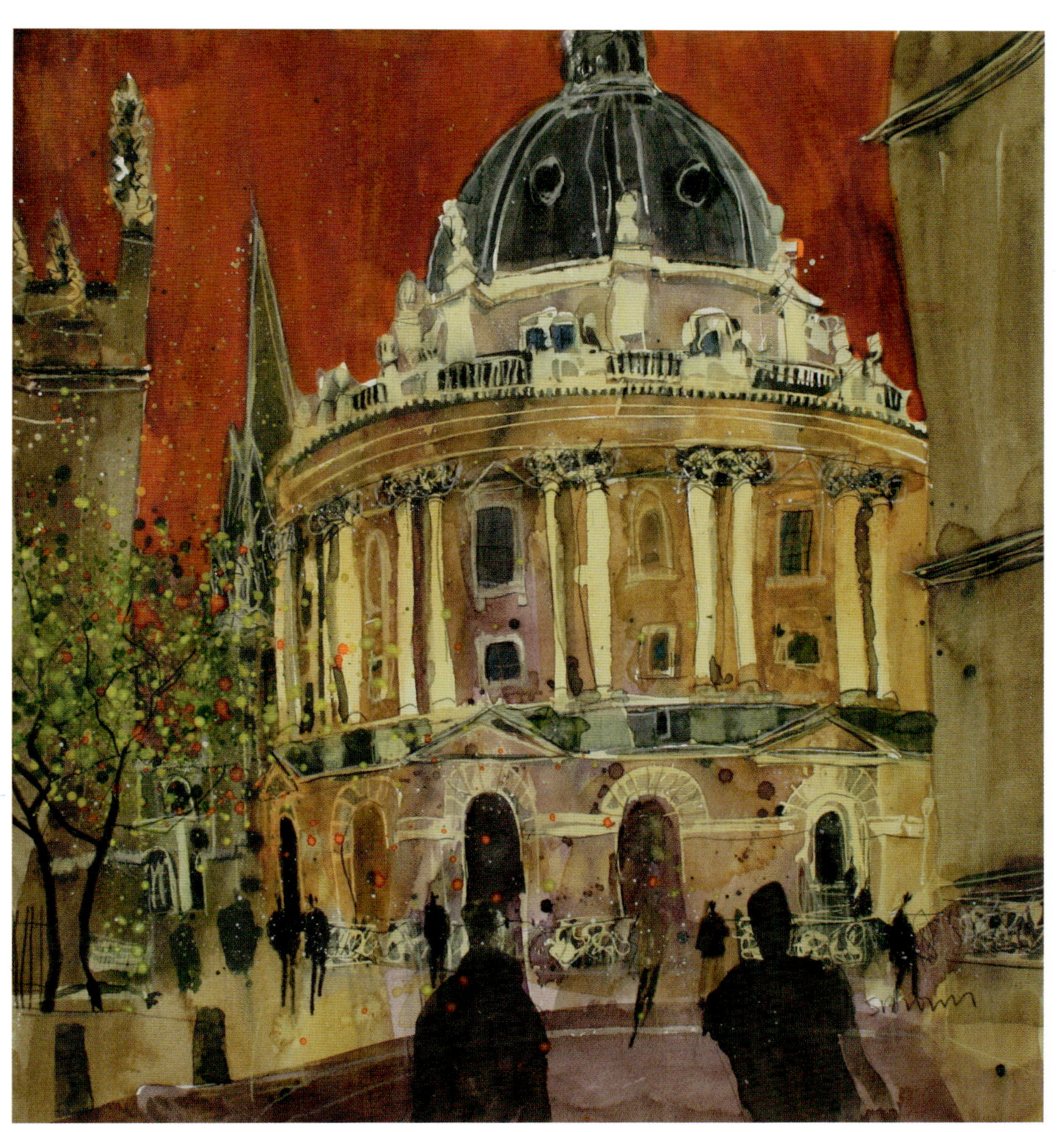

The Radcliffe Camera, Susan Brown

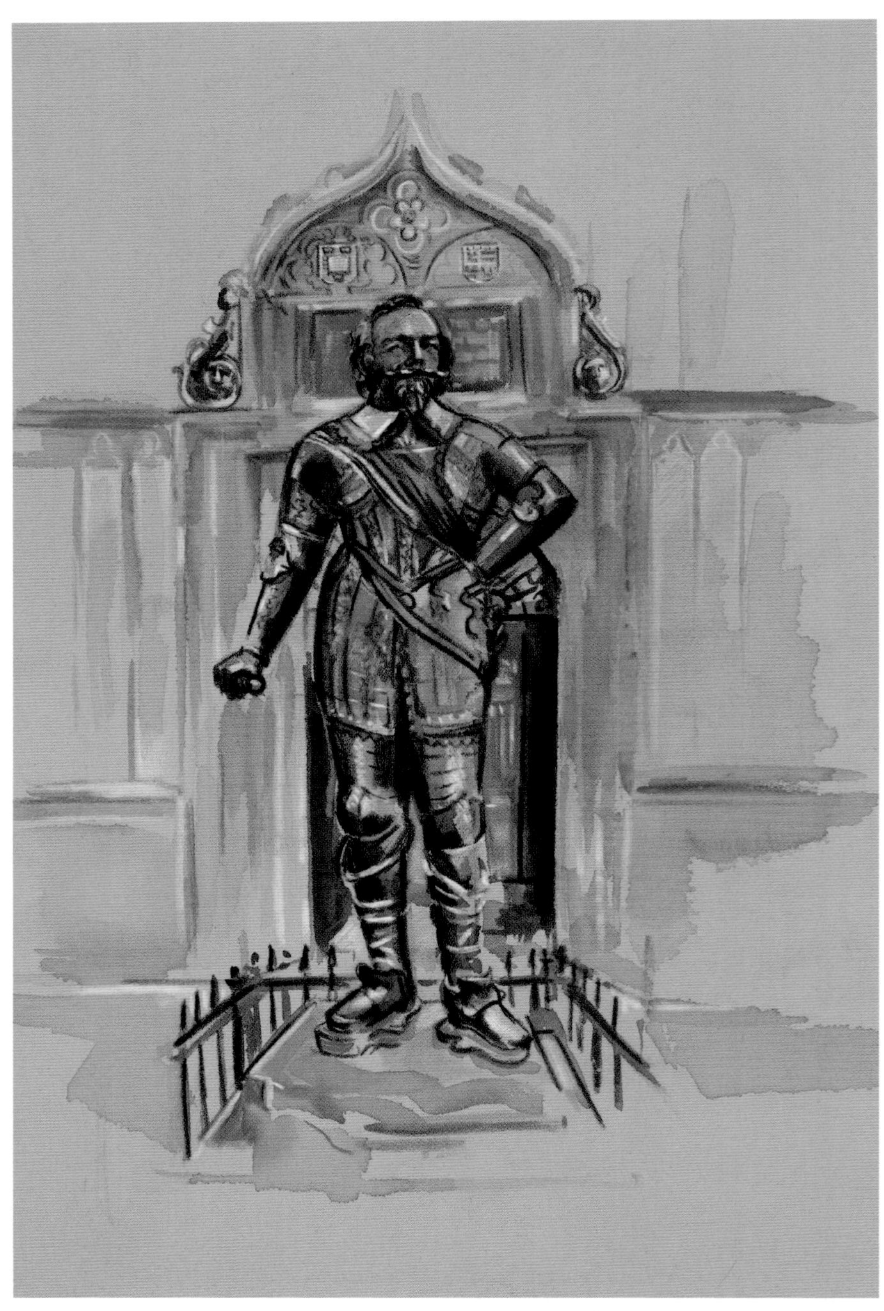

William Herbert, Amanda Beck

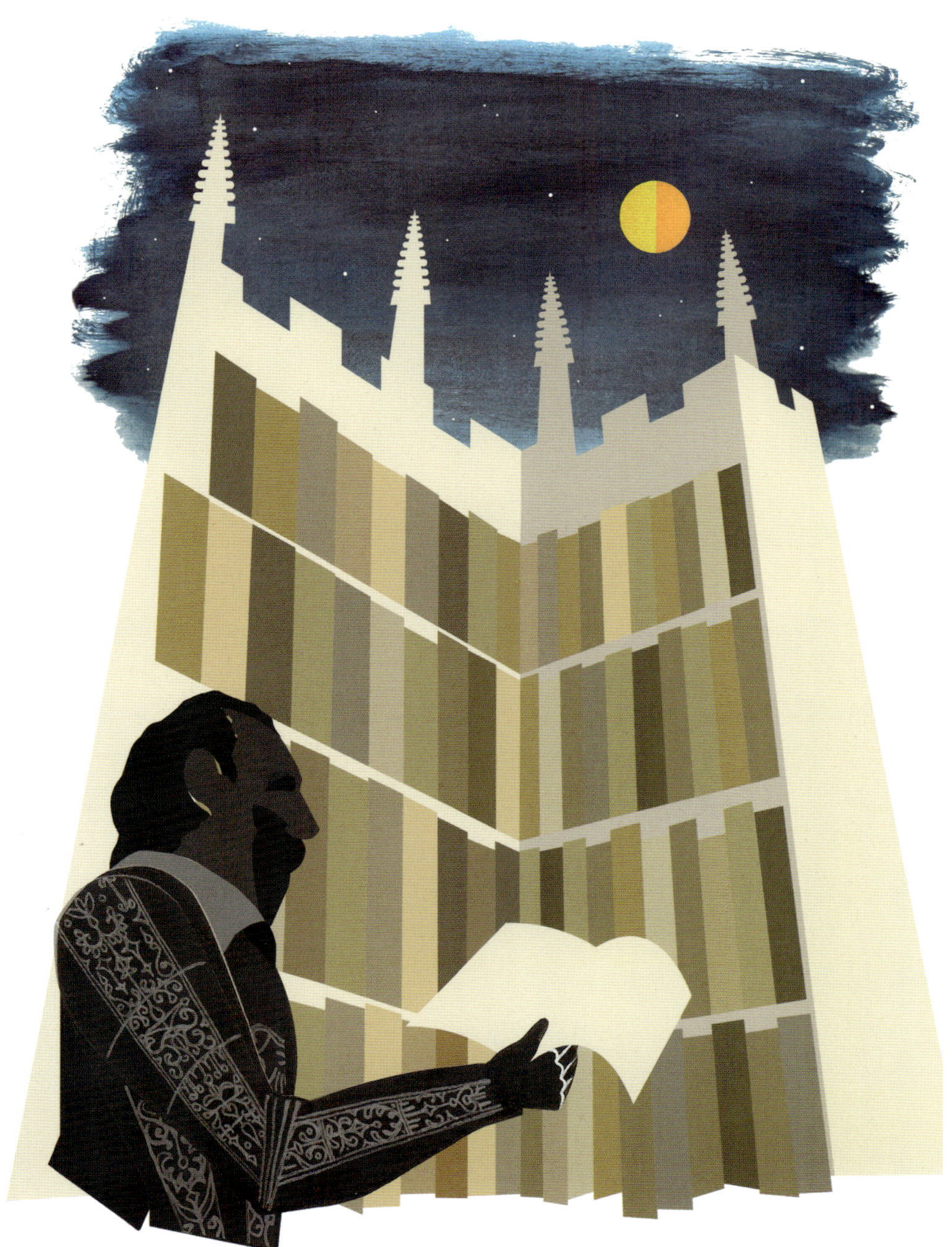

Bodleian Library, Clare Barry

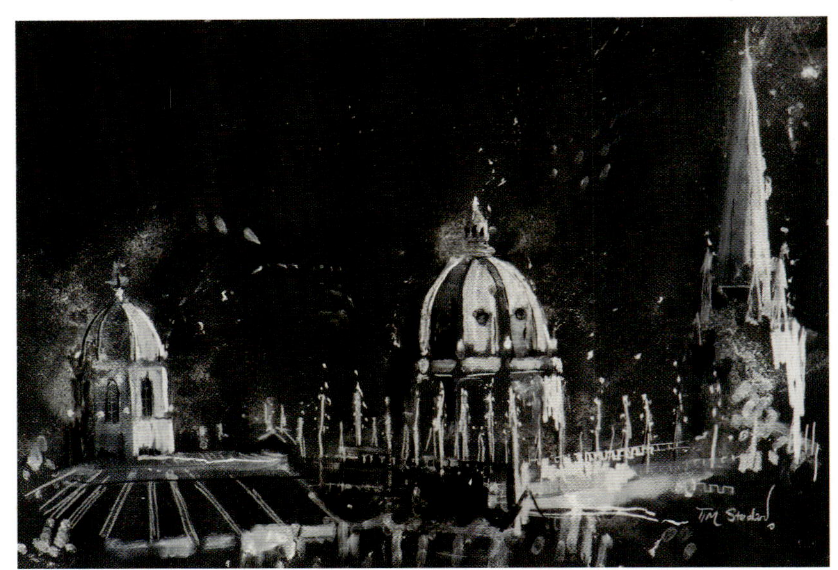

The Dreaming Spires, Tim Steward

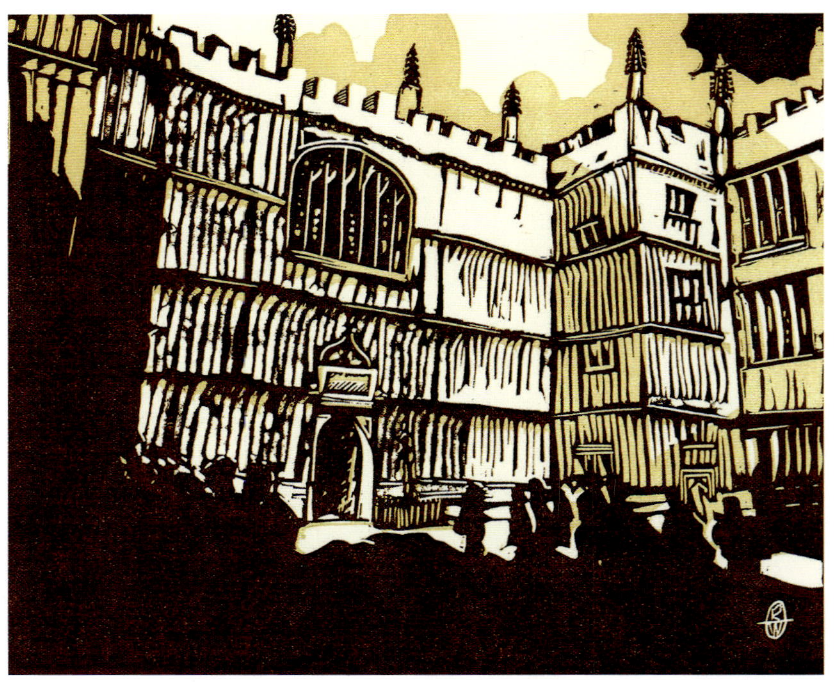

The Old Schools Quad, Robin Wilson

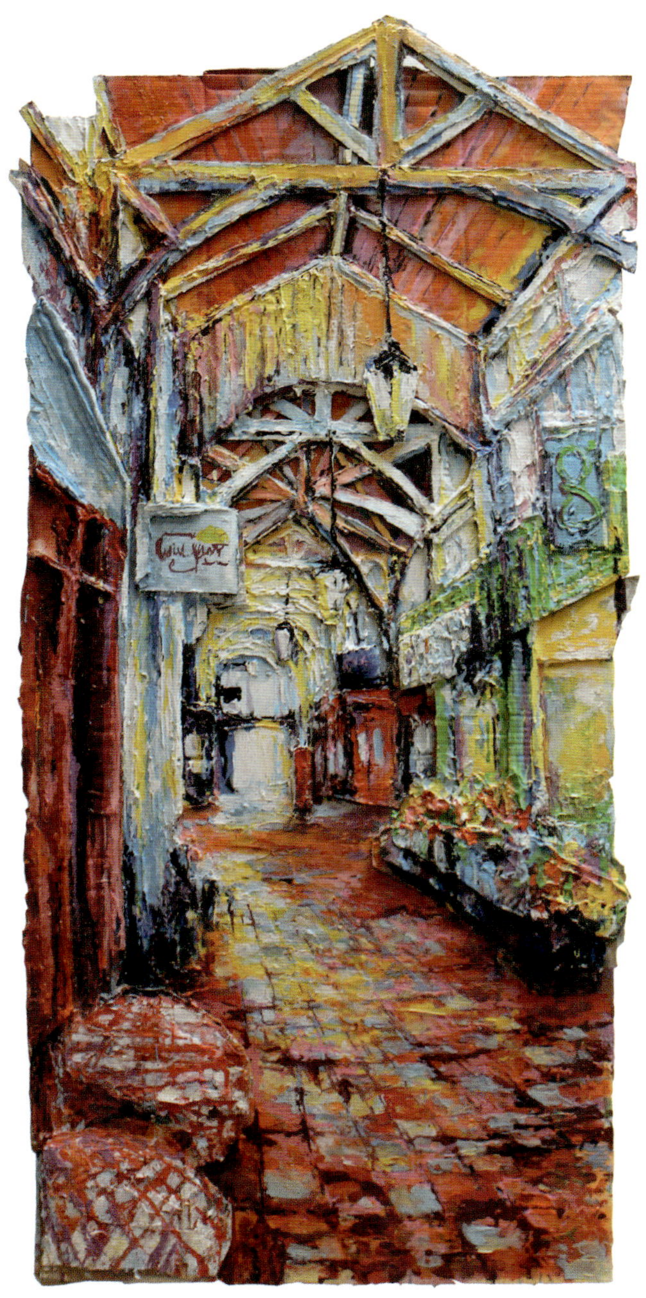

The Covered Market, Andrew 'Mani' Manson

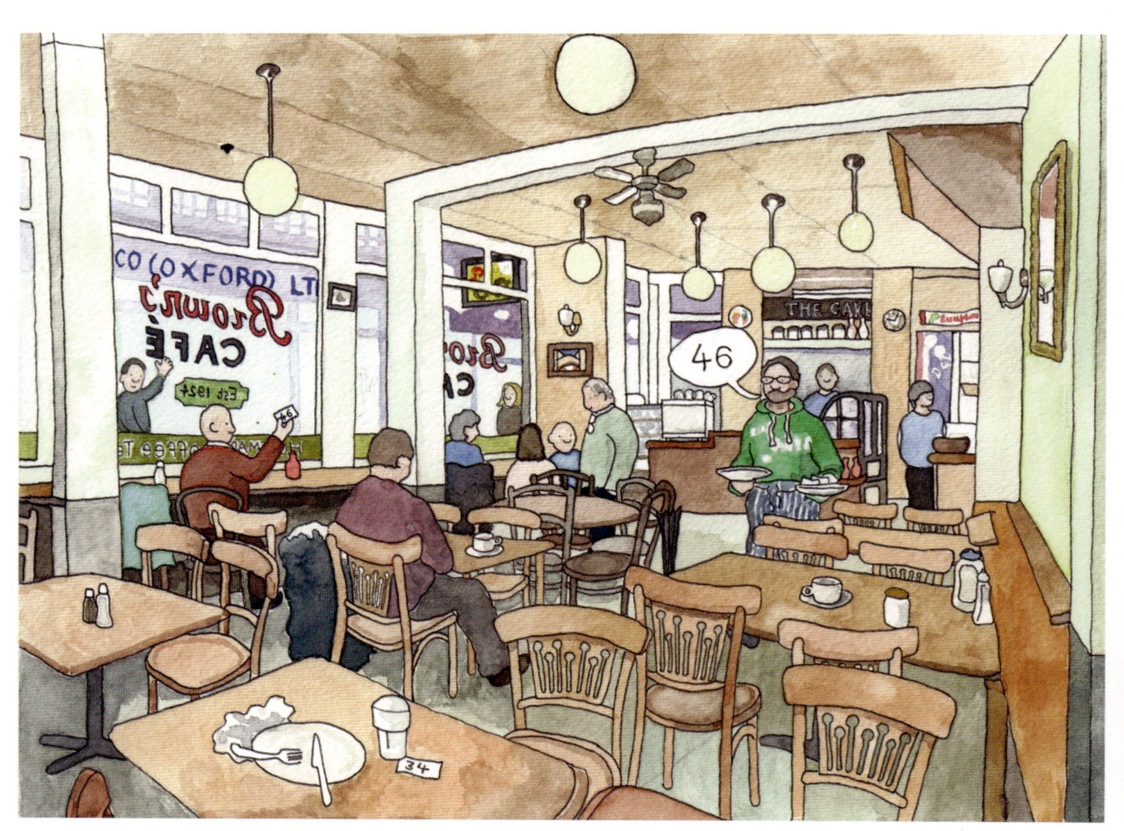

Brown's Café, The Covered Market, Tim Kirtley

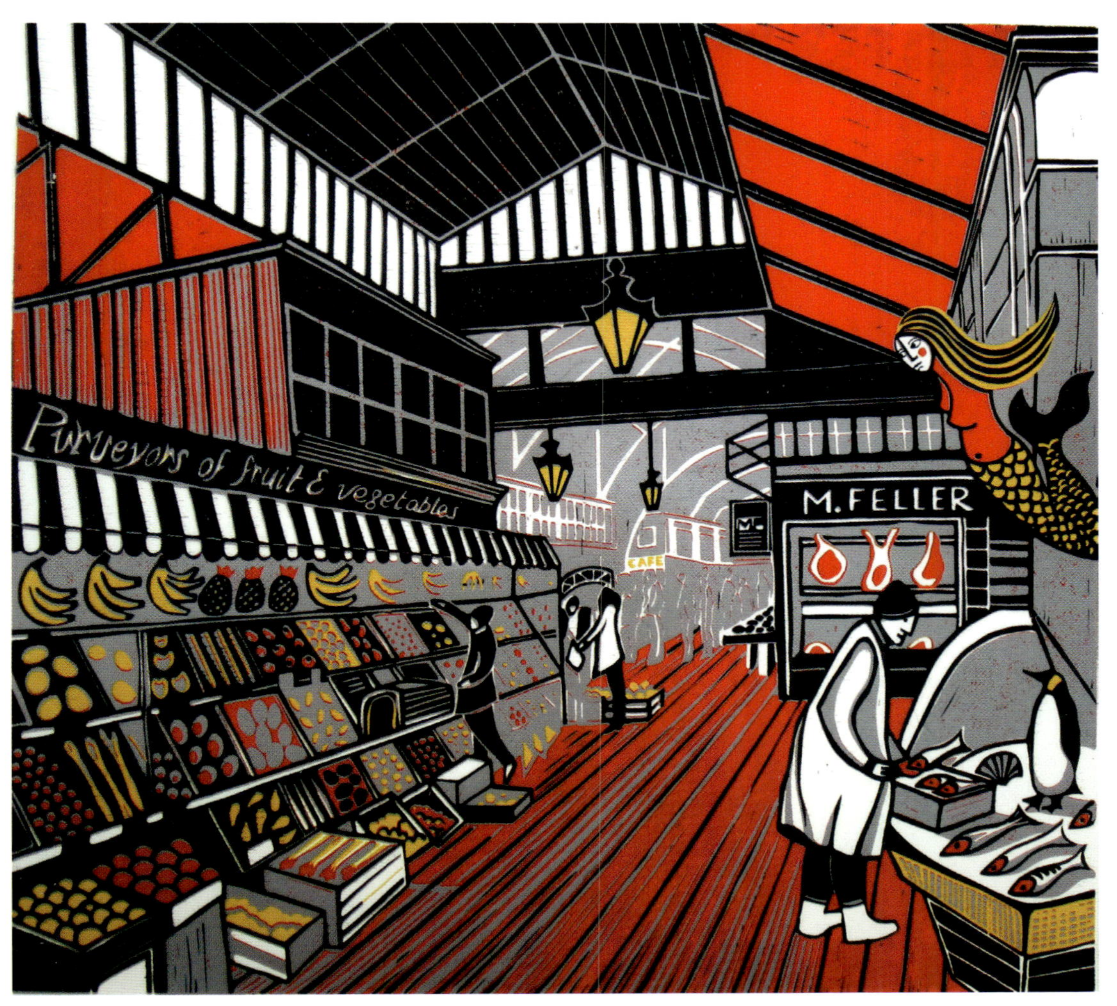

THE COVERED MARKET, SUSAN WHEELER

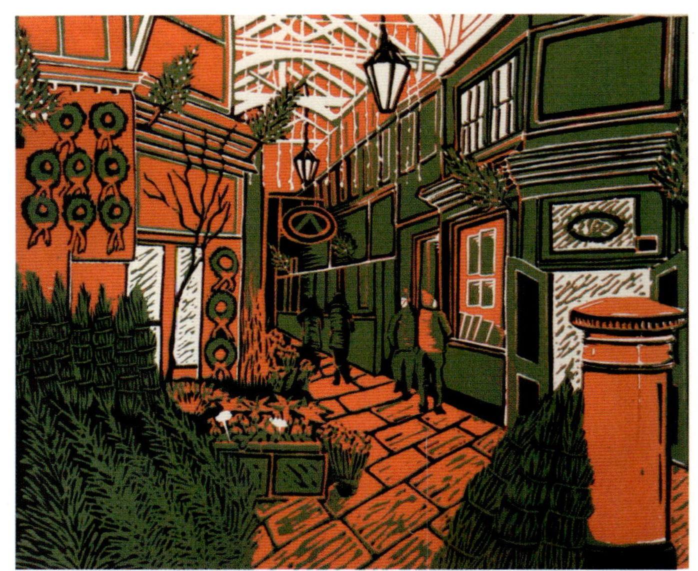

The Covered Market, Gerry Coles

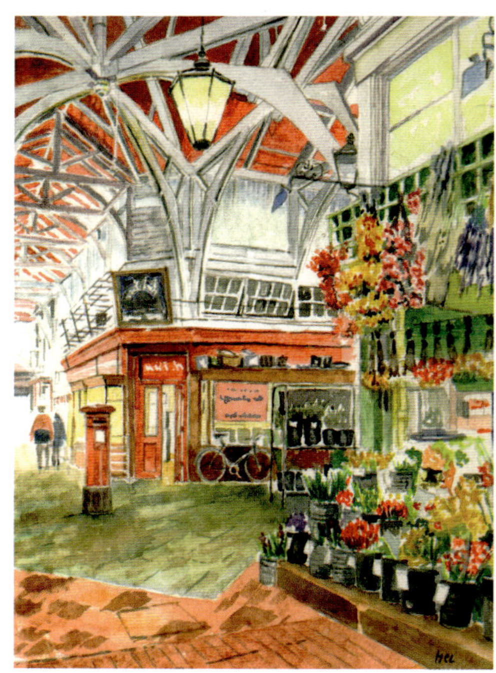

The Covered Market, Mike Lester

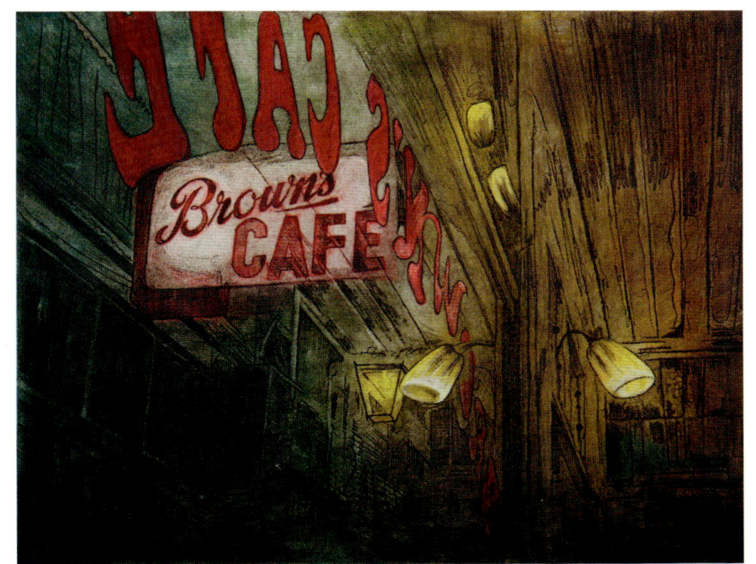

Brown's Café, Elizabeth Moriarty

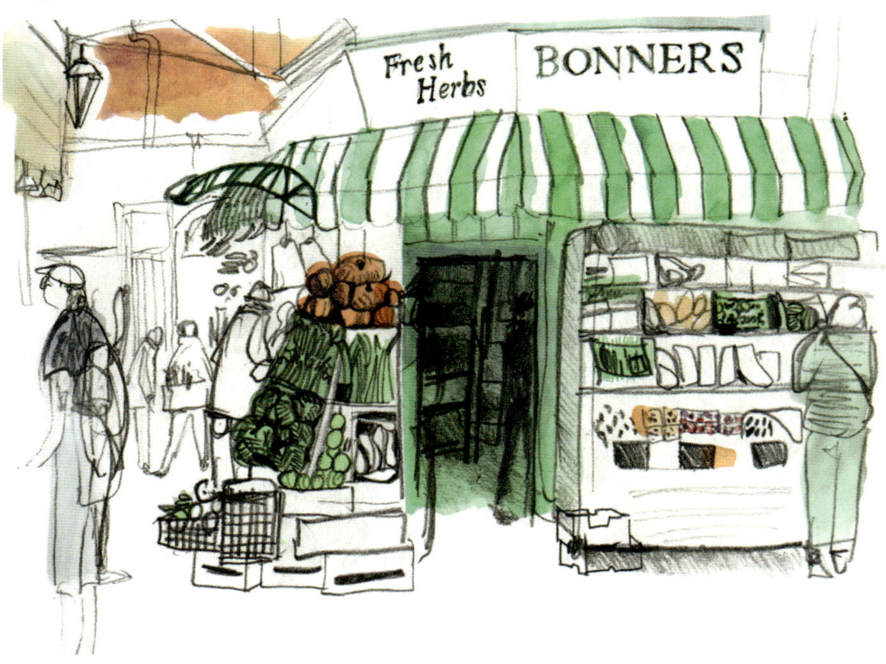

The Covered Market, Louise Hall

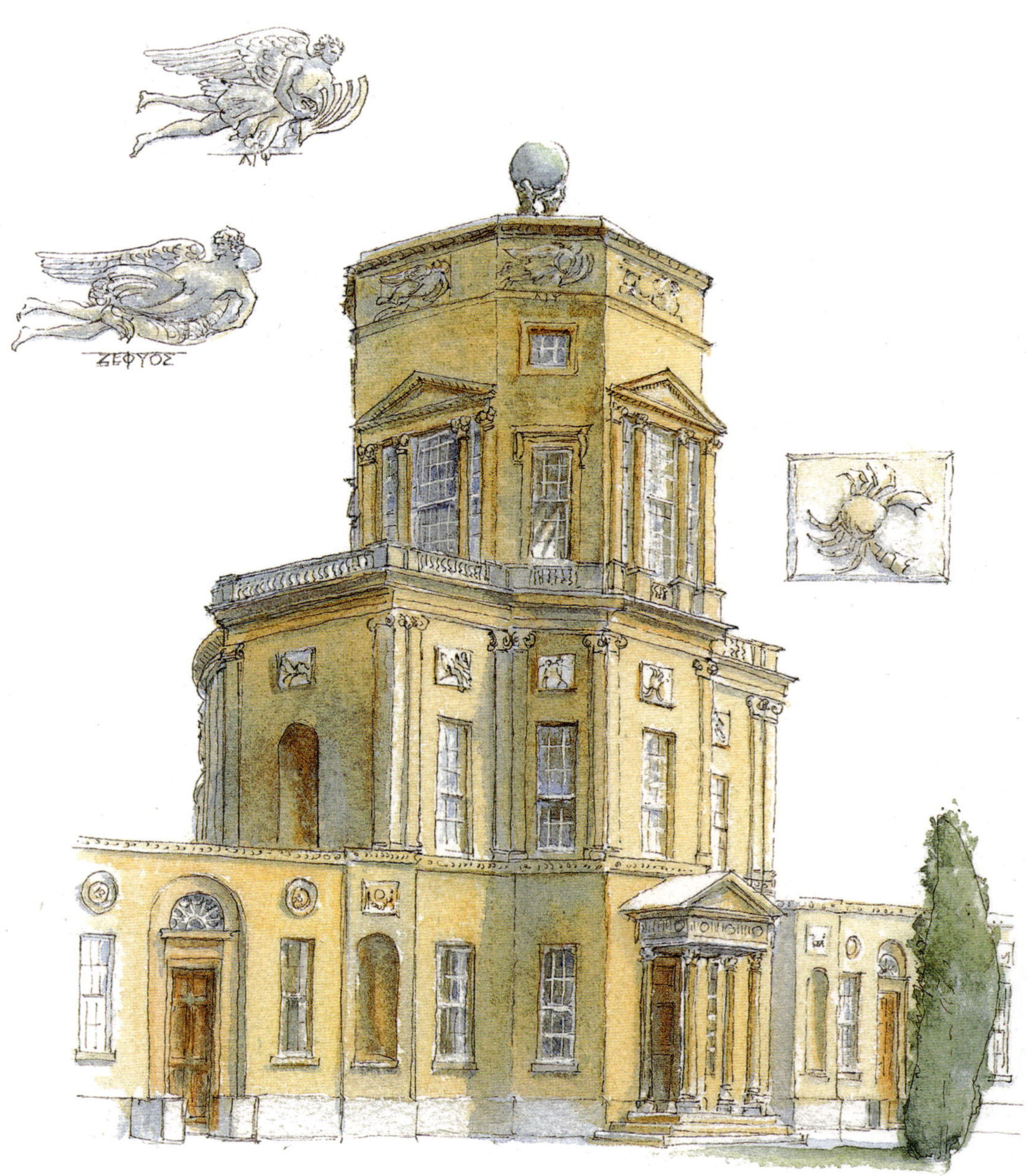

Radcliffe Observatory, Valerie Petts

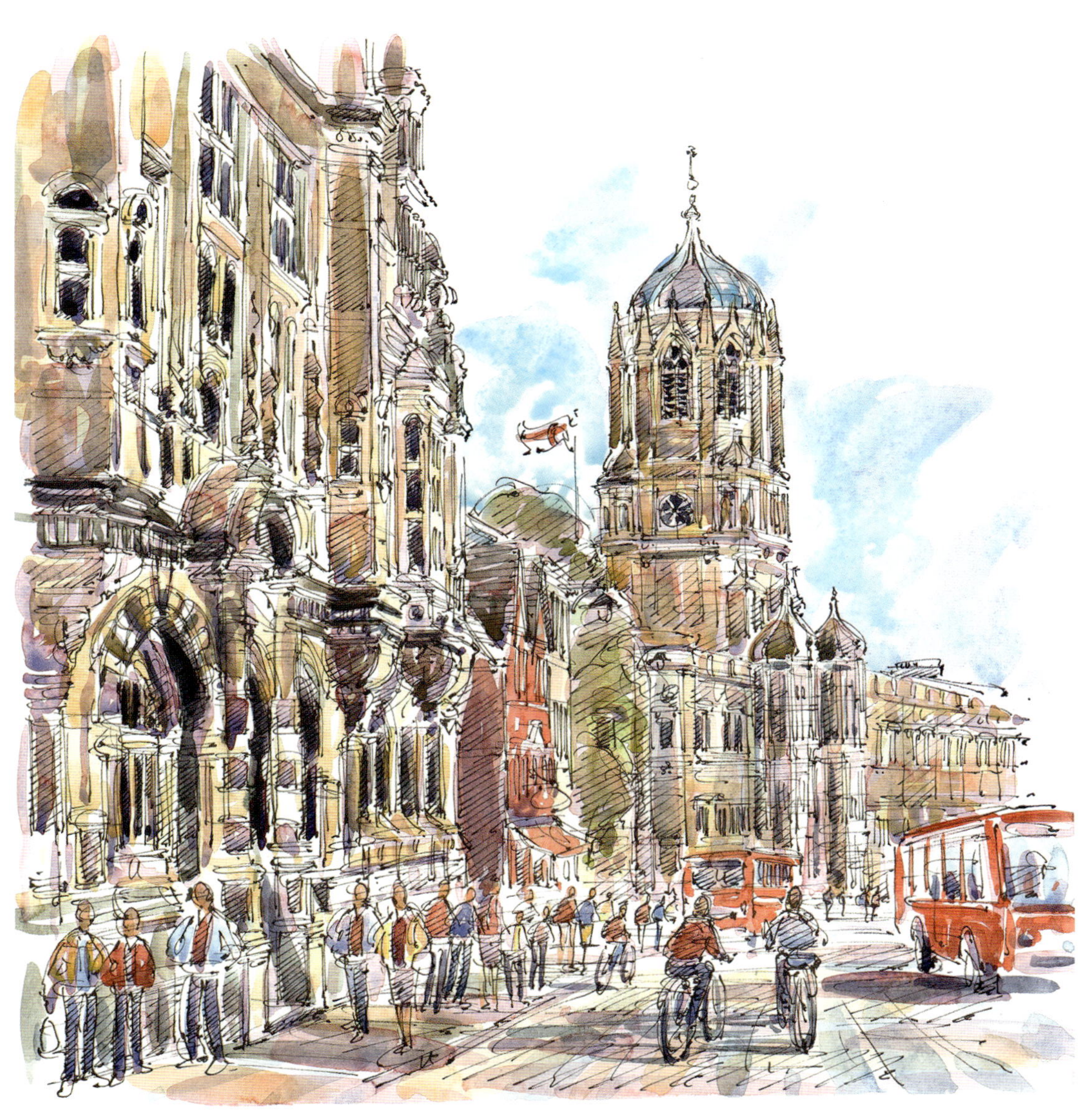

Towards Tom Tower, Richard Briggs

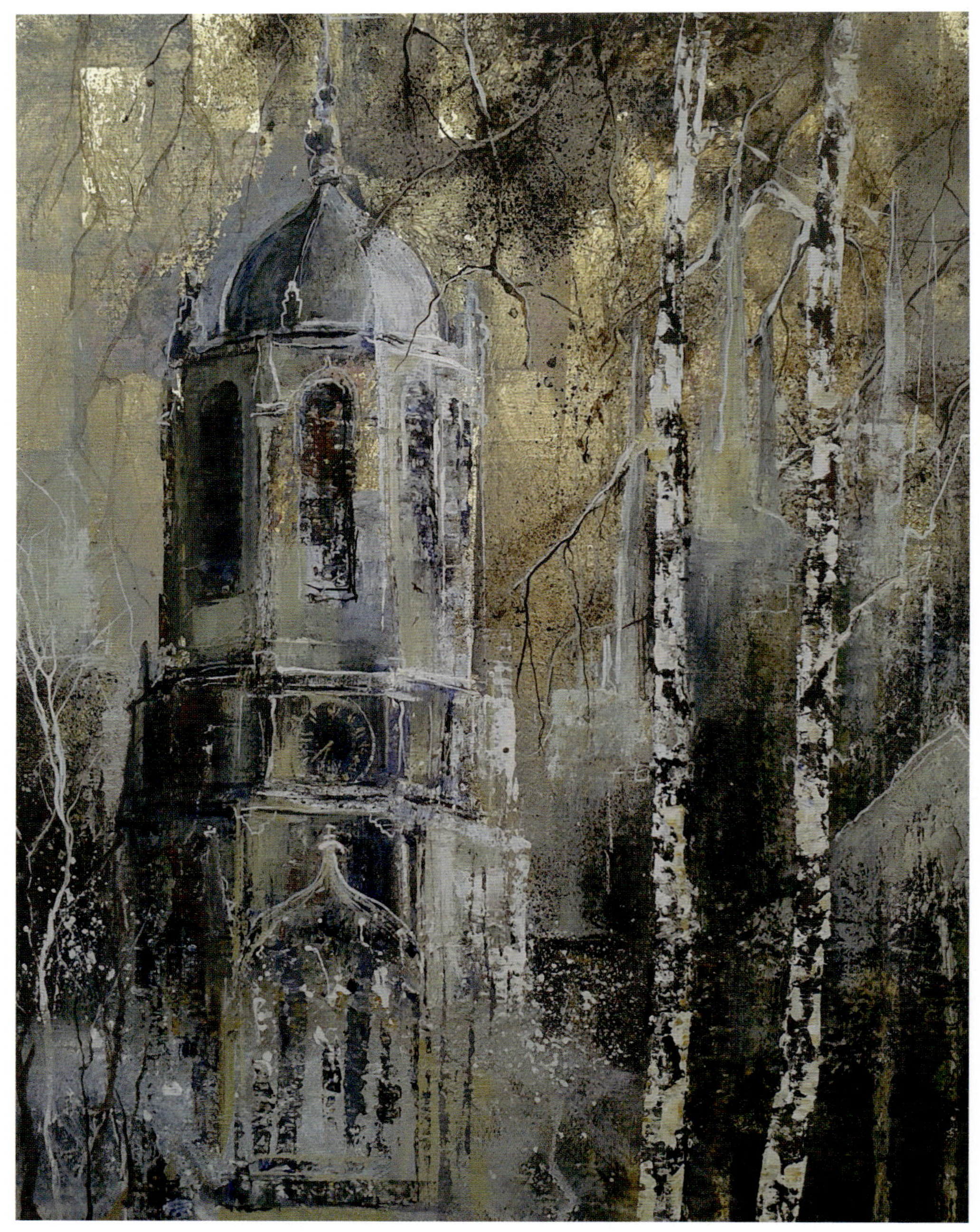

Tom Tower, Christ Church, Bee Bartlett

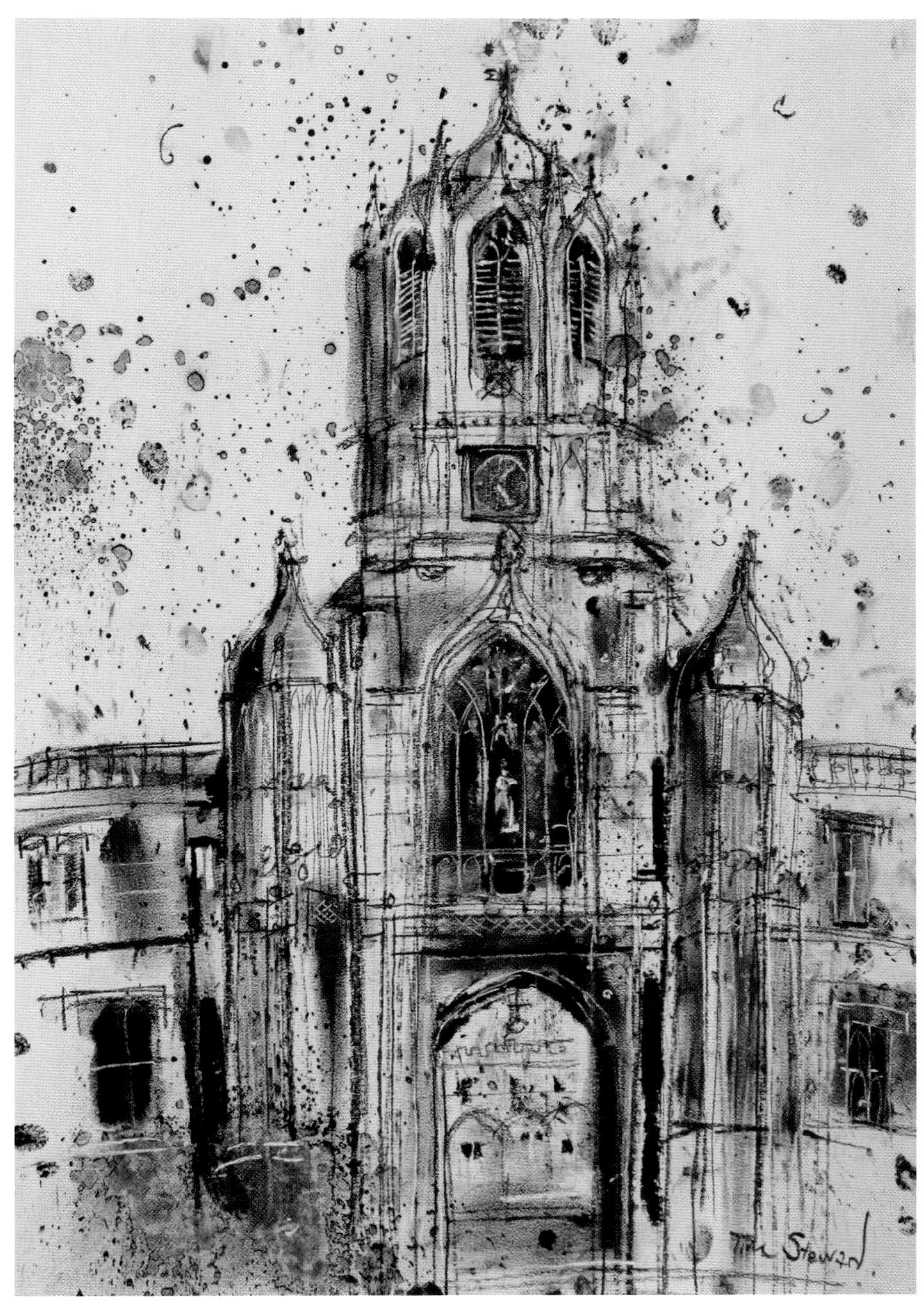

Tom Tower, Tim Steward

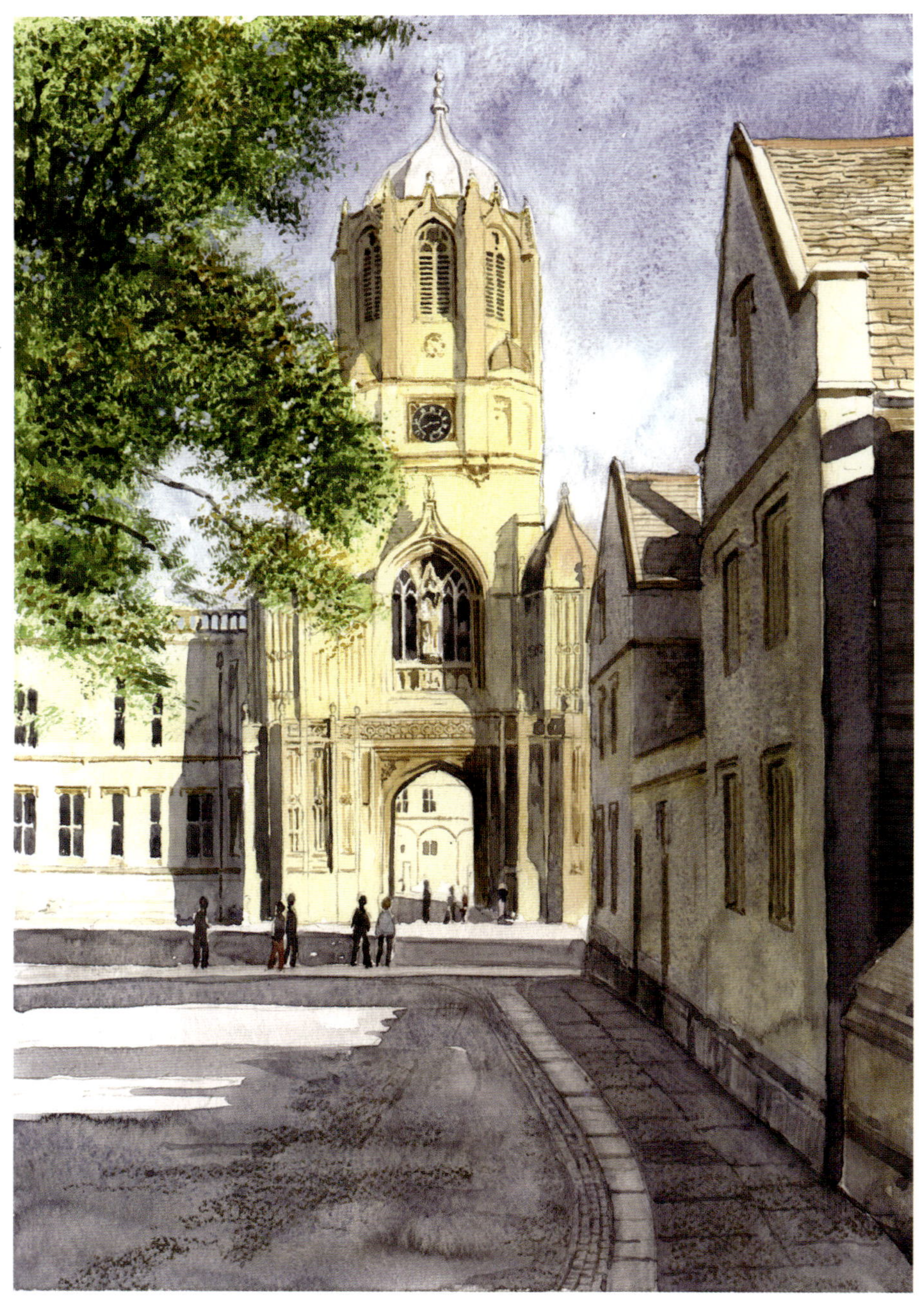

Tom Tower, John Somerscales

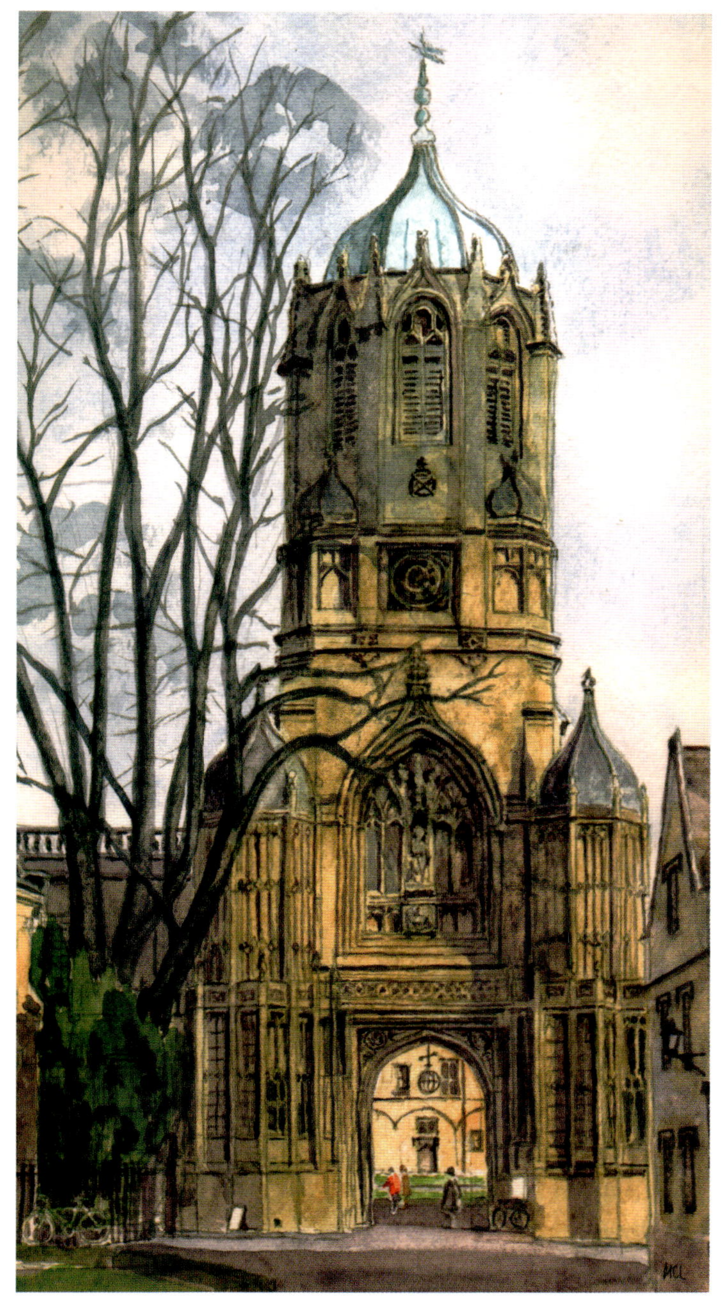

Tom Tower, Charlie Davies

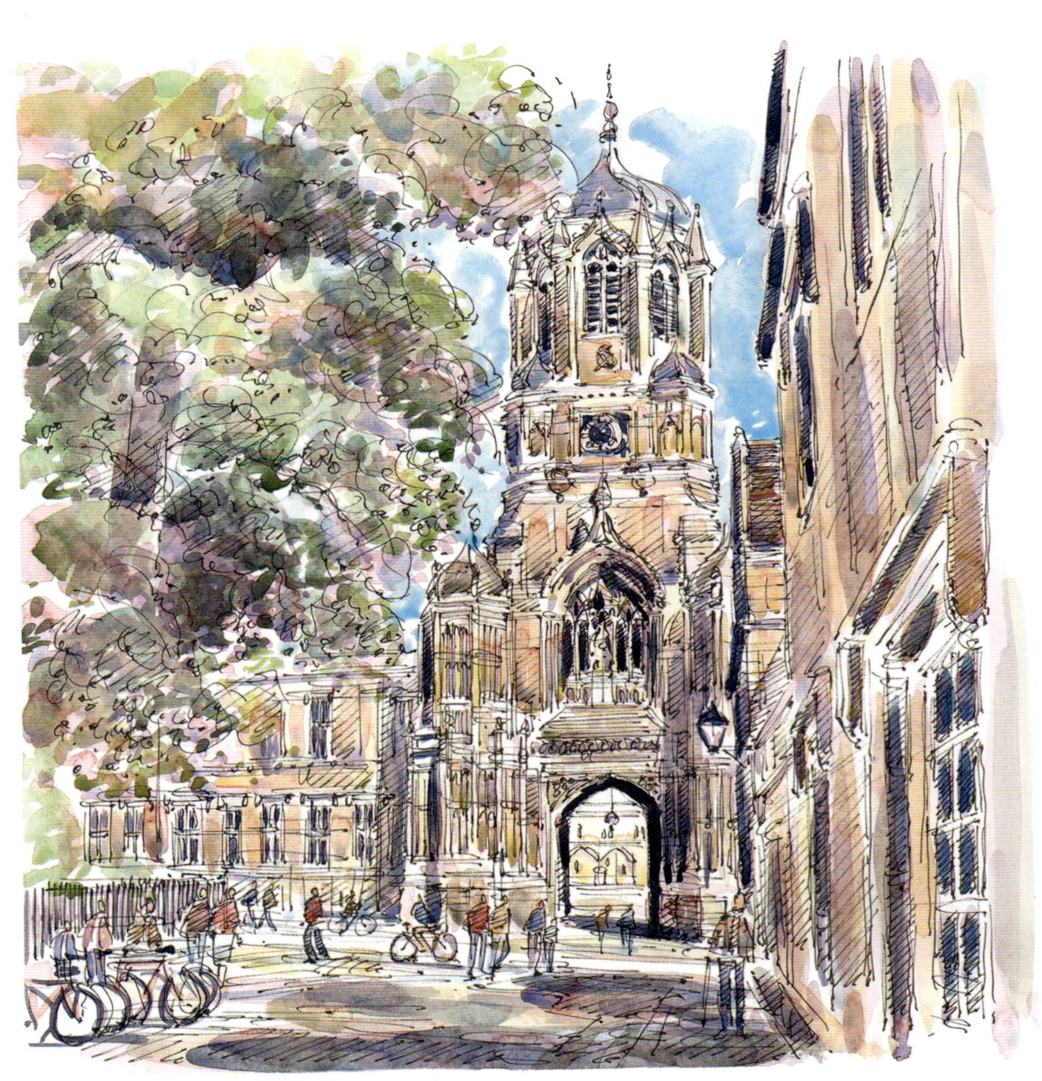

Tom Tower, Richard Briggs

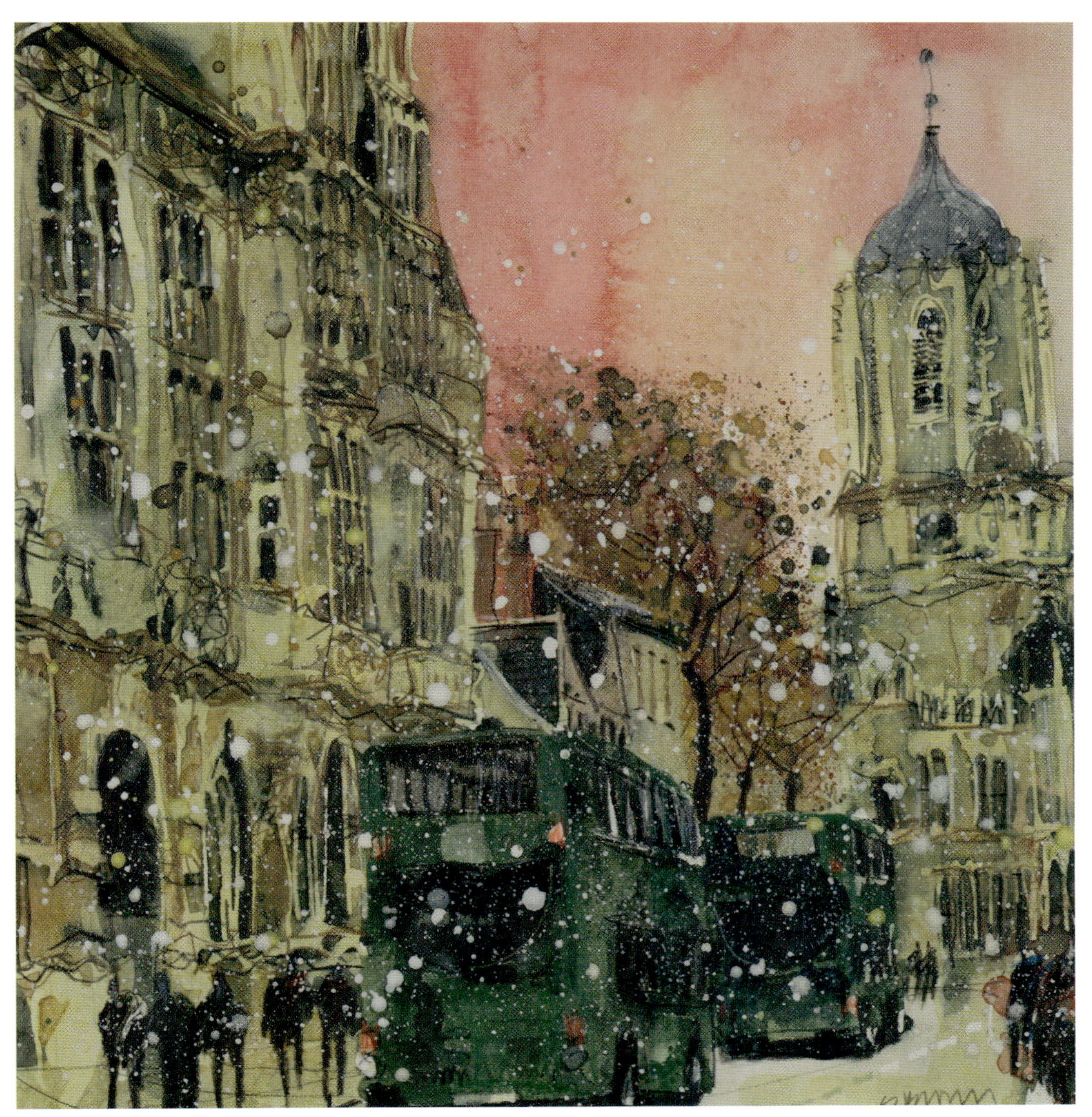

Christ Church, Susan Brown

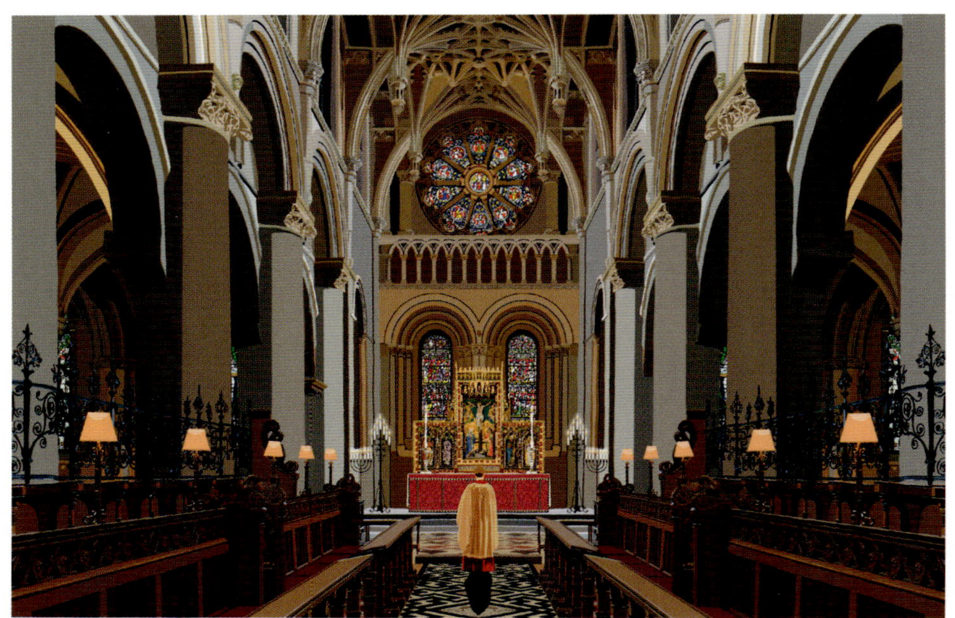

Christ Church, Richard O'Neill

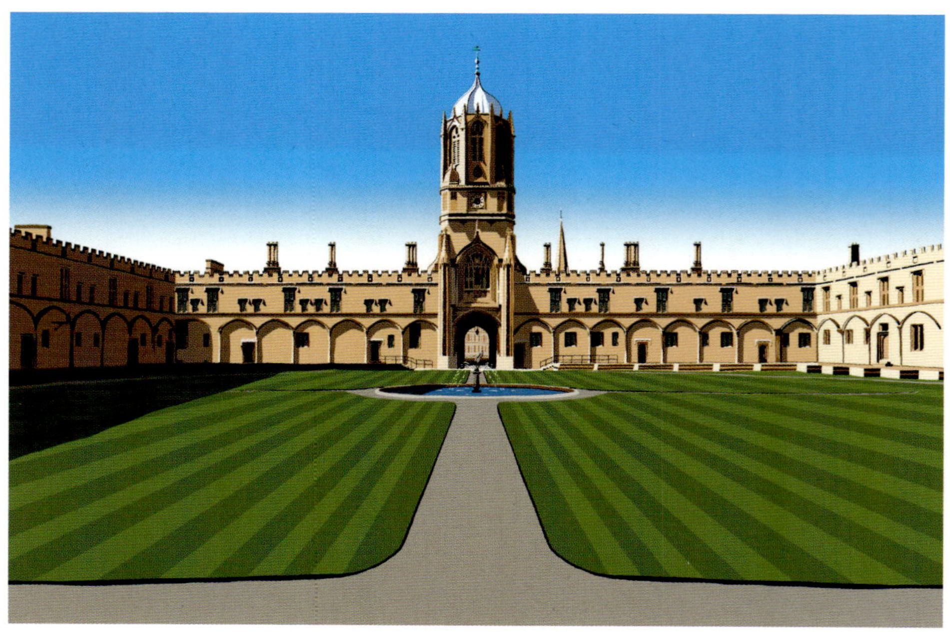

Christ Church, Richard O'Neill

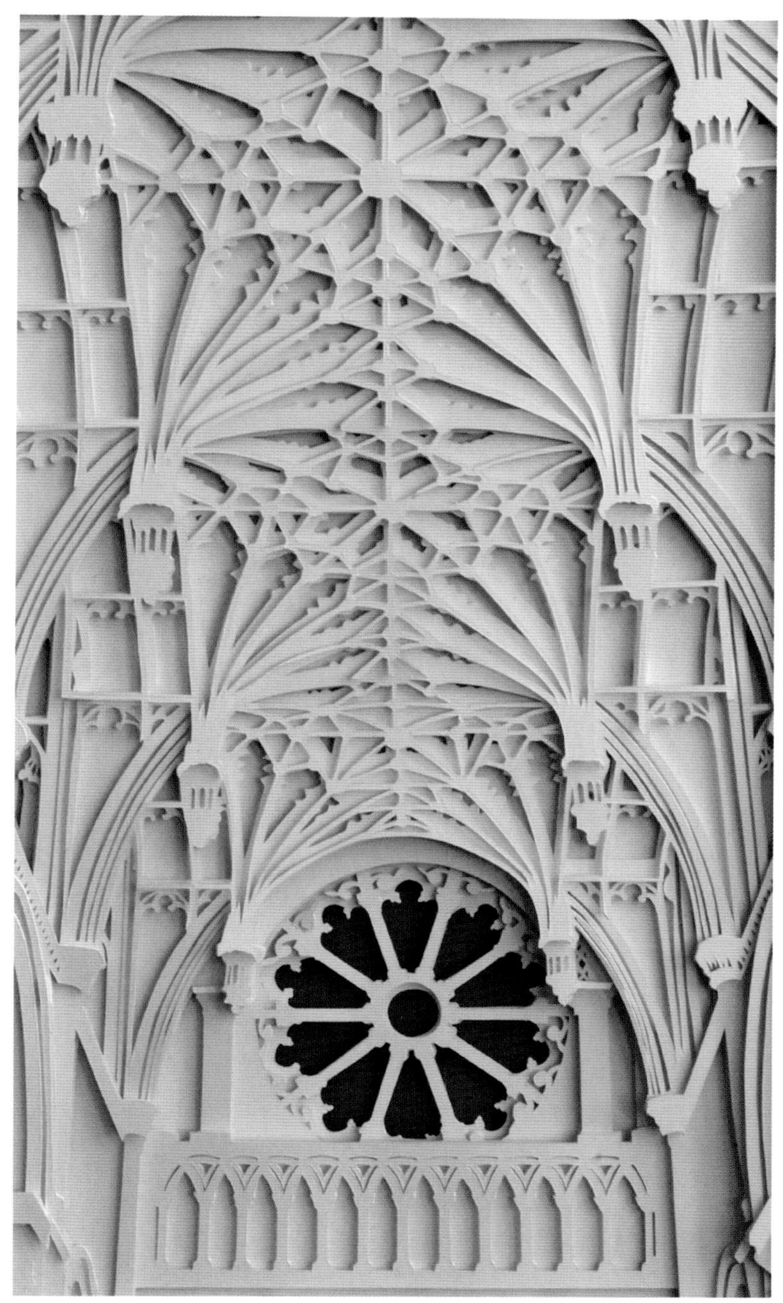

Christ Church, Kate Hipkiss

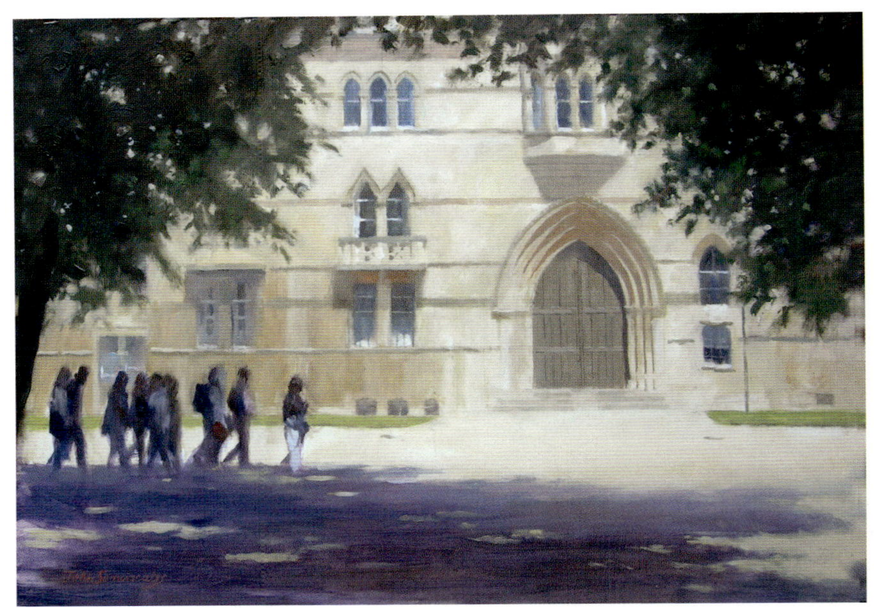

Christ Church, John Somerscales

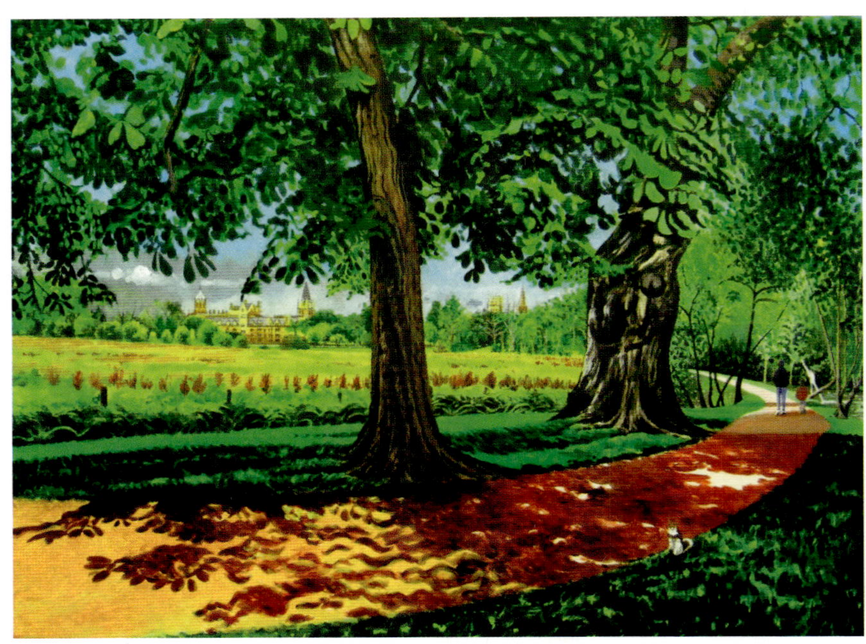

Christ Church Meadow, Daniel Drury

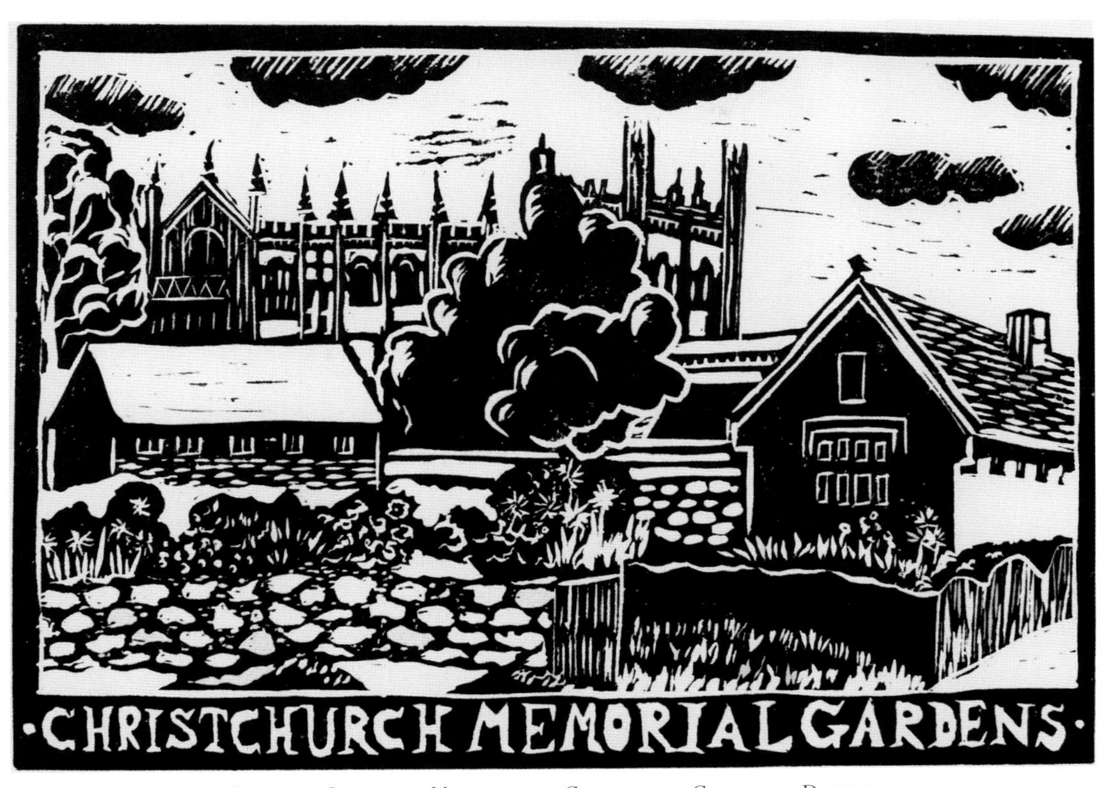

Christ Church Memorial Gardens, Charlie Davies

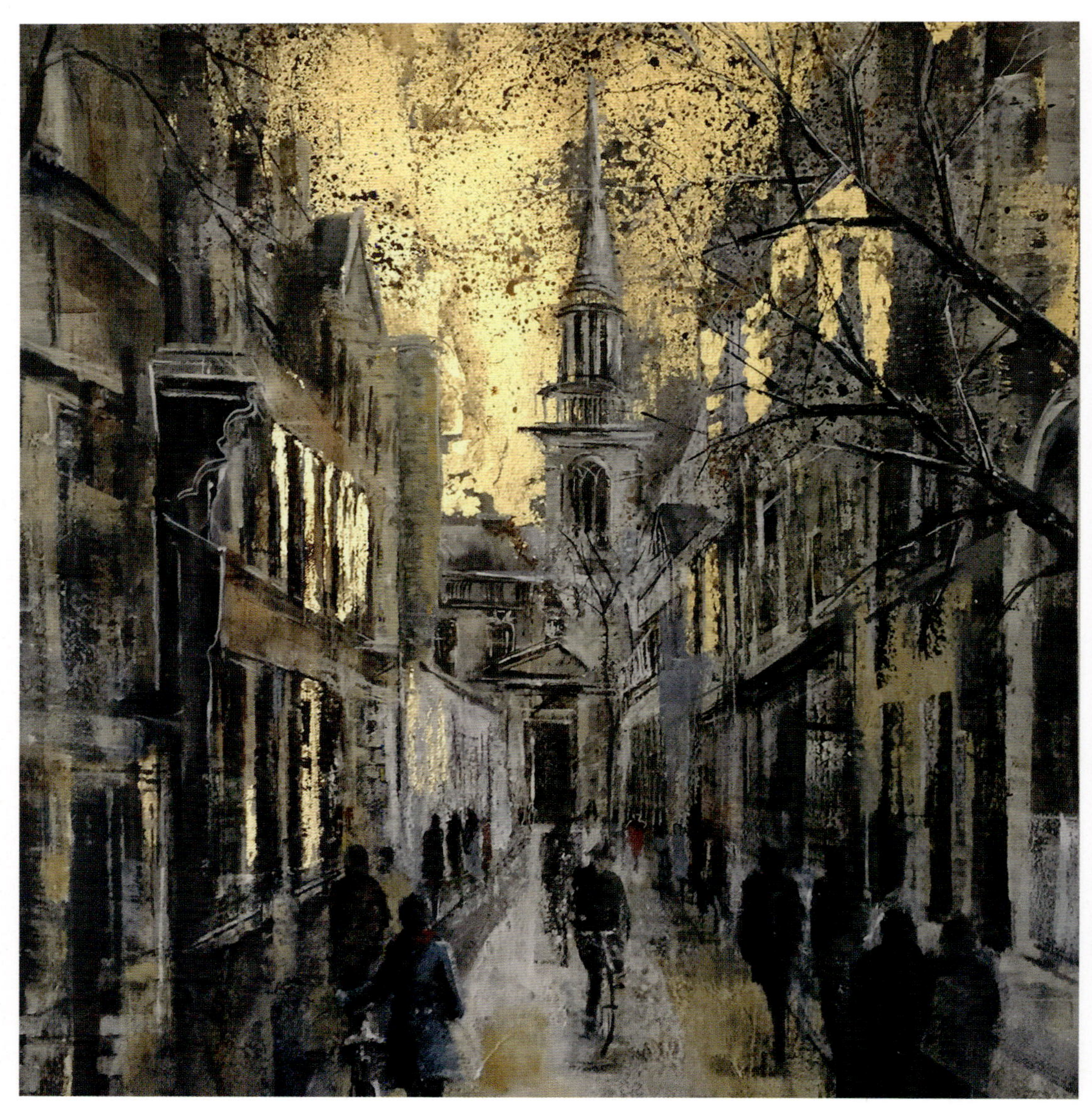

Turl Street, Bee Bartlett

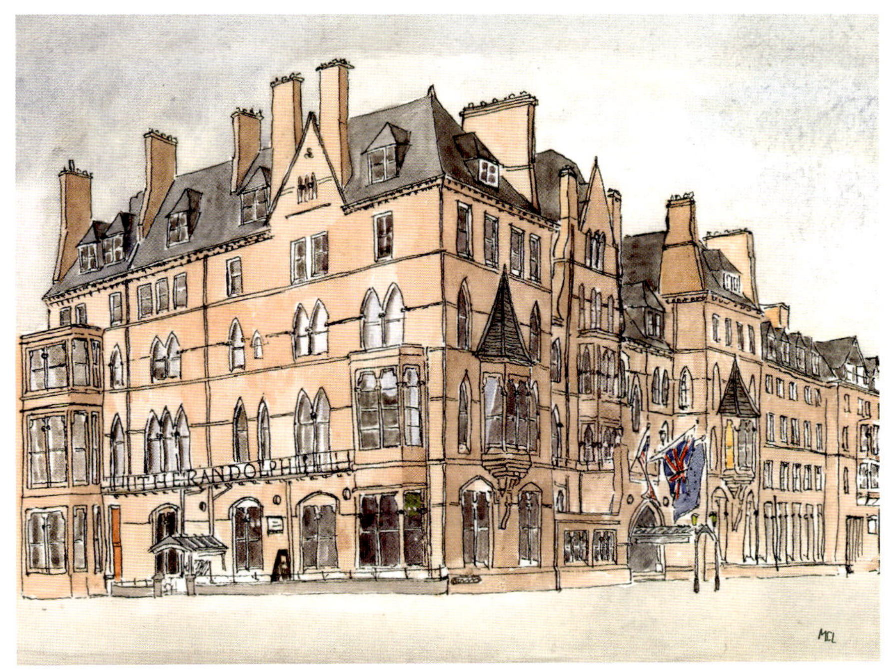

THE RANDOLPH HOTEL, MIKE LESTER

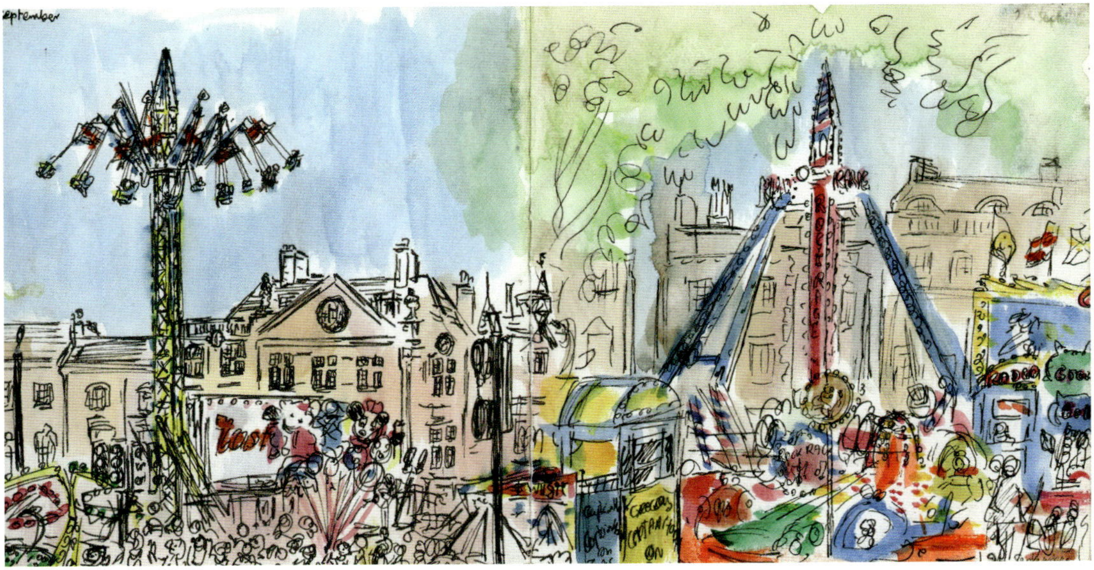

ST GILES' FAIR, IMOGEN FOXELL

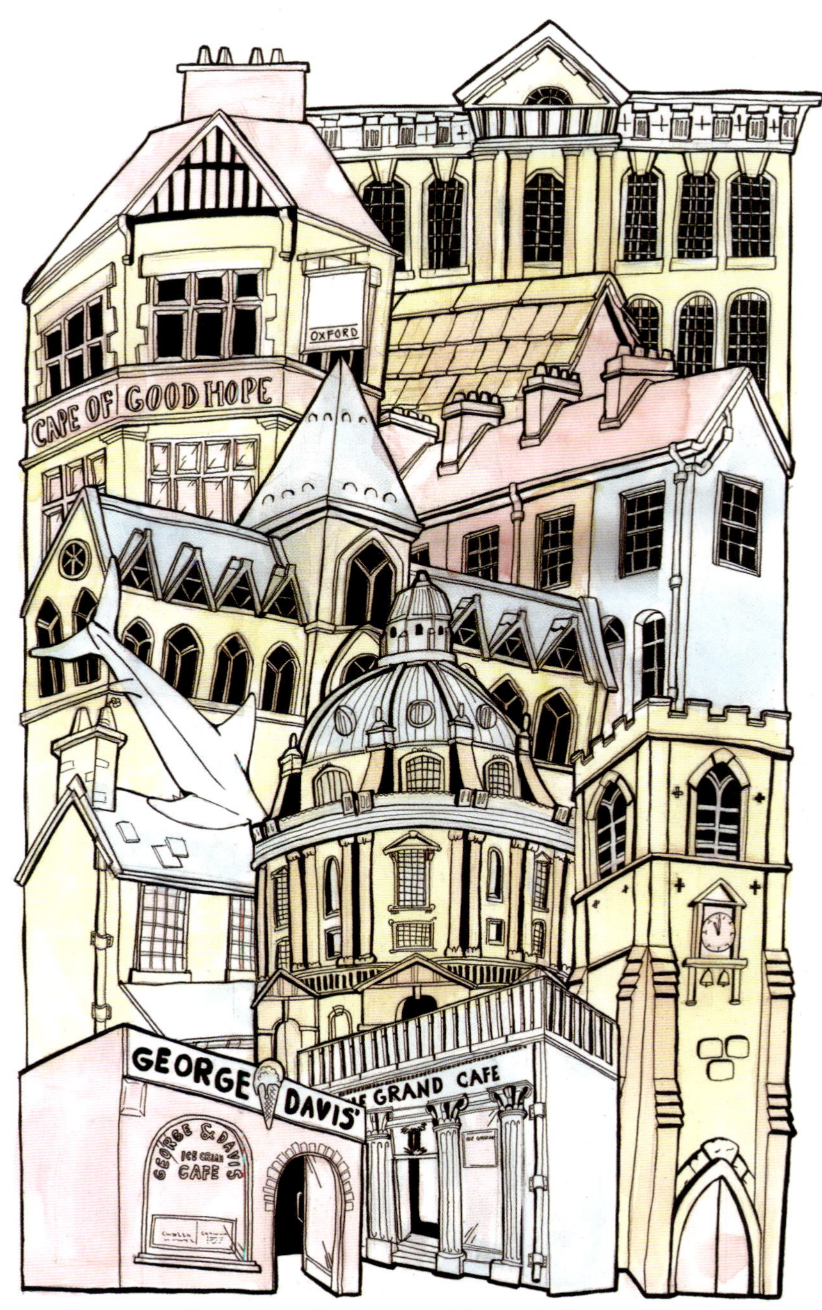

STACKING CITYSCAPE, MARK COLLIASS

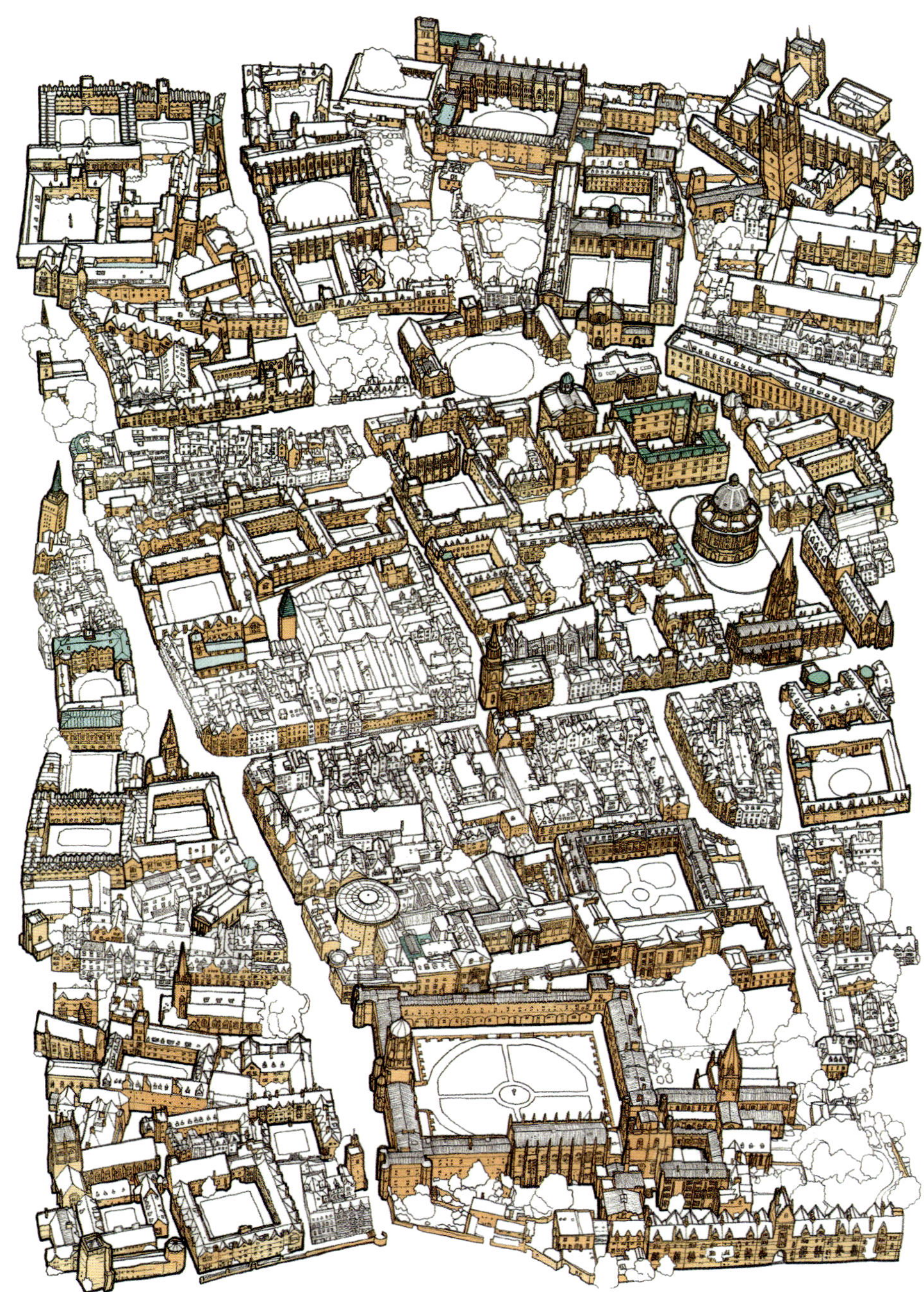

A Reimagined Cityscape, William Bright

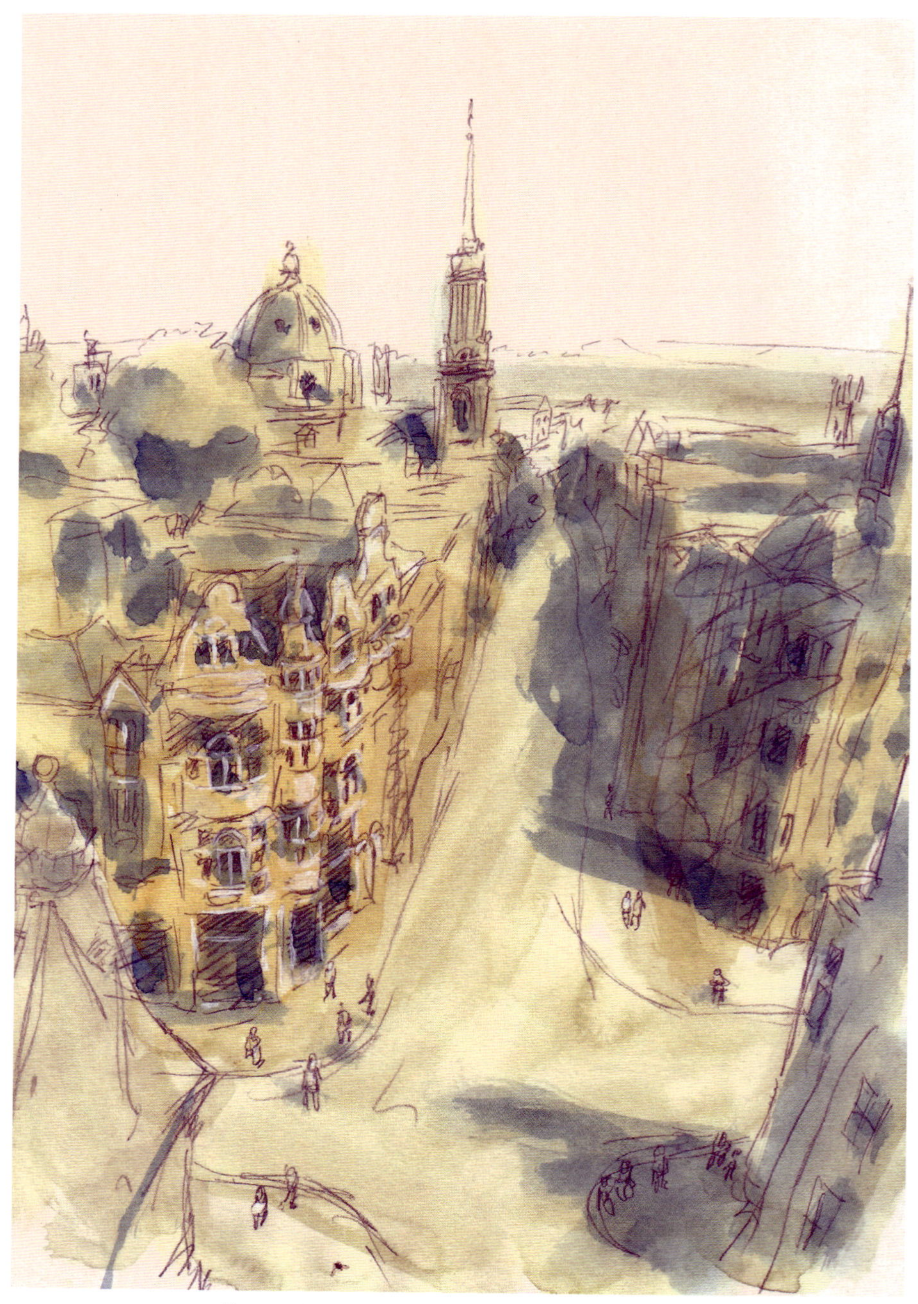

From Carfax Tower, Steve Appleton

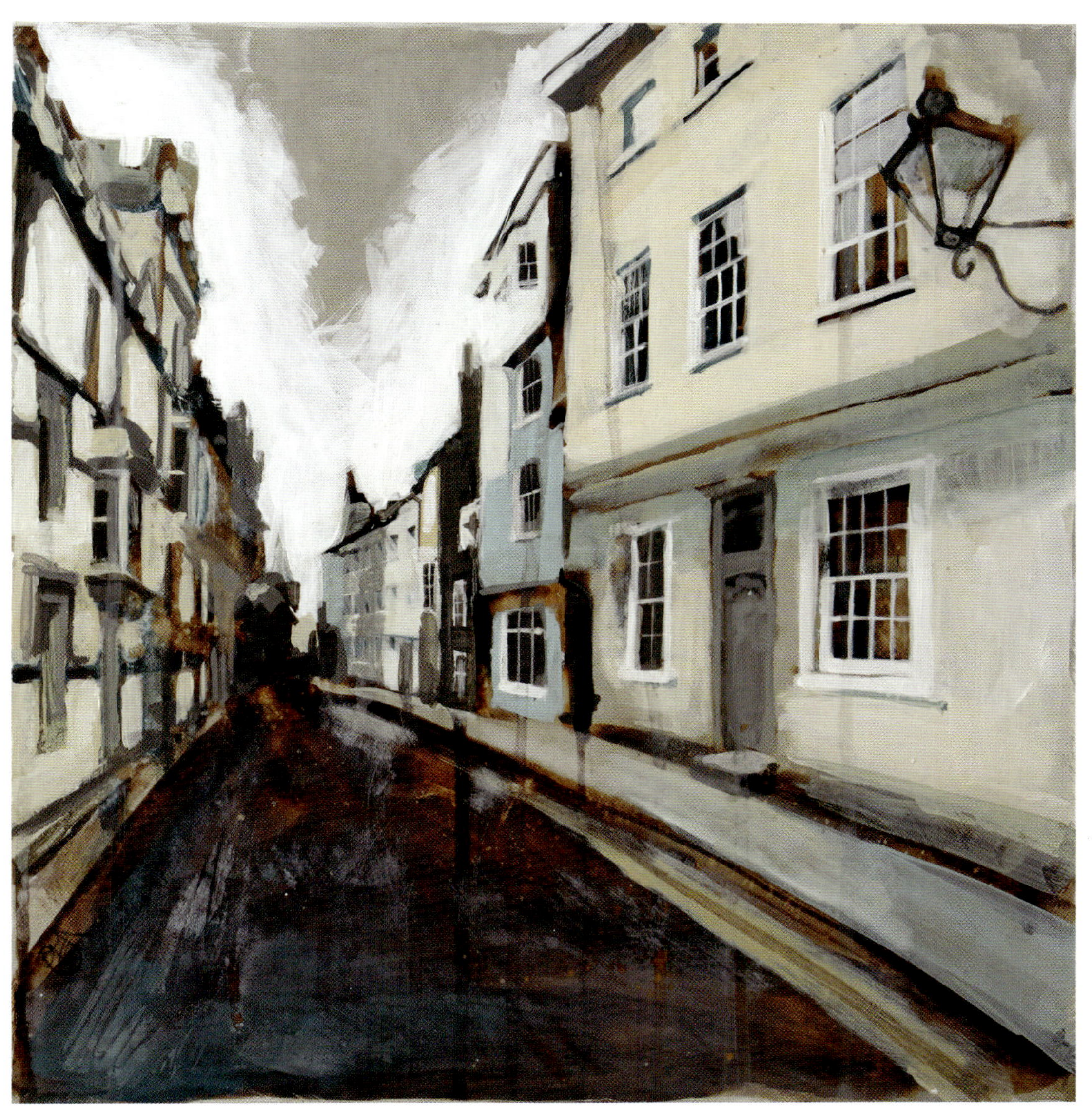

Ship Street, Camilla Dowse

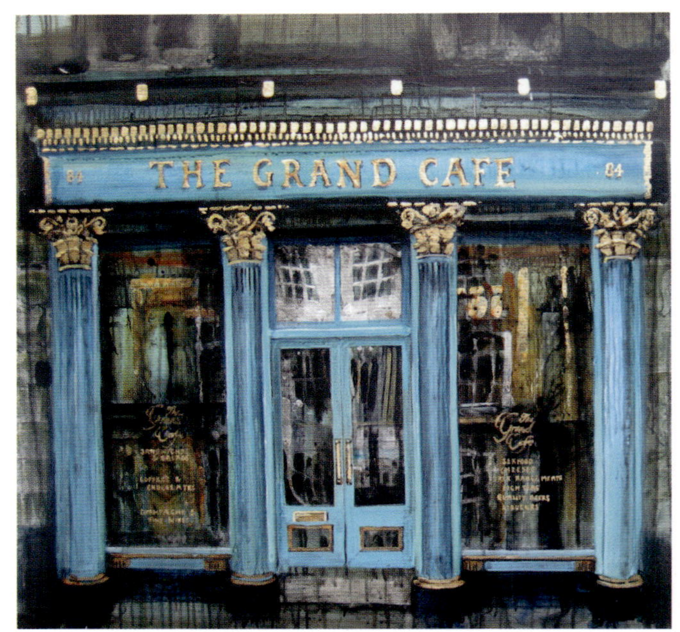

The Grand Café, Melissa Jane Sturgeon

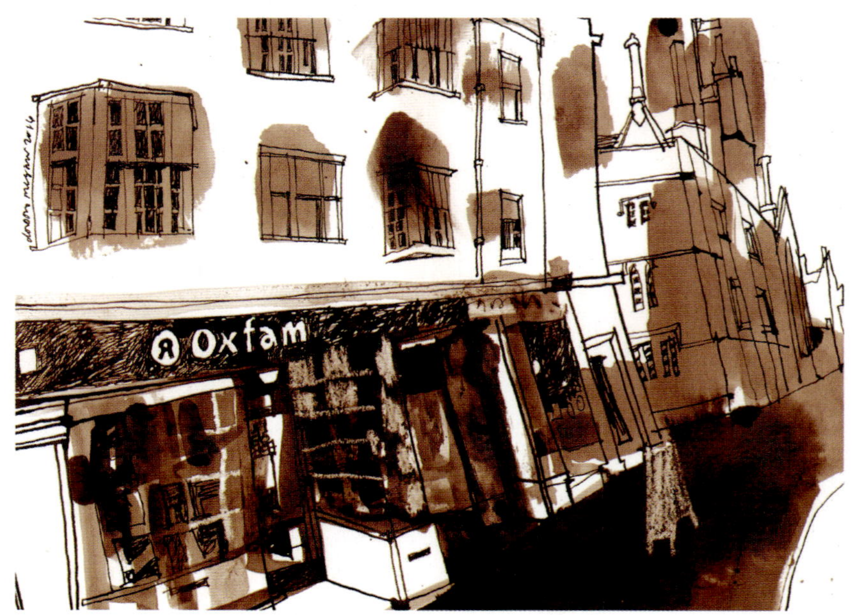

Oxfam Turl Street, Dorothy Megaw

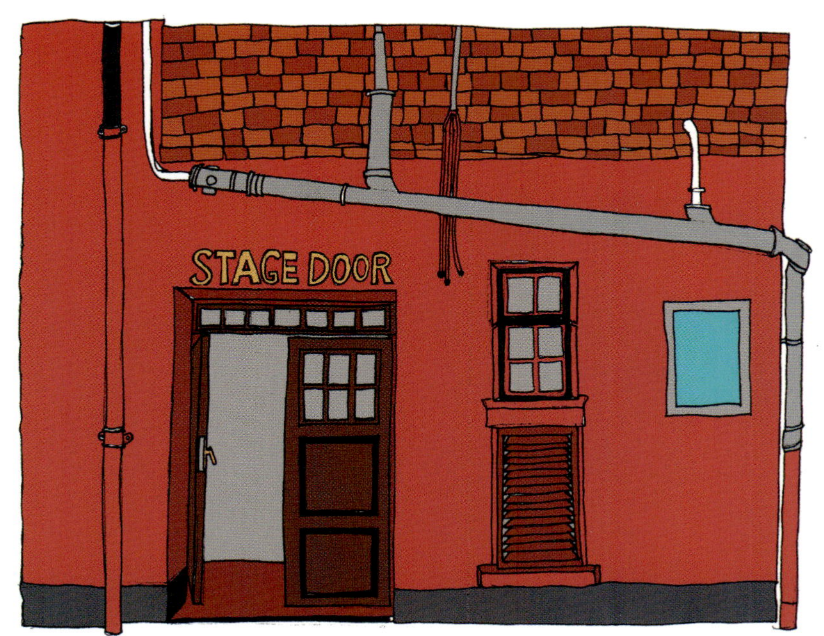

New Theatre Oxford, Joe Davis

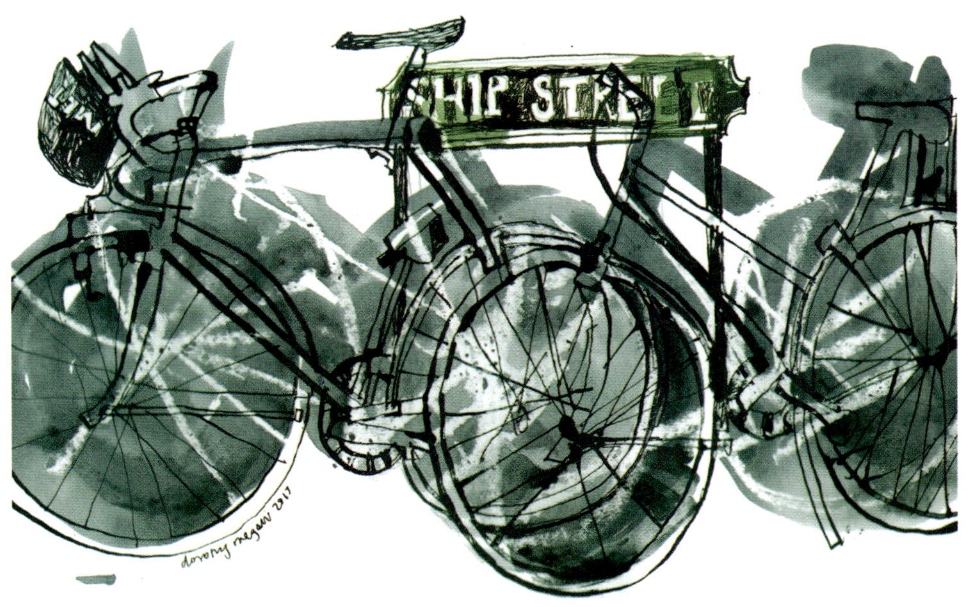

Ship Street, Dorothy Megaw

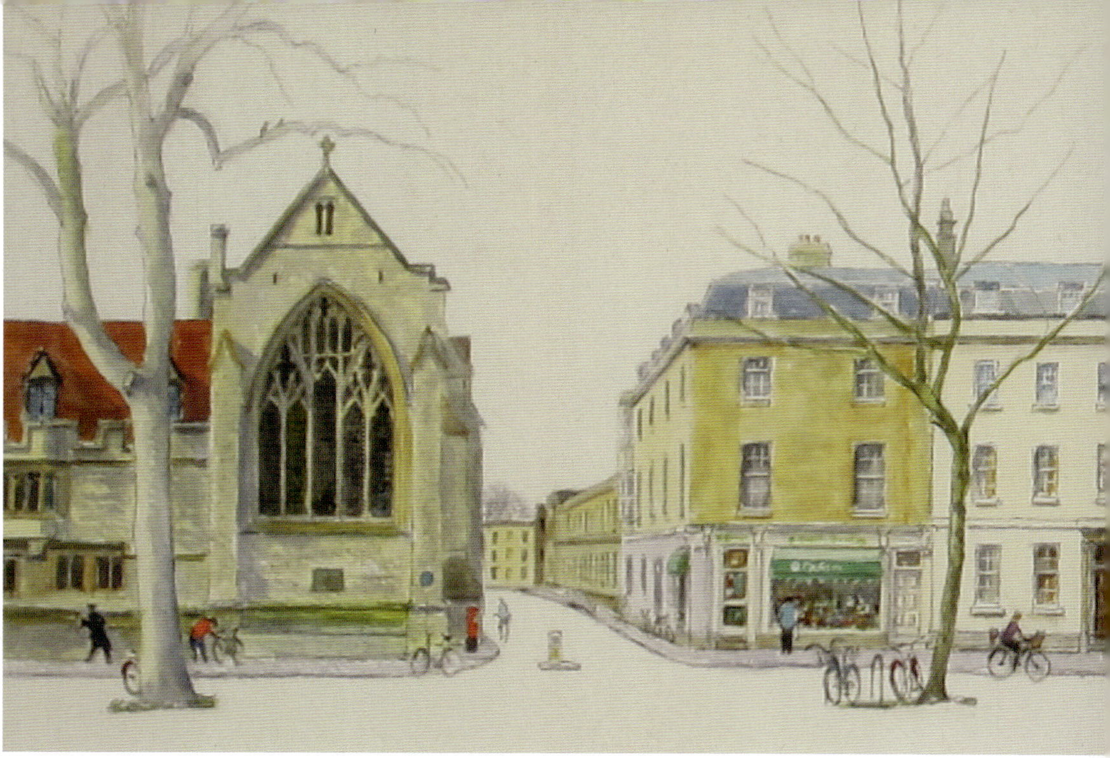

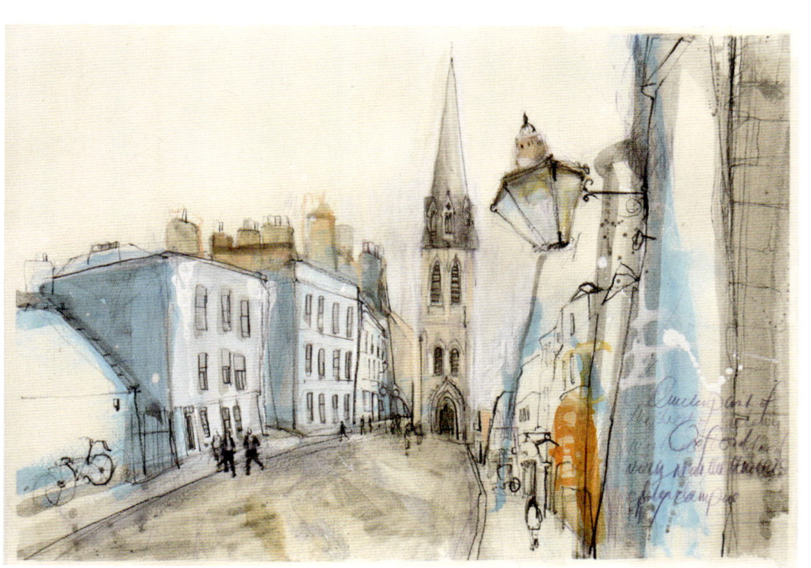

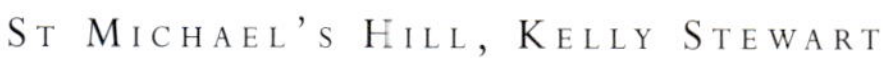

St Michael's Hill, Kelly Stewart

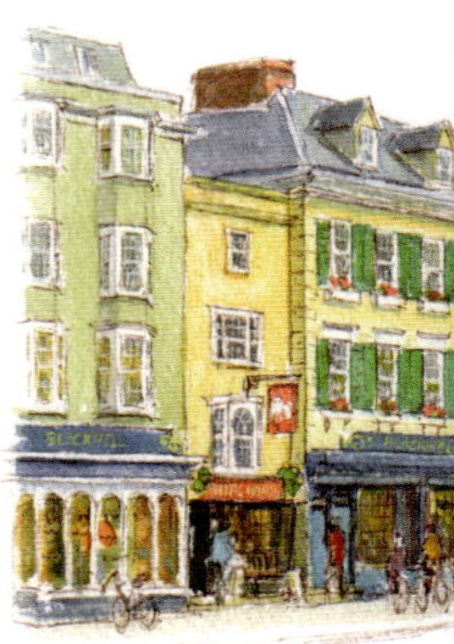

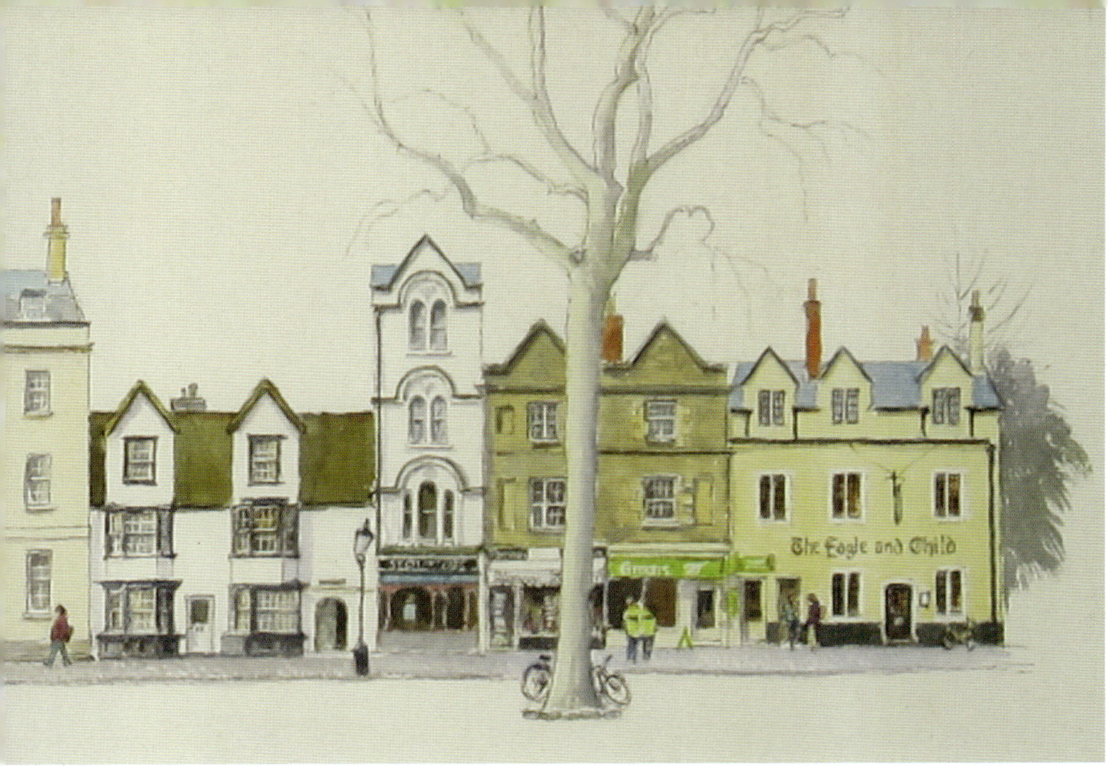

St Giles', Valerie Petts

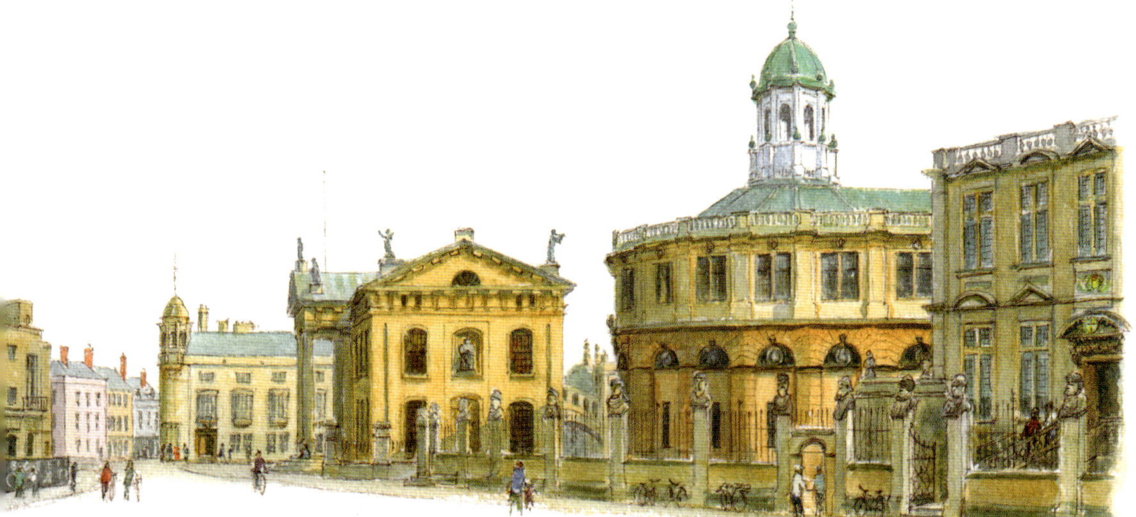

The Broad, Valerie Petts

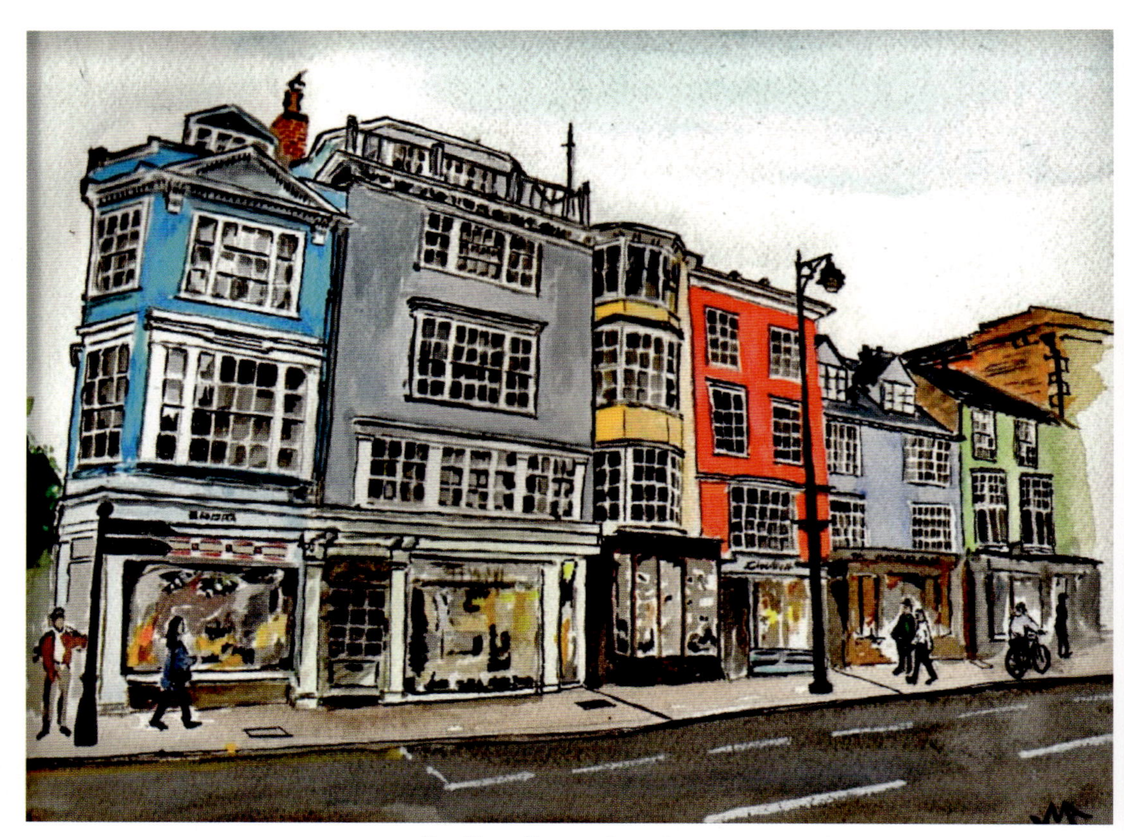

On The High, Jon Alsop

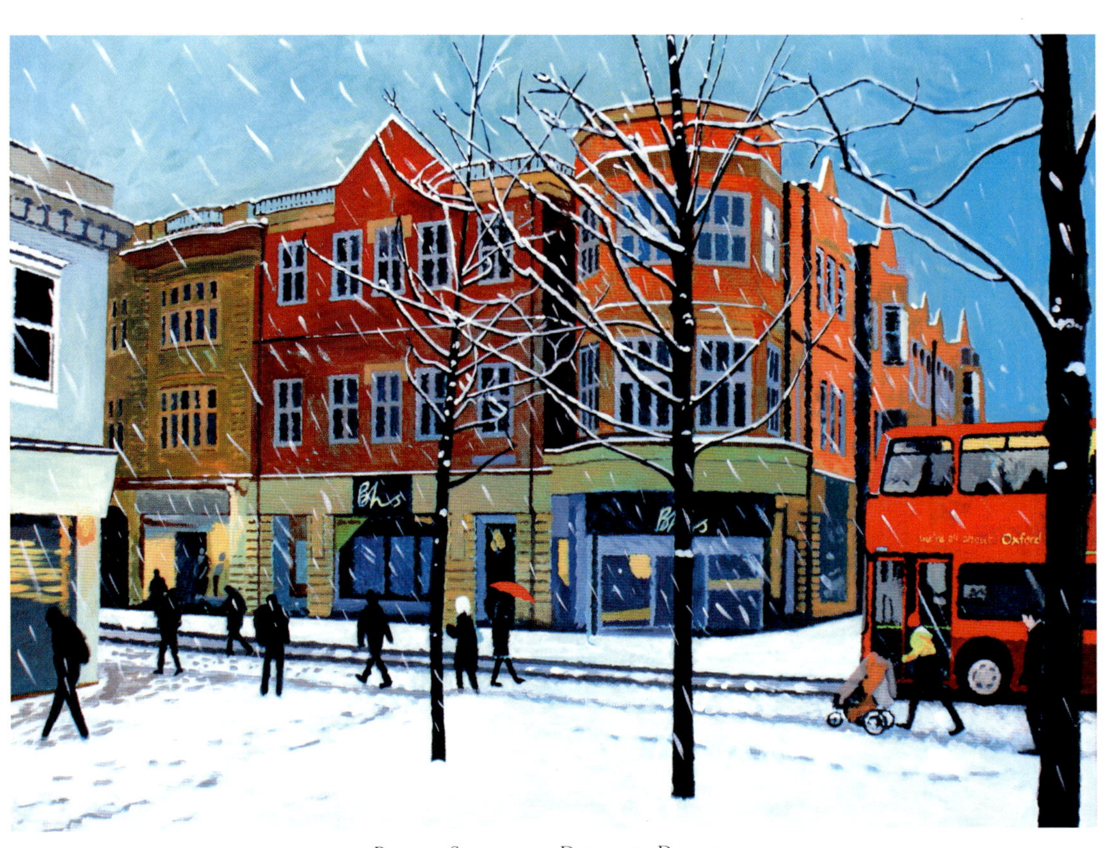

Bonn Square, Daniel Drury

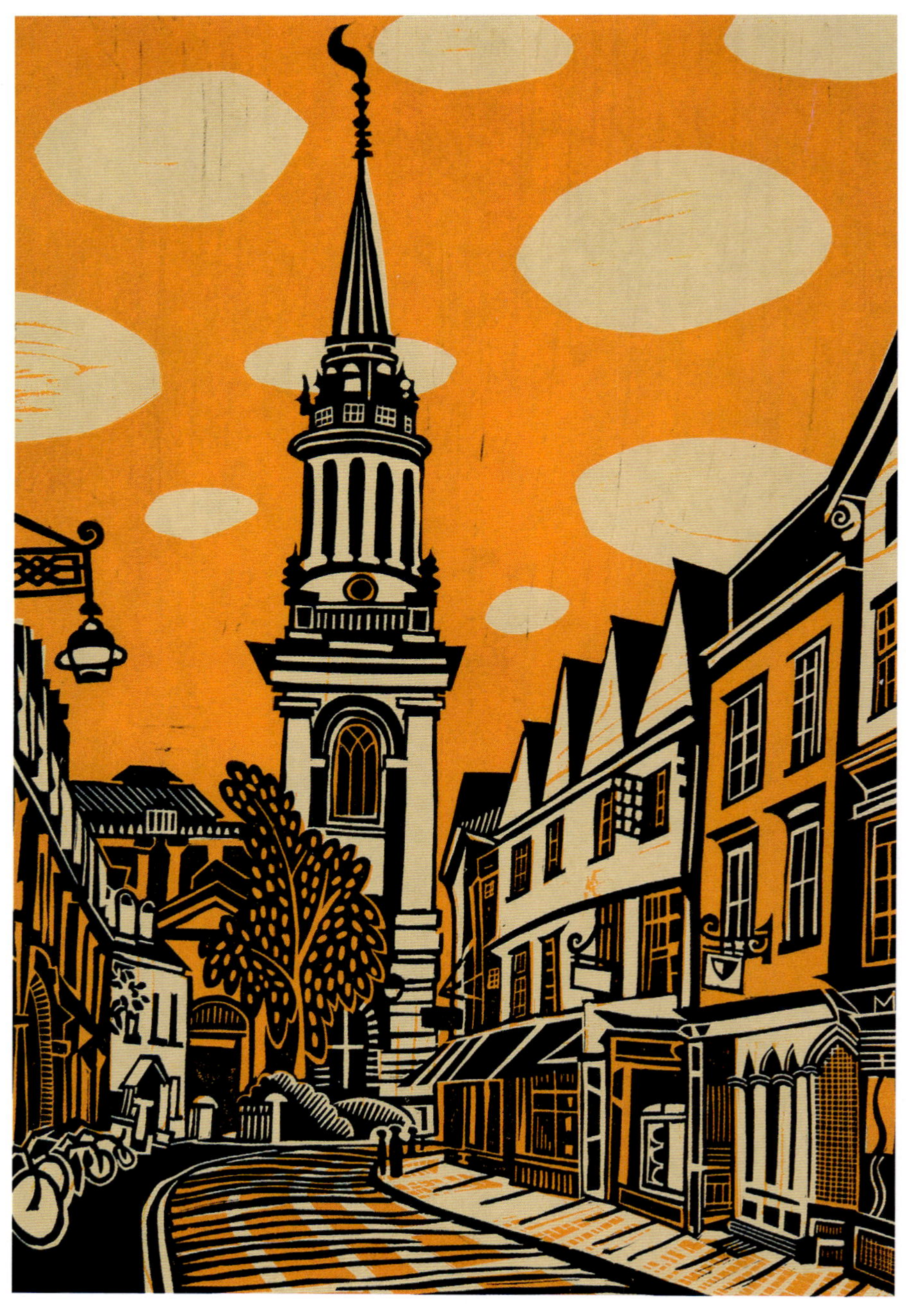

Lincoln College, Susan Wheeler

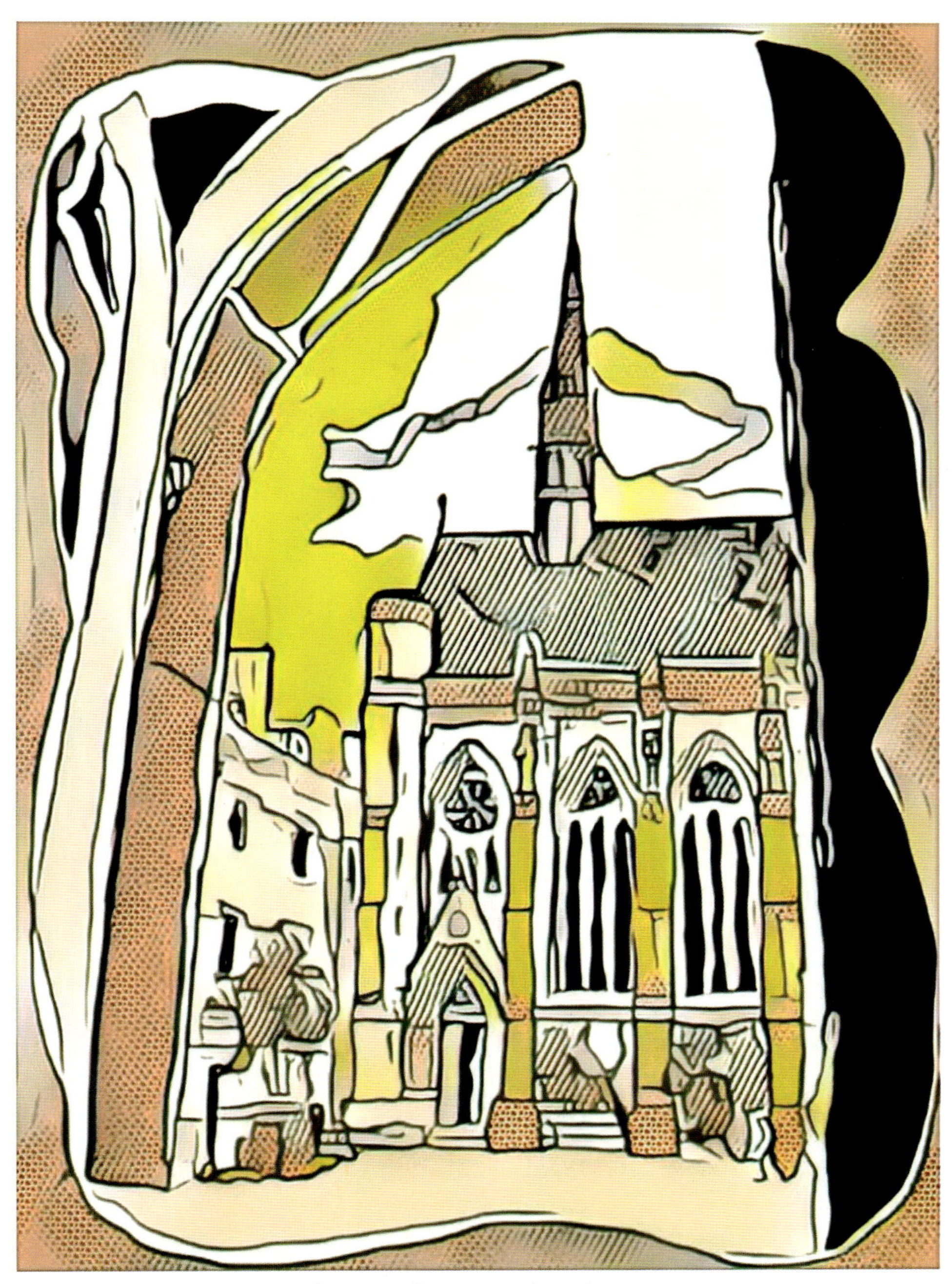

Exeter College, Jon Alsop

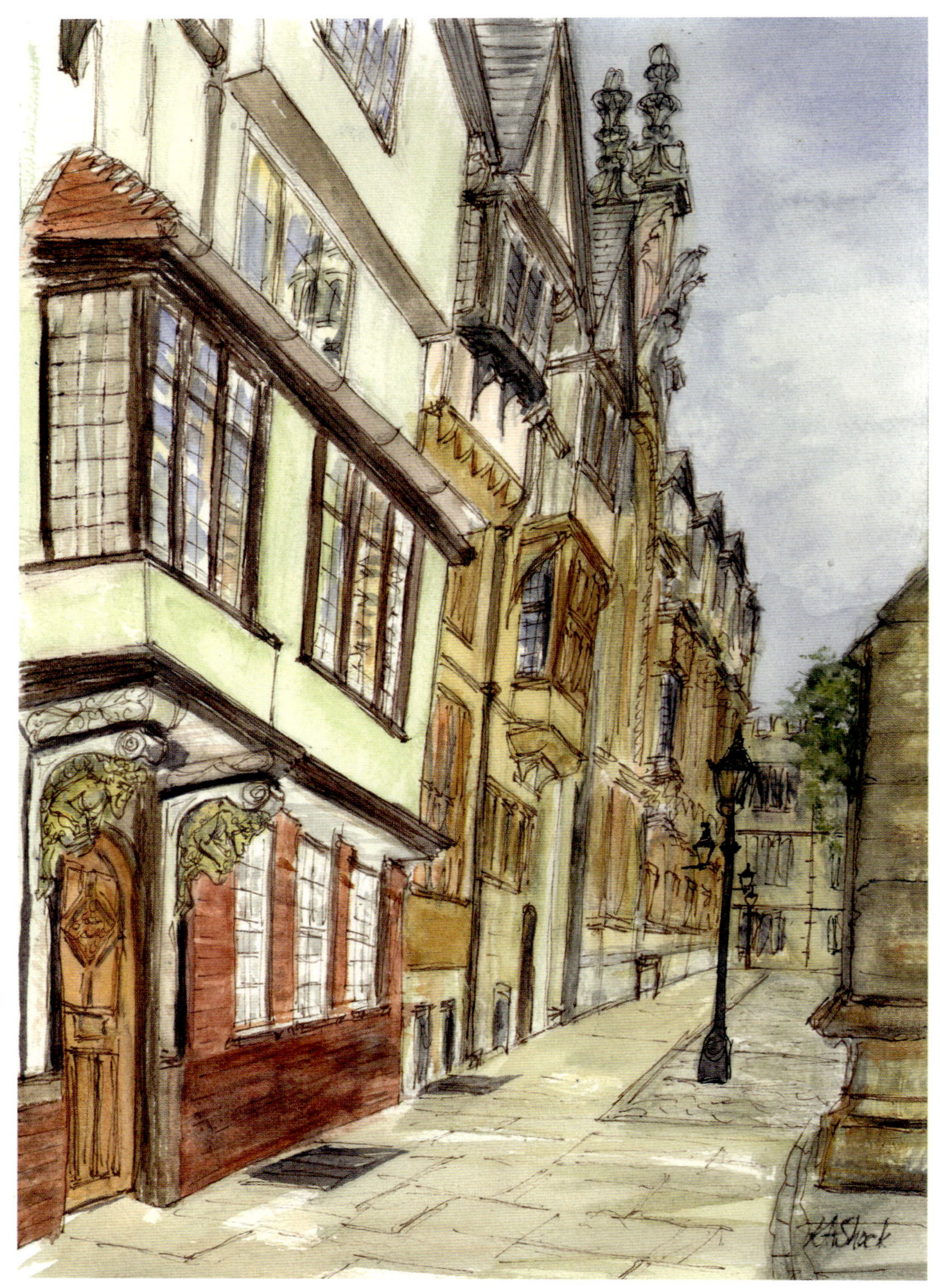

St Mary's Passage, Katherine Shock

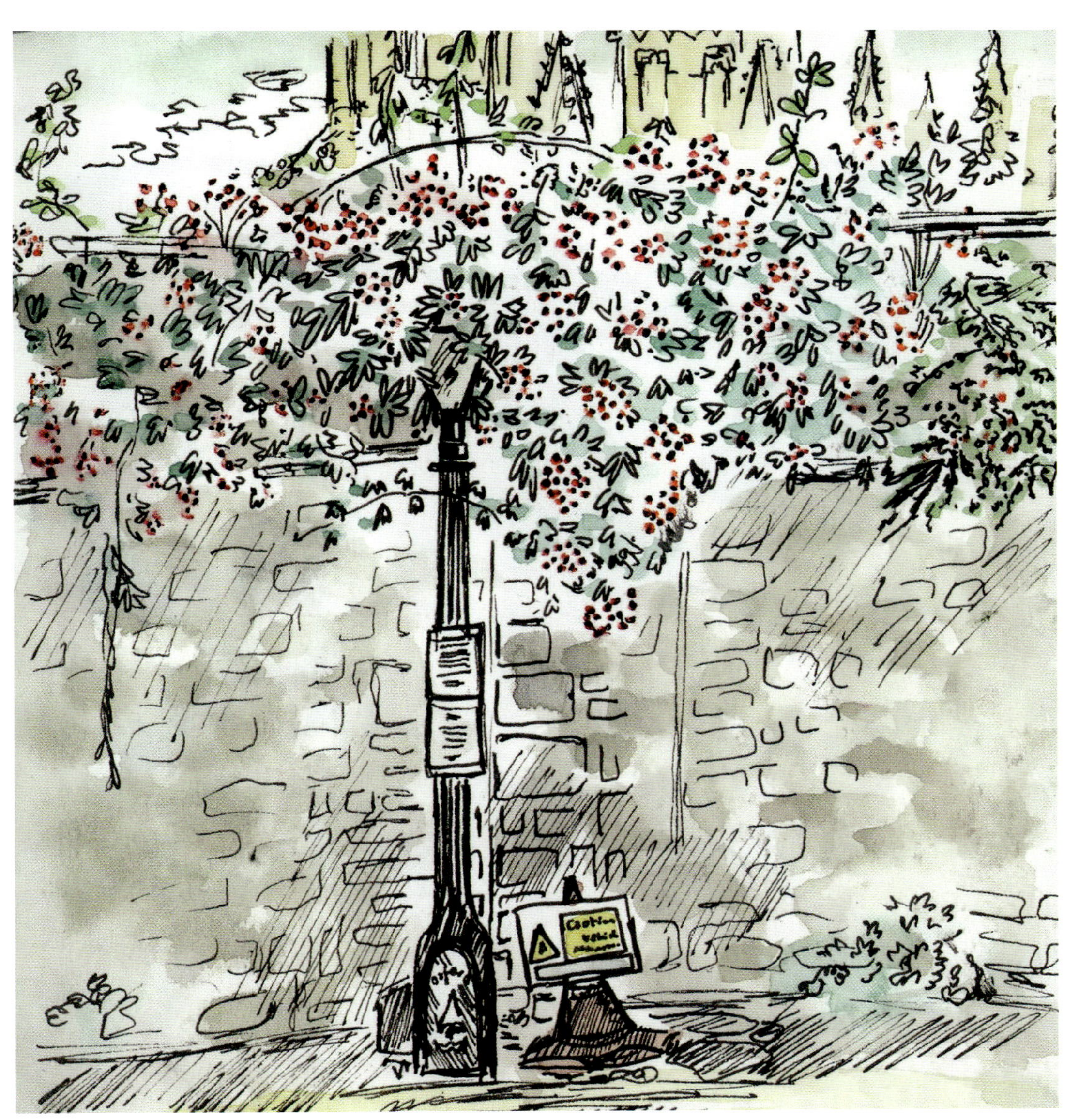

Lamppost in Queen's Lane, Imogen Foxell

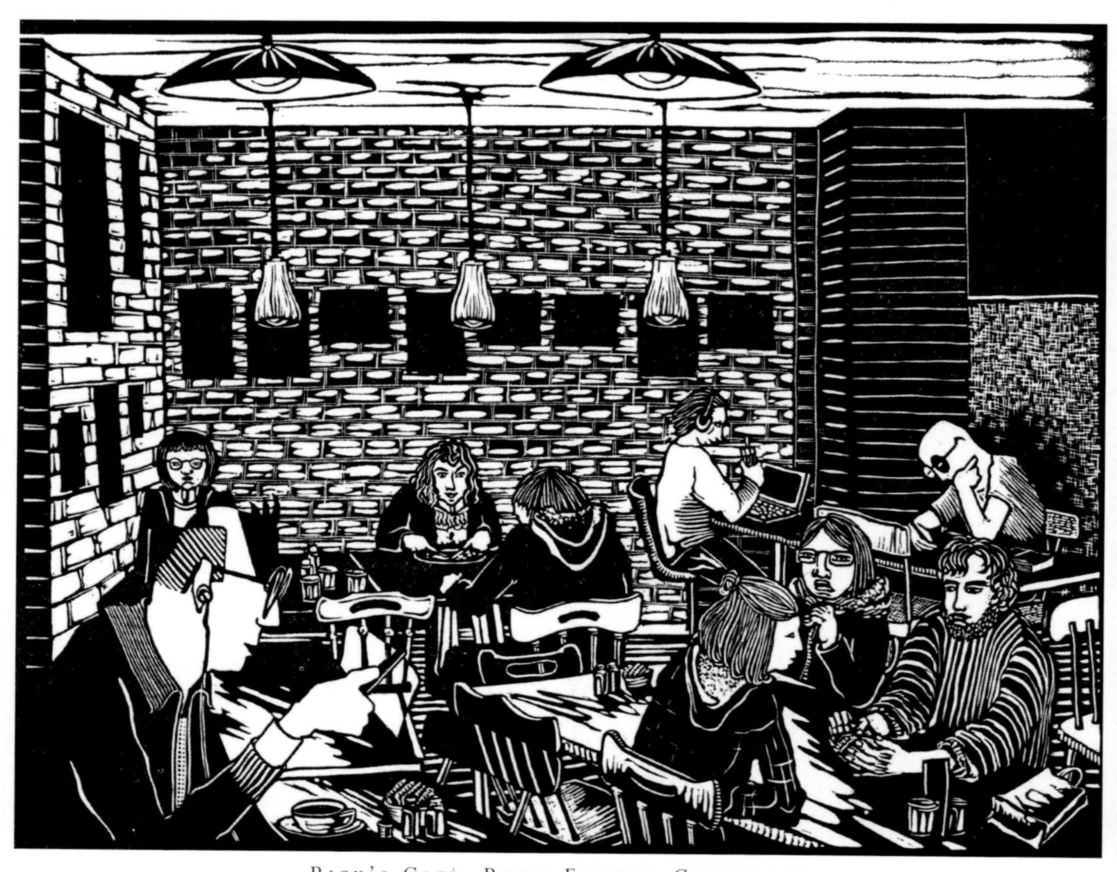

Rick's Café, Rosie Fairfax-Cholmeley

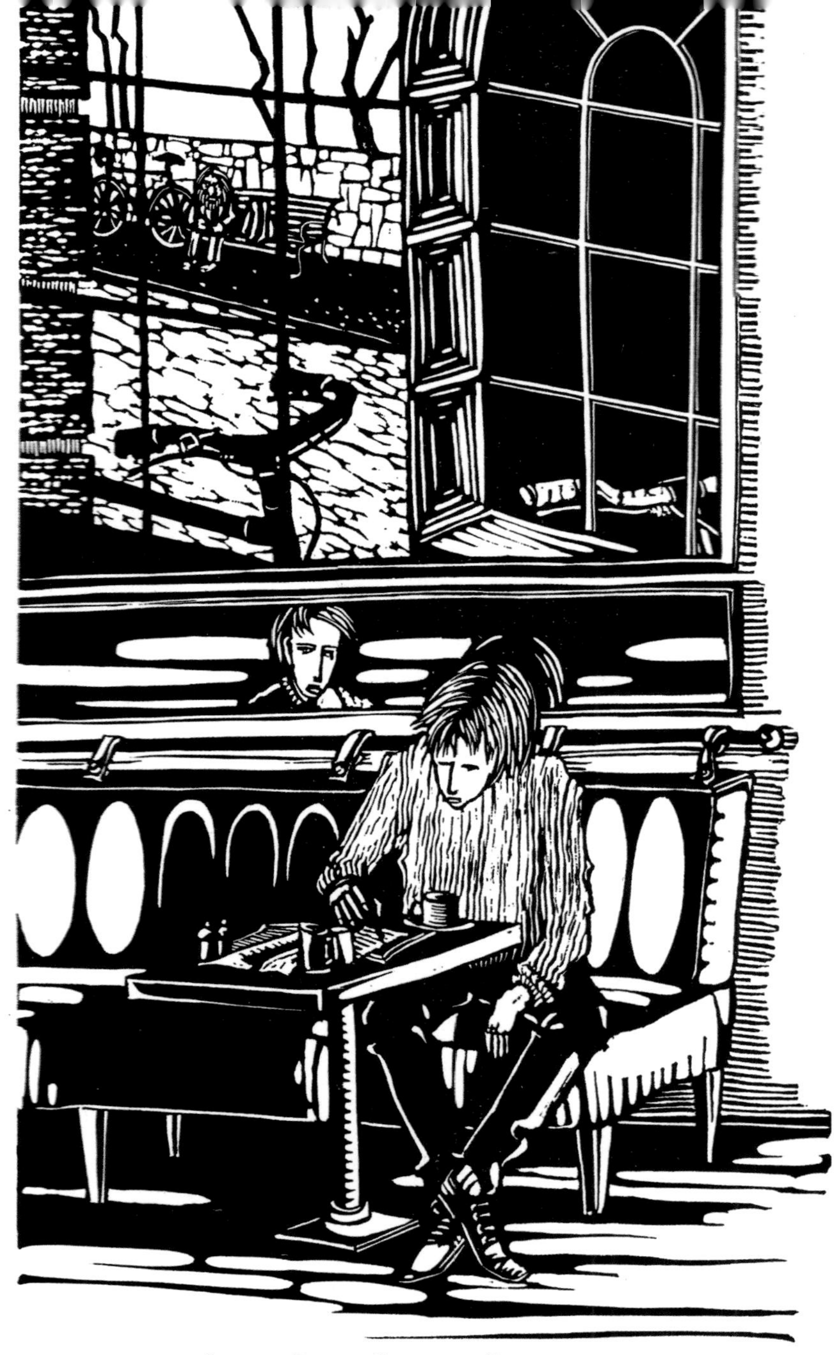

Quod, Rosie Fairfax-Cholmeley

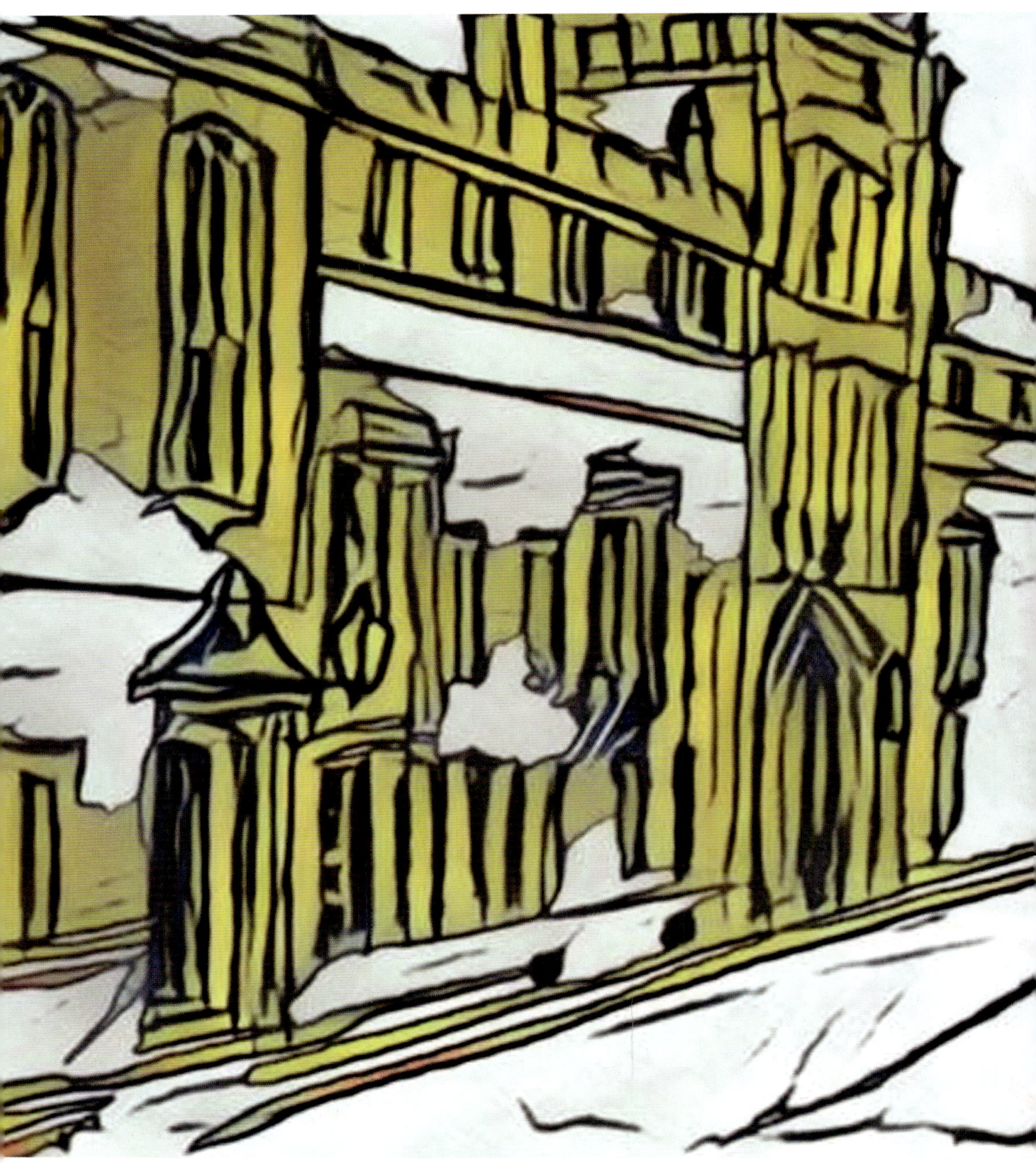

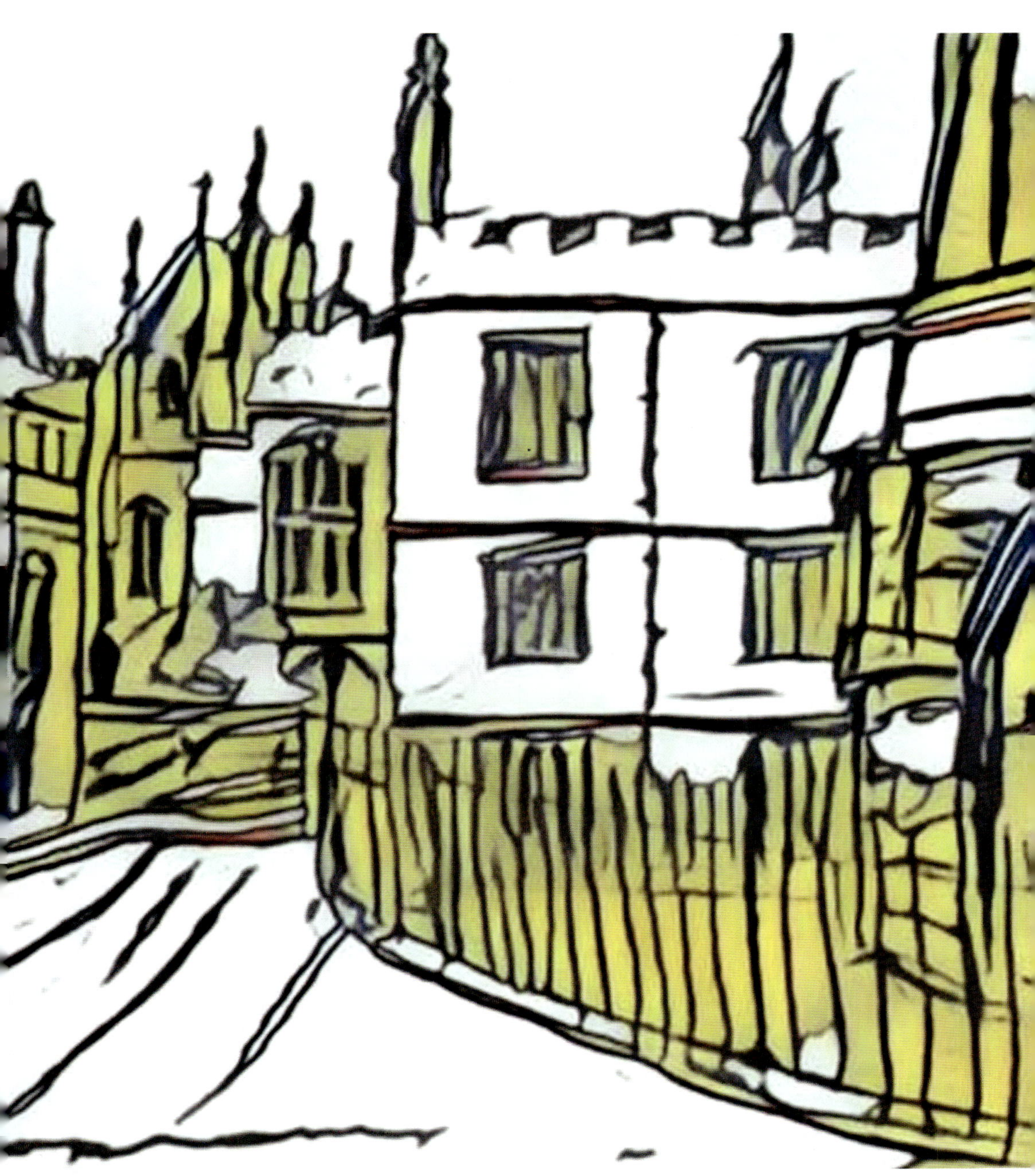

Brasenose College, Jon Alsop

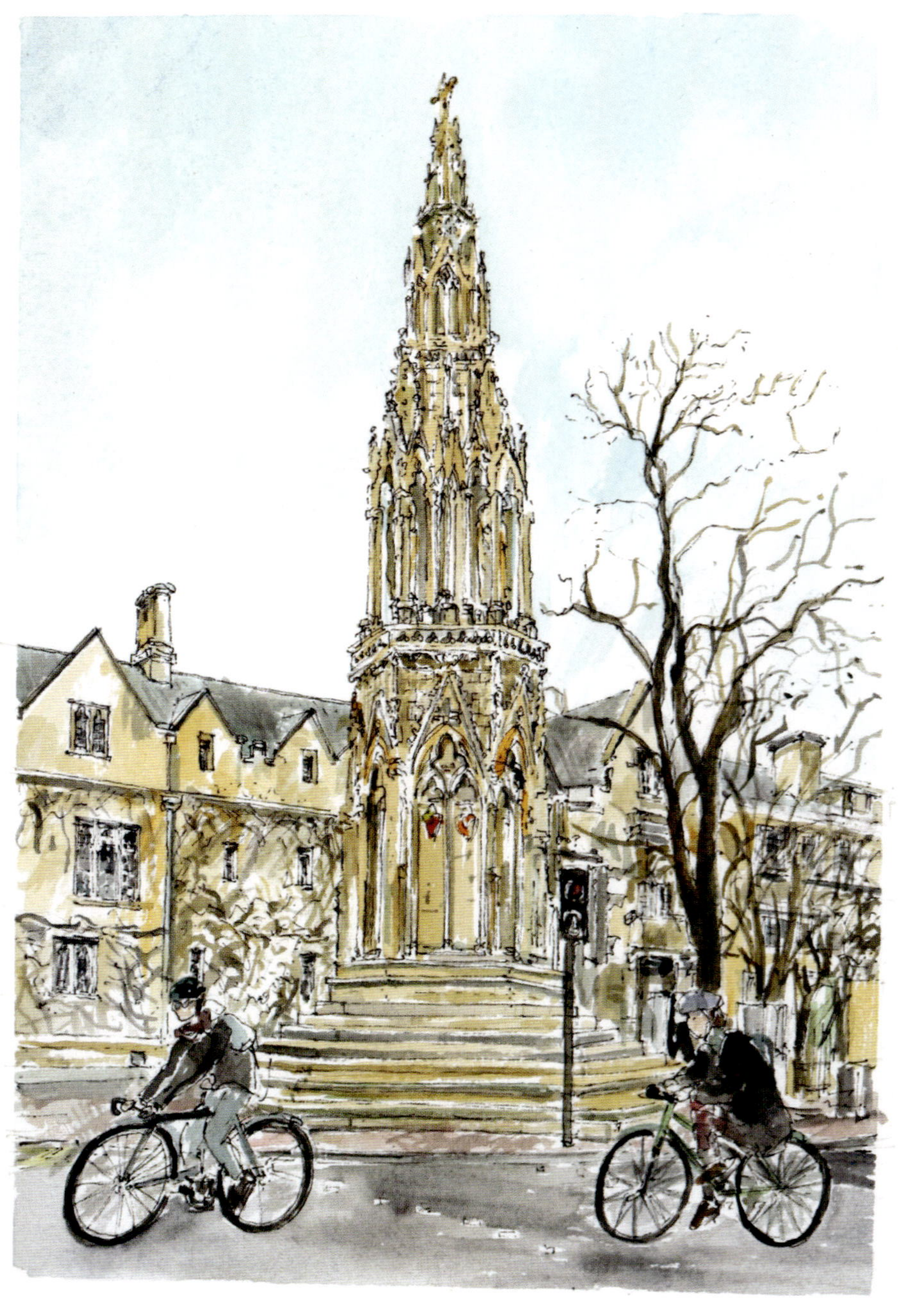

Martyrs' Memorial, Fiona Miller

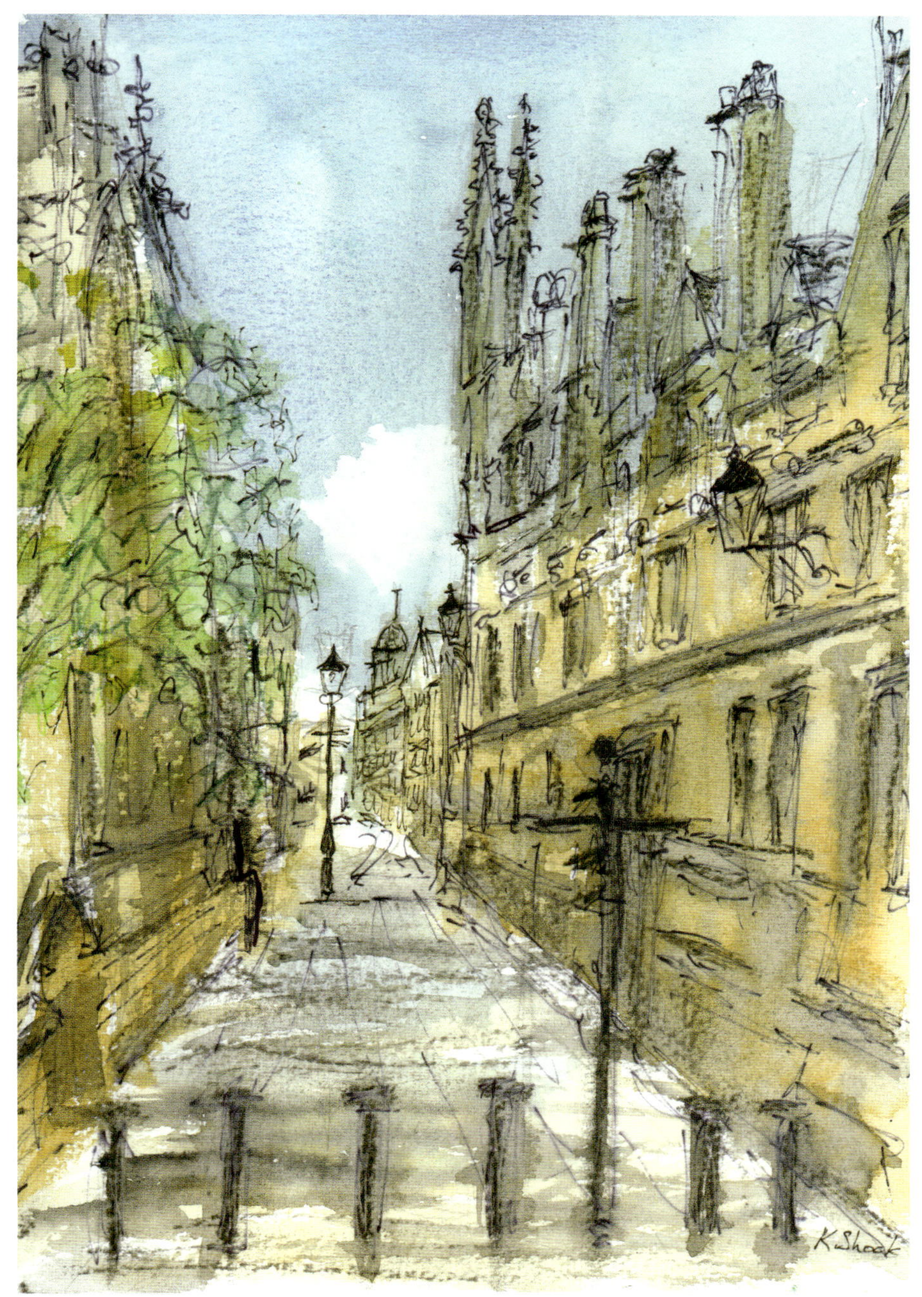

CATTE STREET, KATHERINE SHOCK

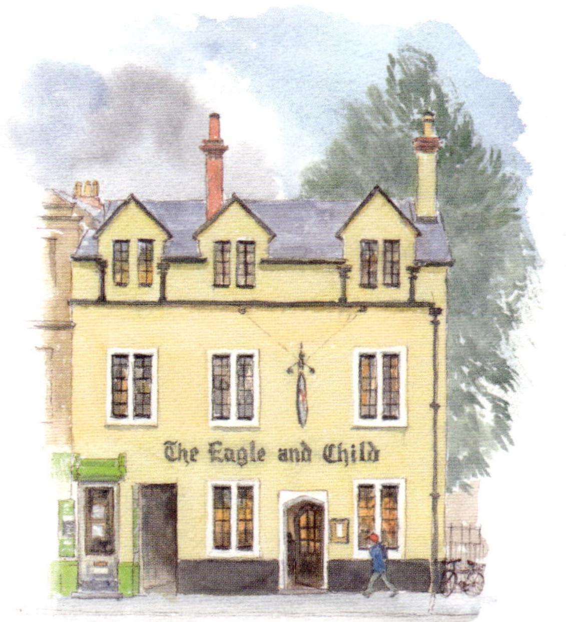

THE EAGLE AND CHILD, VALERIE PETTS

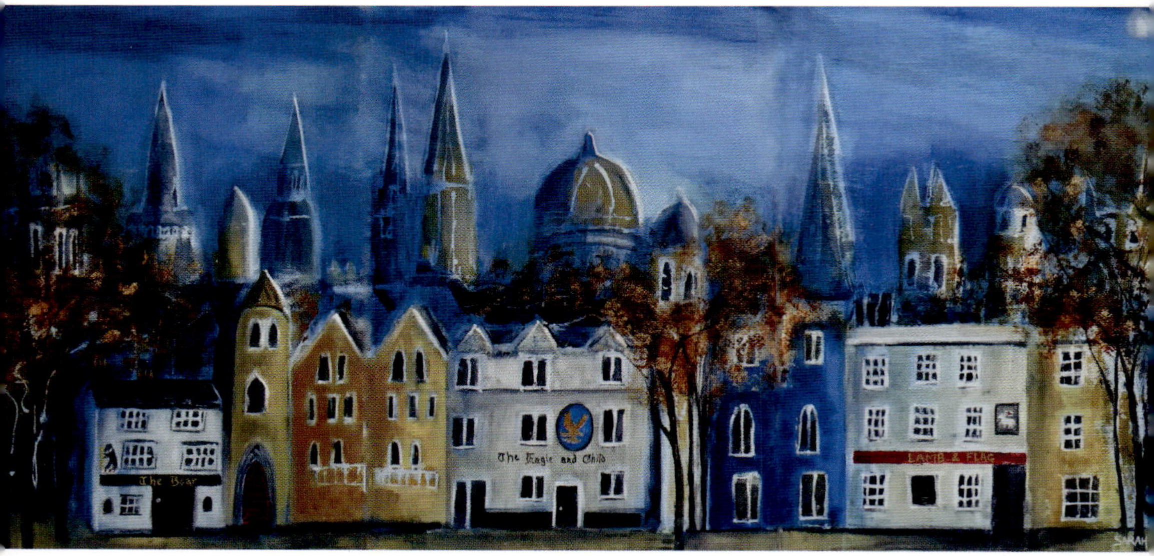

THE EAGLE AND CHILD, SARAH BOND

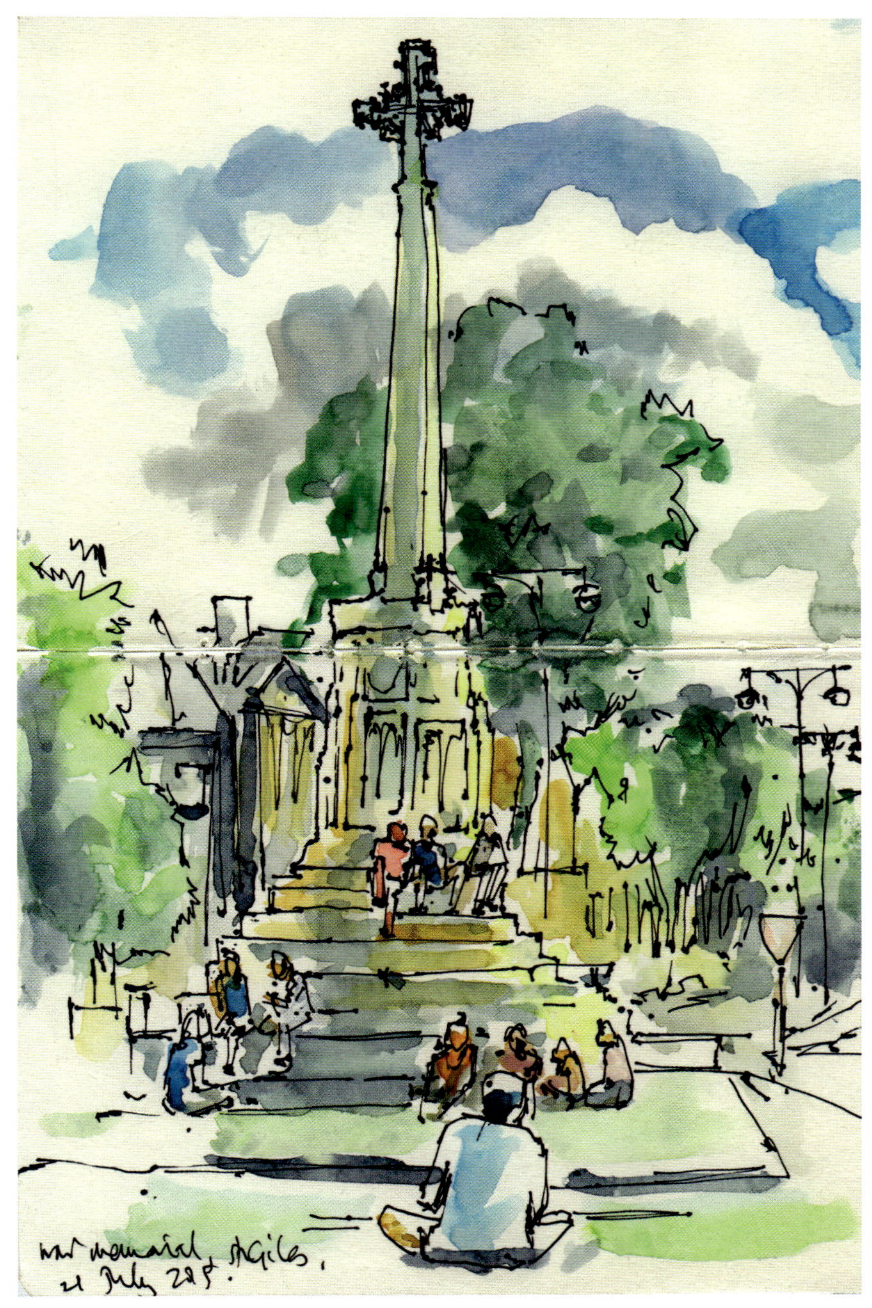

War Memorial, St Giles', Catriona Hopton

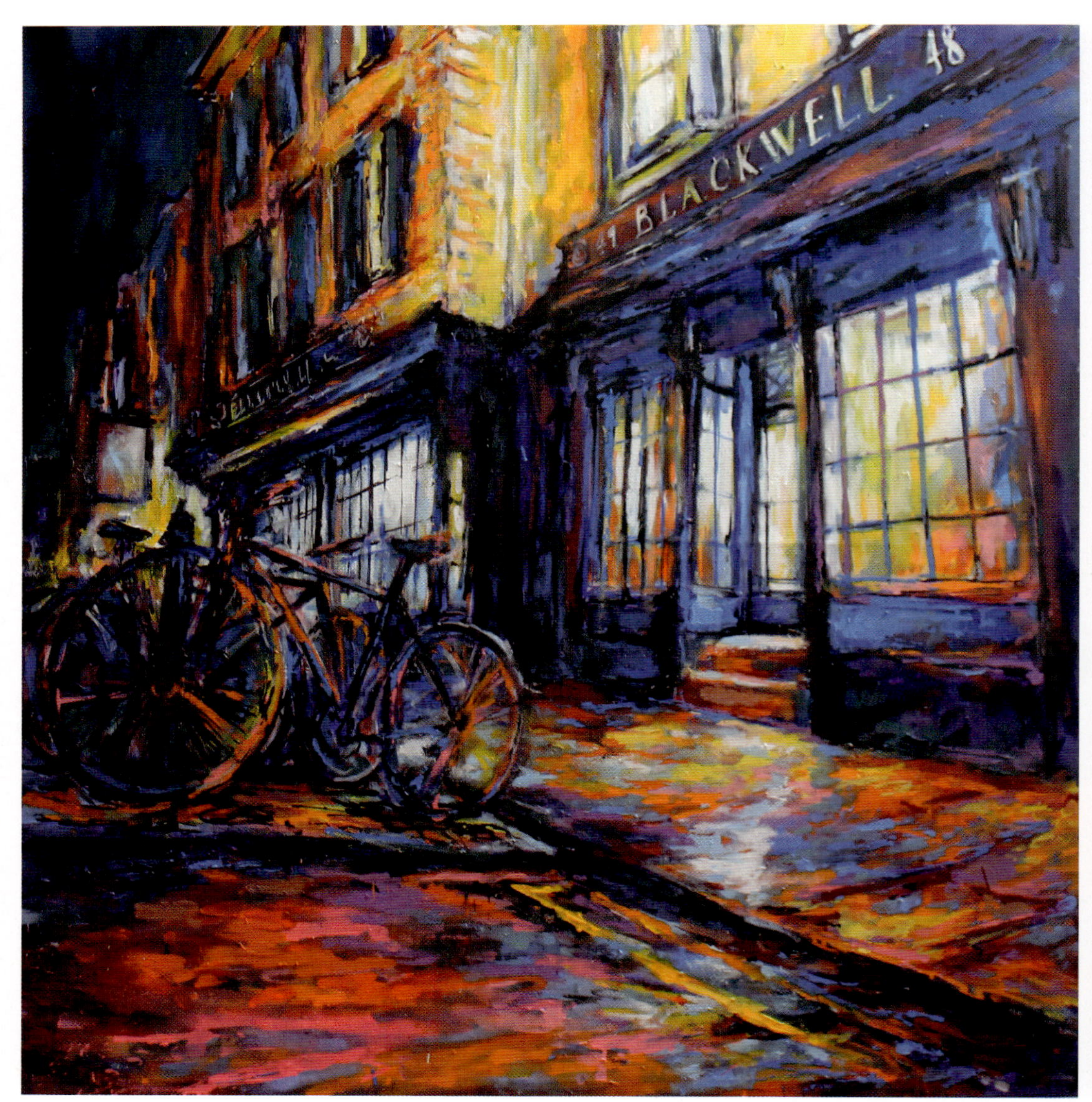

Blackwell's by Night, Andrew 'Mani' Manson

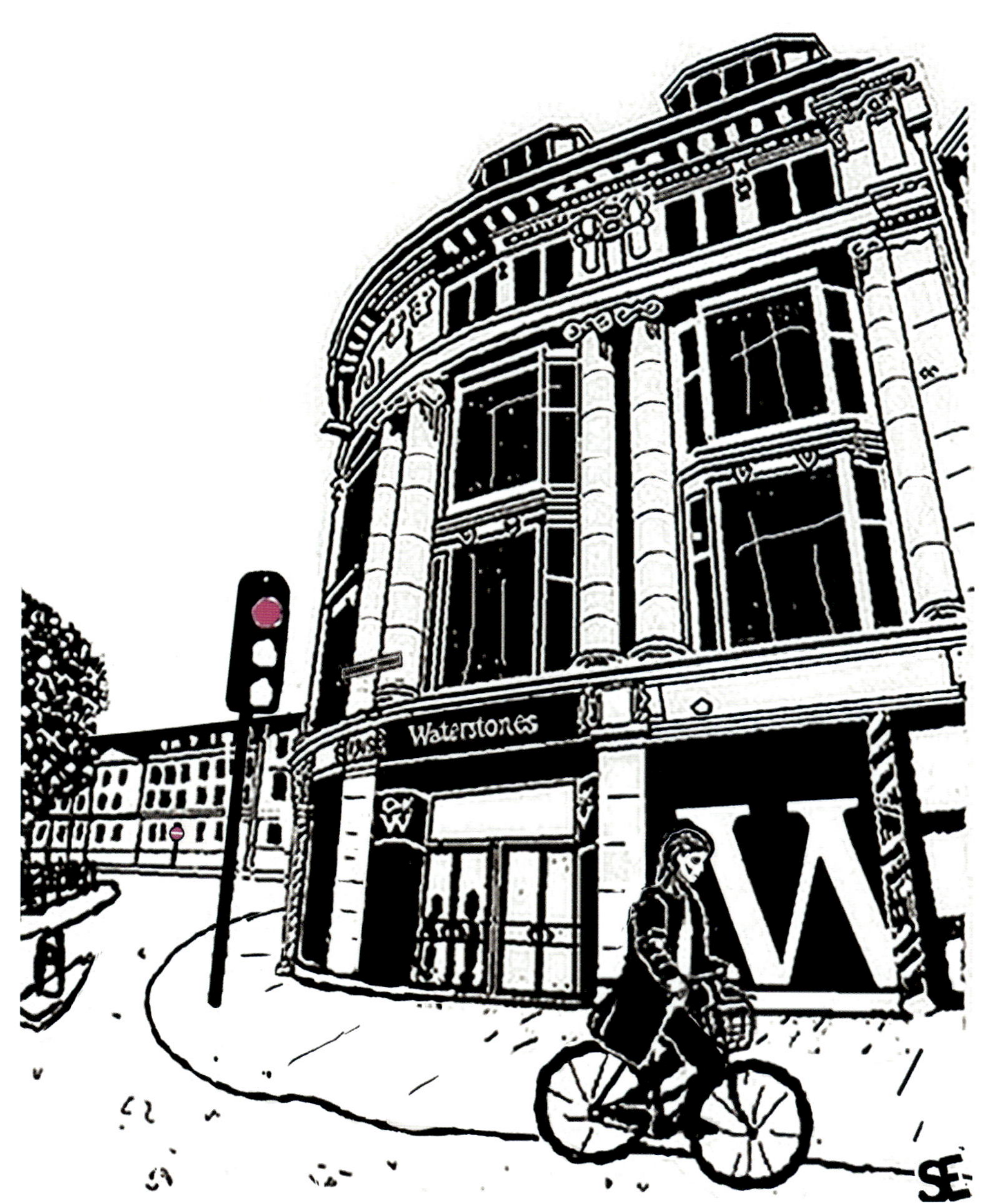

Waterstones, Simon East

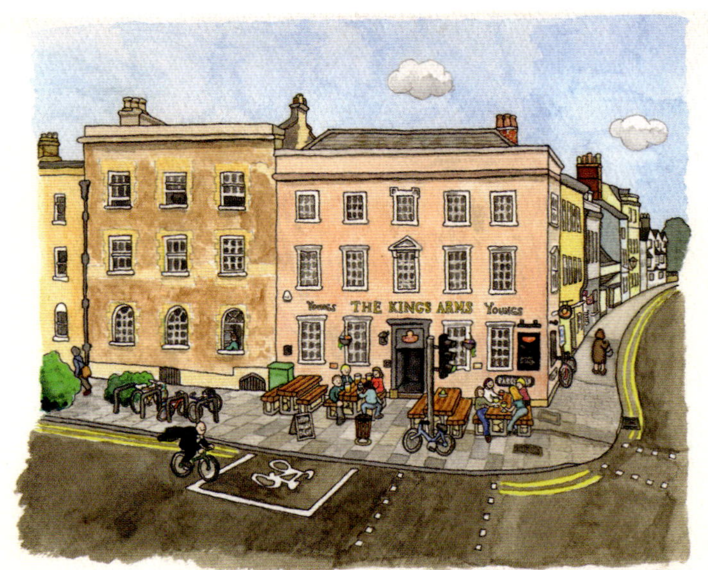

The Kings Arms, Tim Kirtley

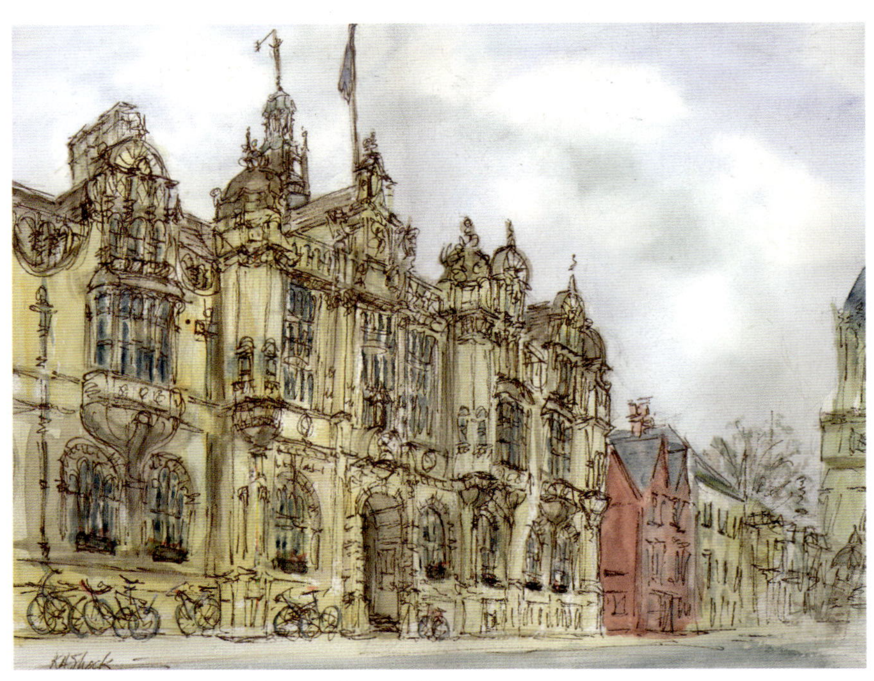

Town Hall, Katherine Shock

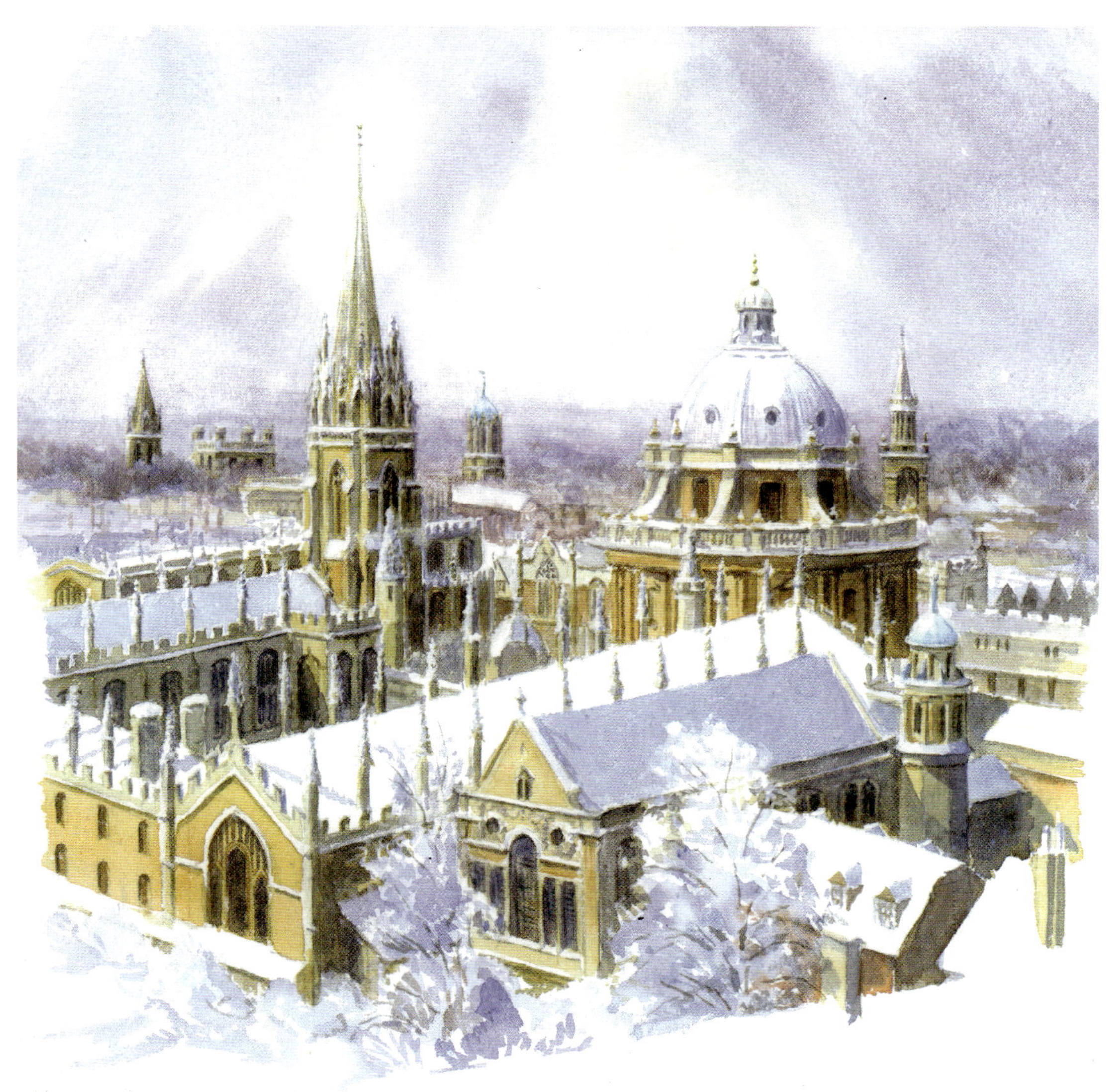

Winter in Oxford, Valerie Petts

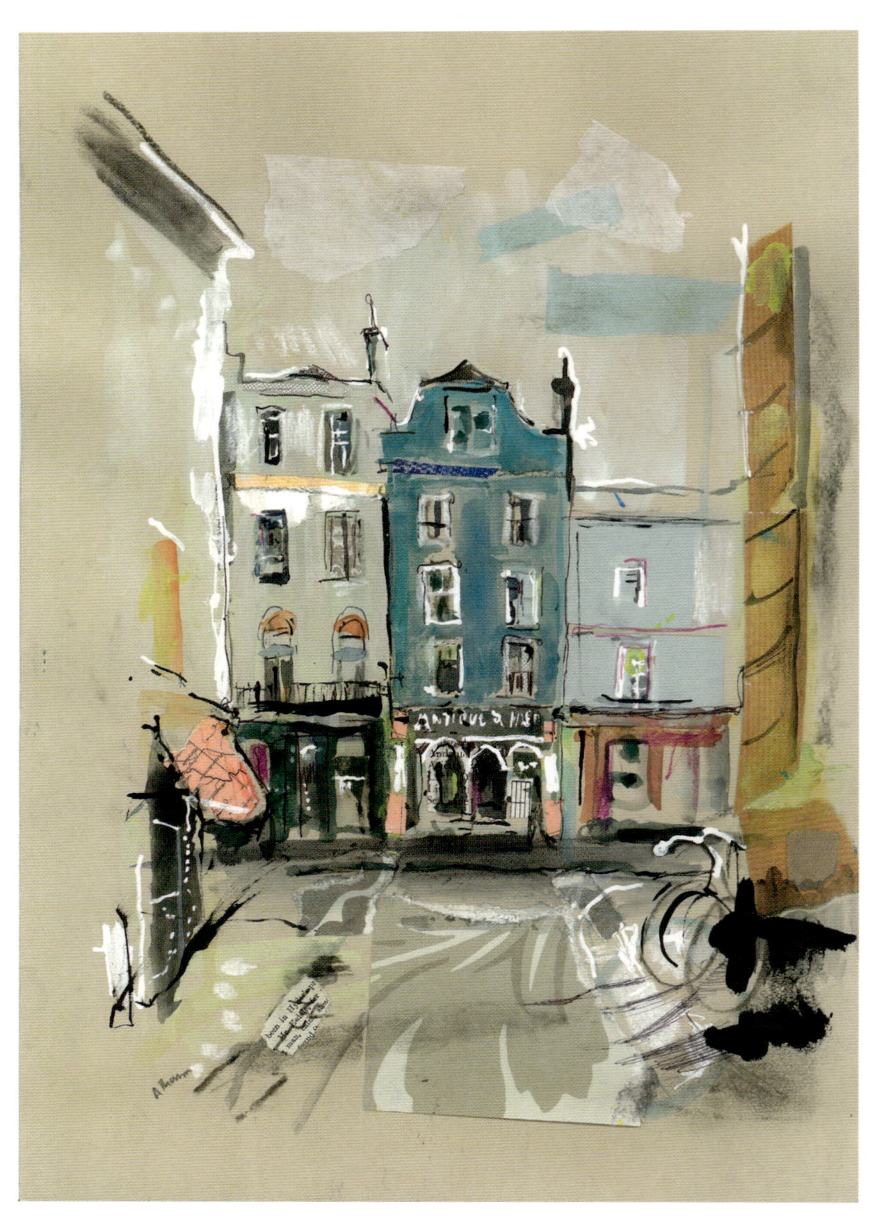

Antiques on High Street, Alice Thomson

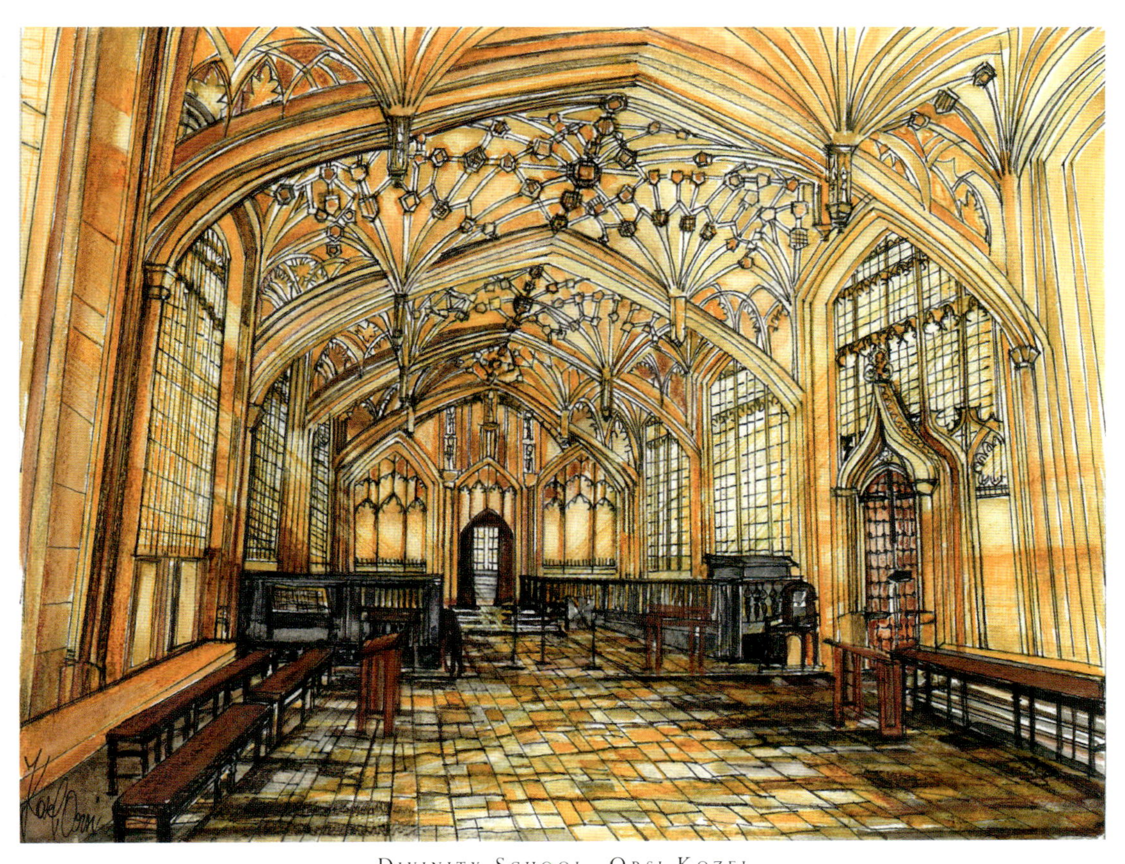

Divinity School, Orsi Kozel

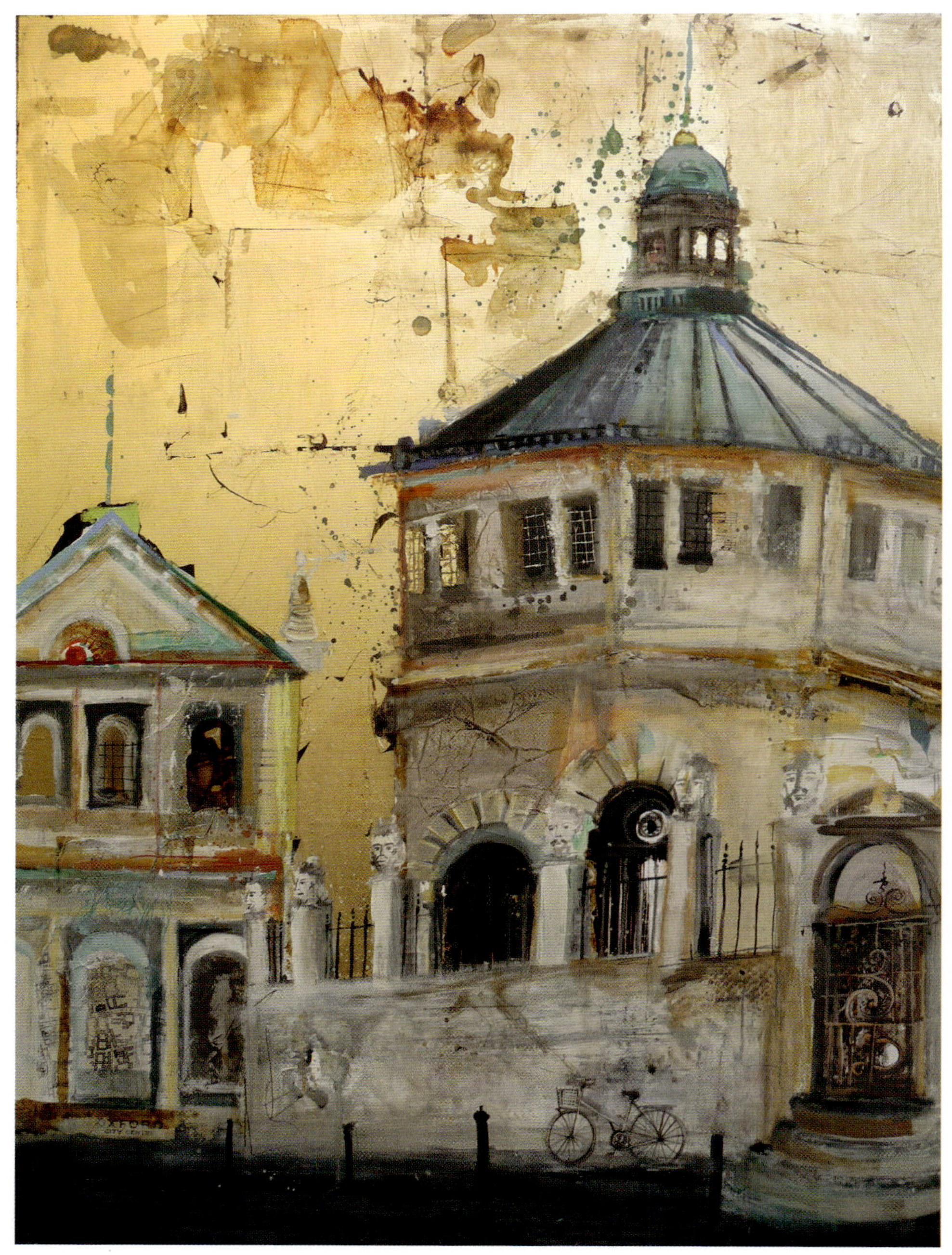

Broad street, Emmie van Biervliet

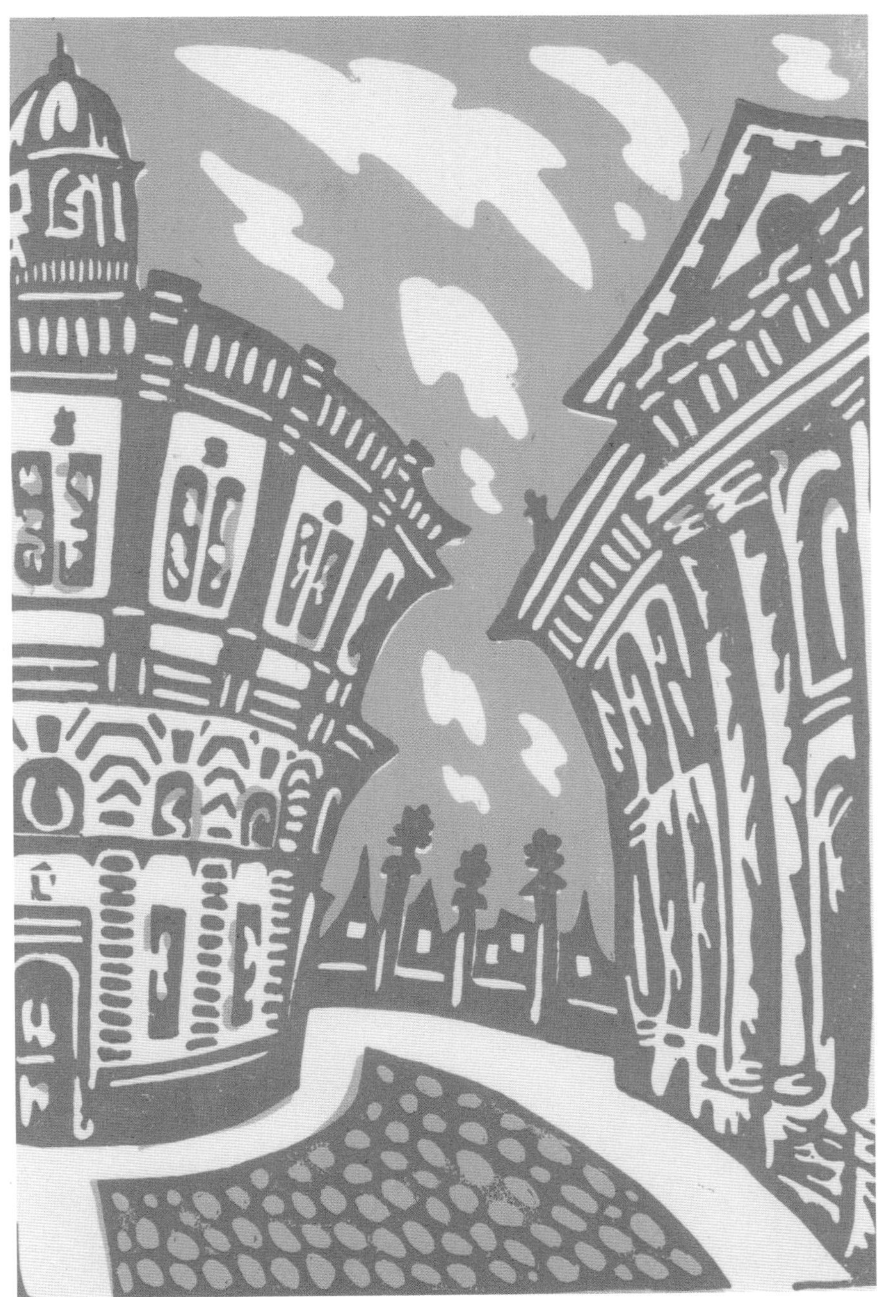

The Sheldonian Theatre, Jan Ritchie

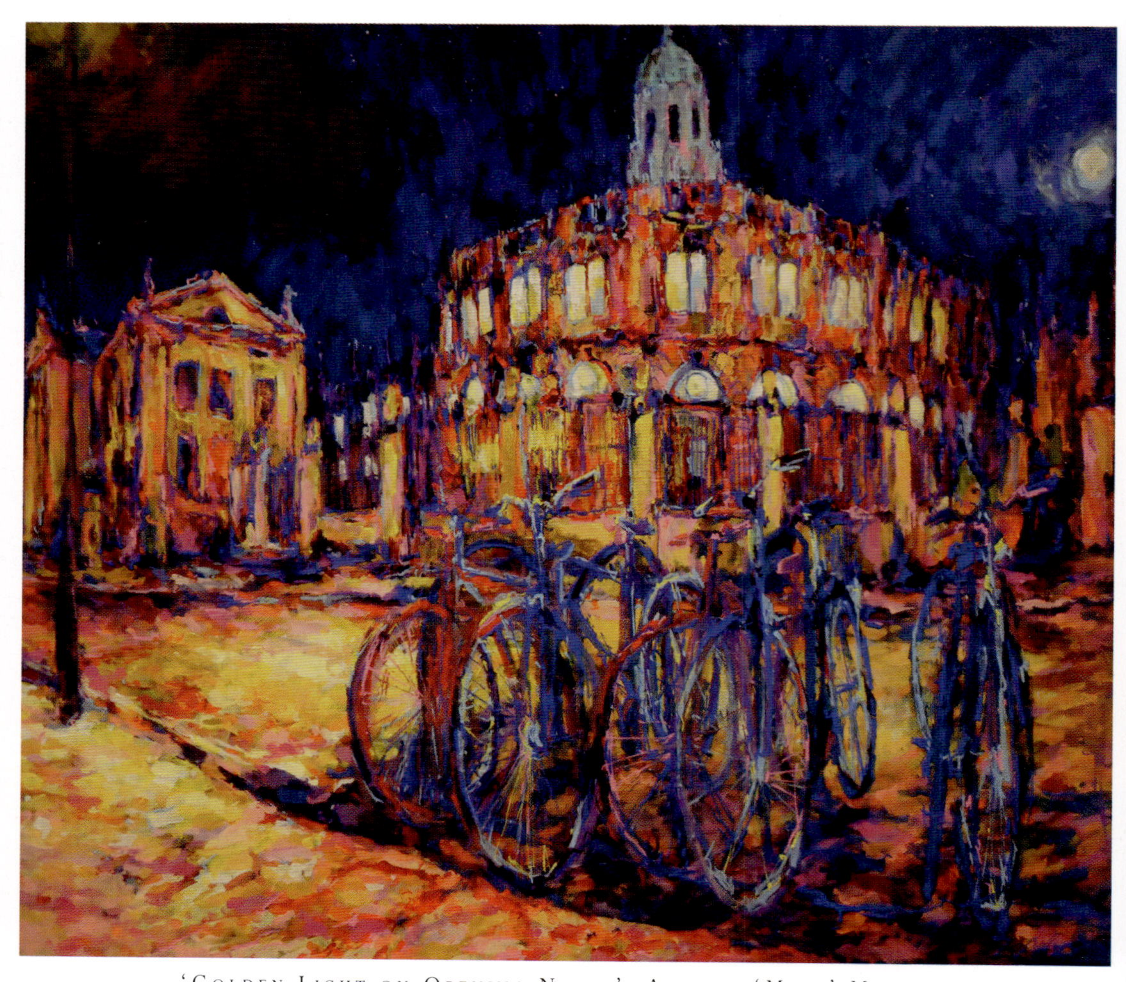

'Golden Light on Opening Night', Andrew 'Mani' Manson

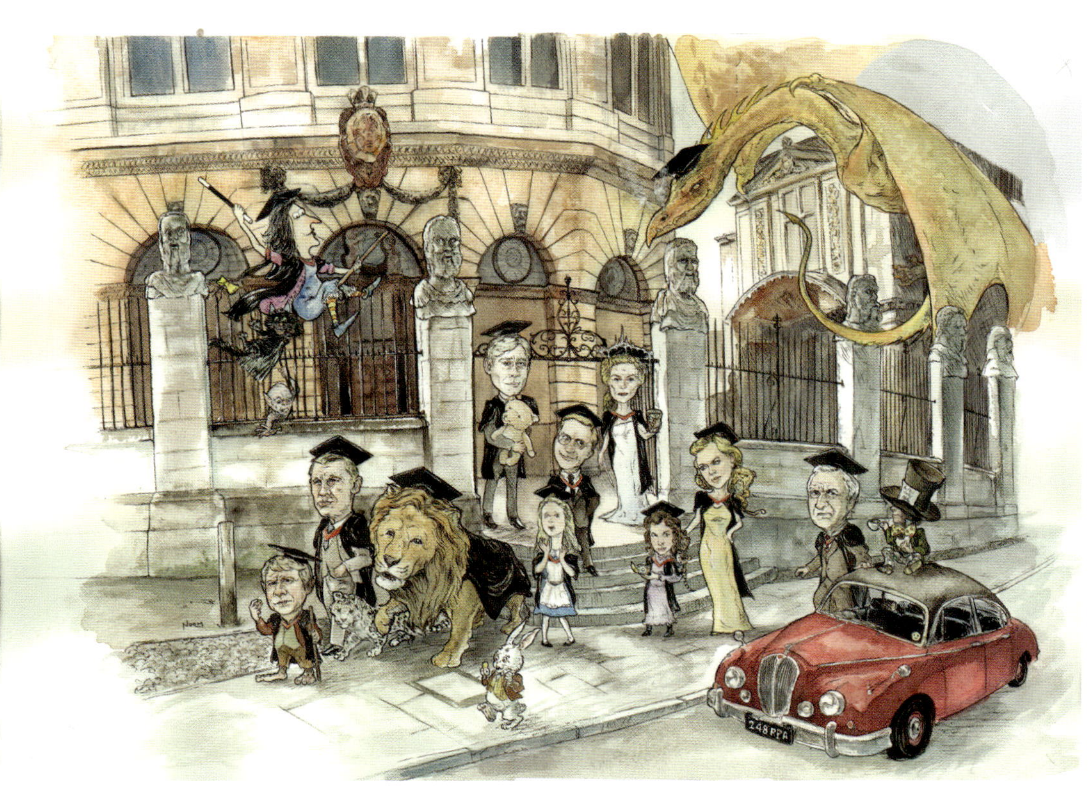

THE SHELDONIAN THEATRE, NORM CHUNG

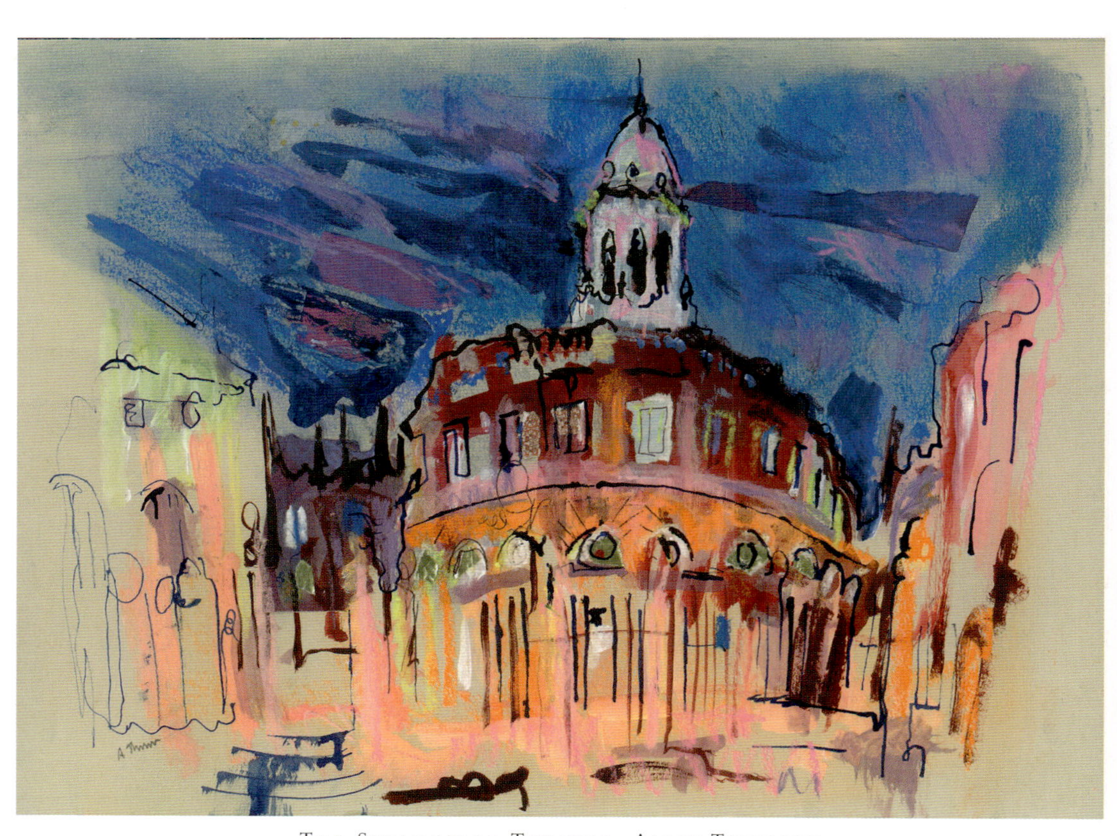

The Sheldonian Theatre, Alice Thomson

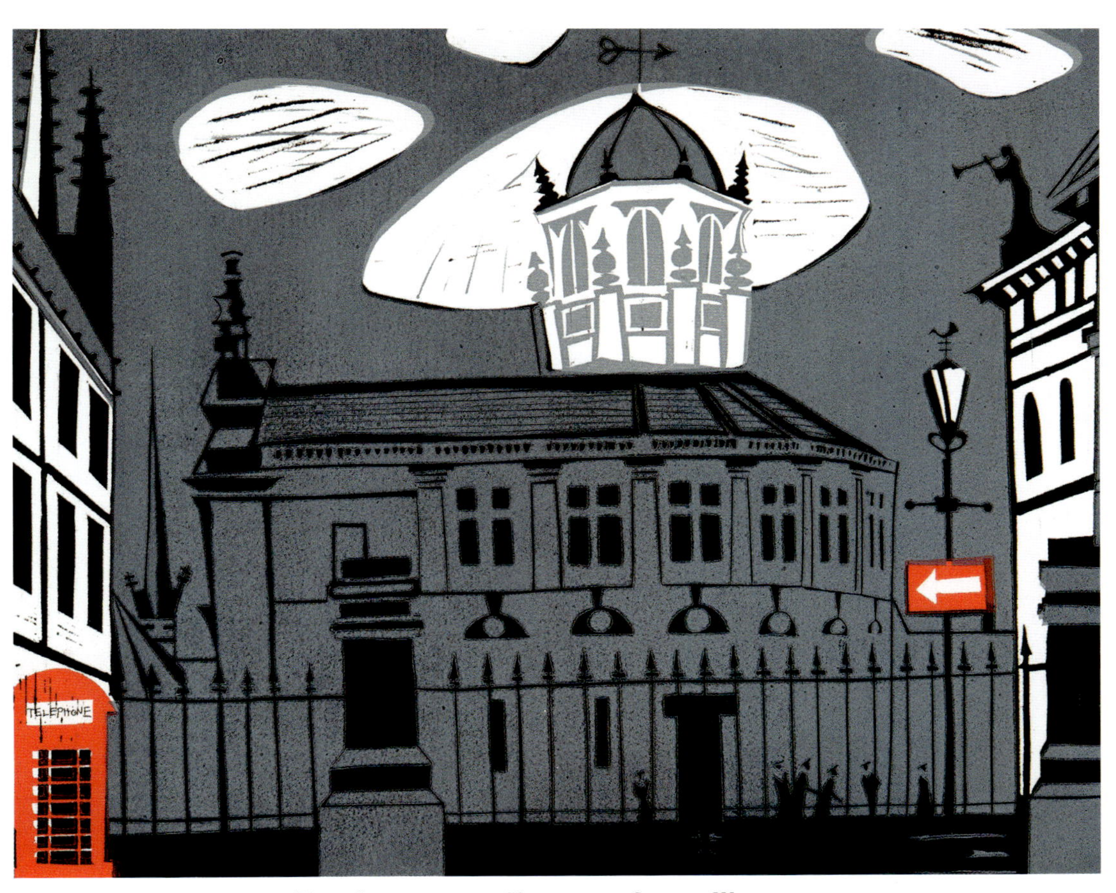

The Sheldonian Theatre, Susan Wheeler

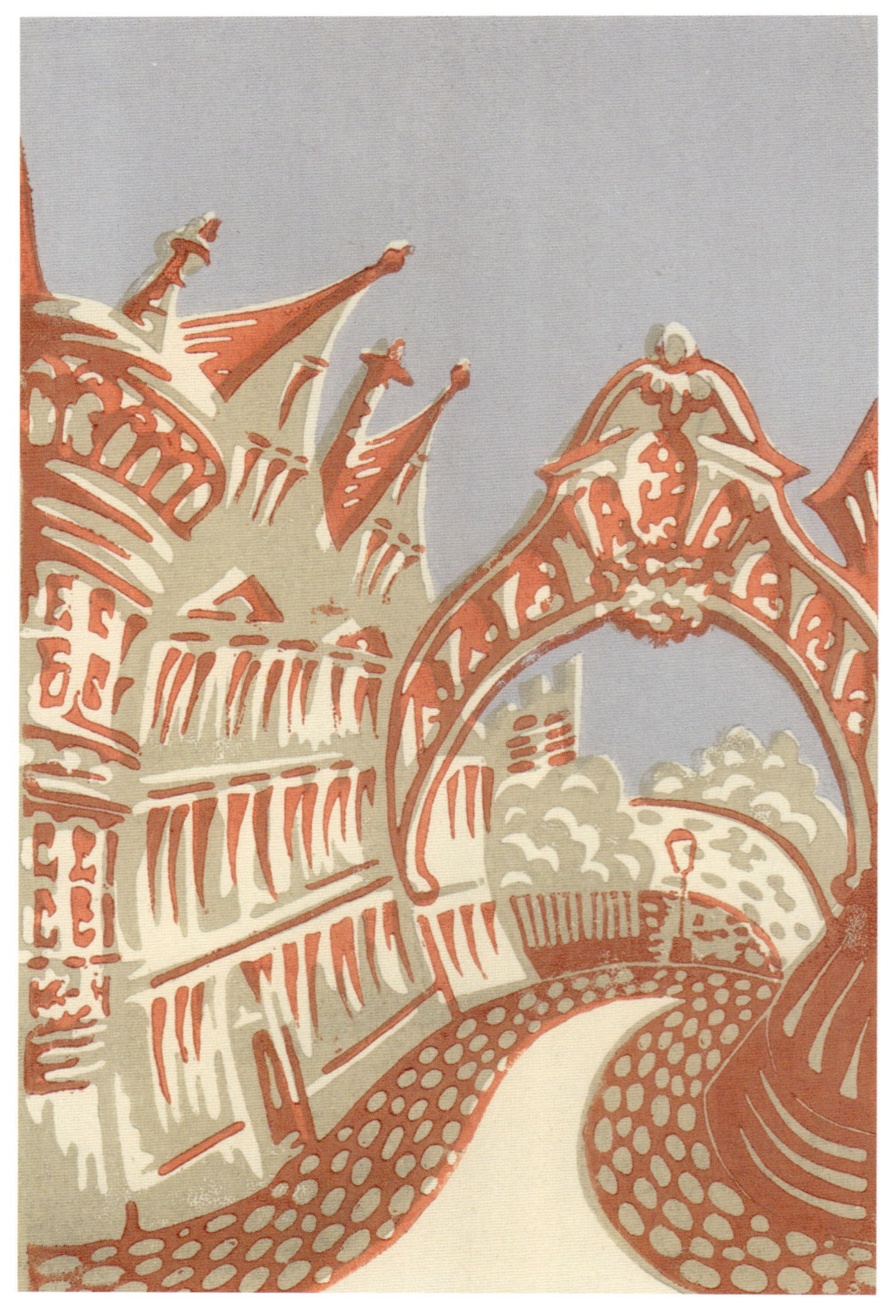

Bridge of Sighs, Jan Ritchie

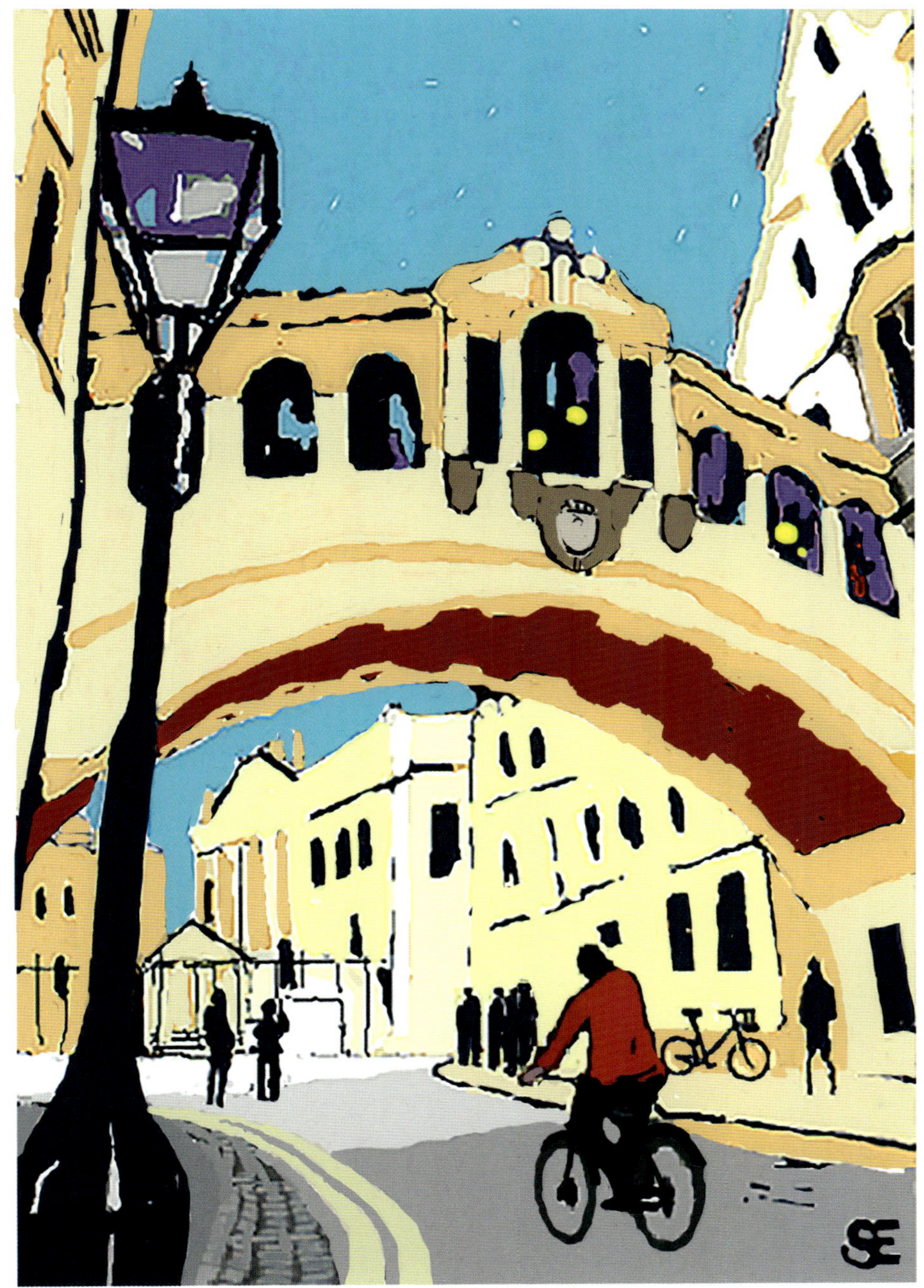

Bridge of Sighs, Simon East

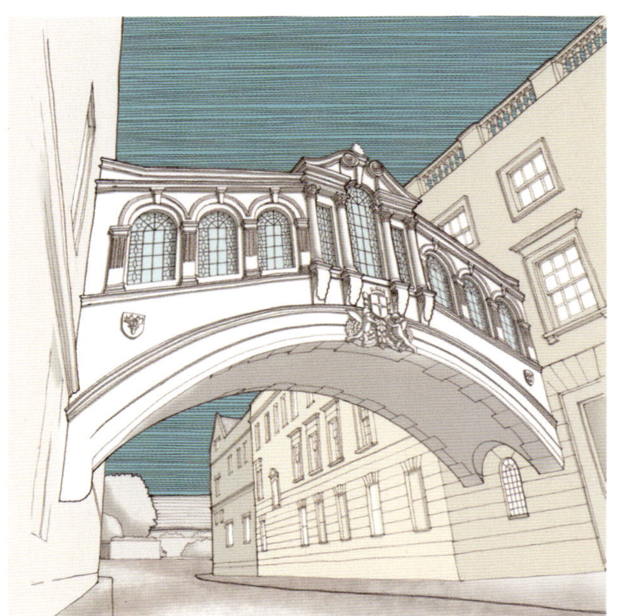

Bridge of Sighs, Robert Kann

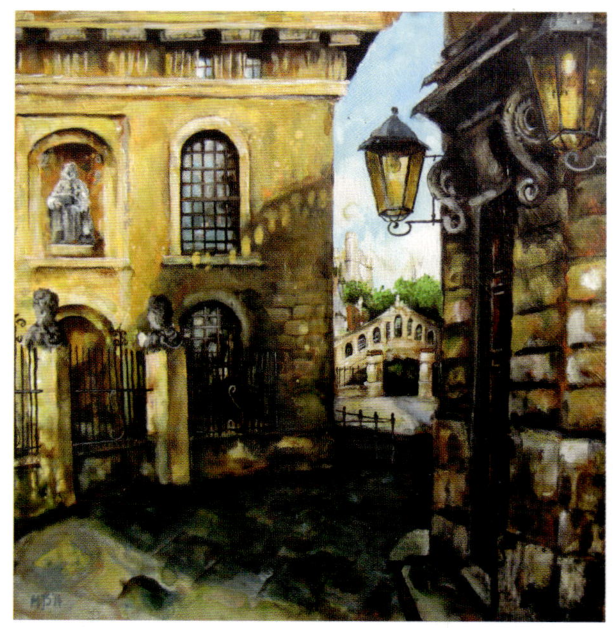

Shadows of the Sheldonian, Melissa Jane Sturgeon

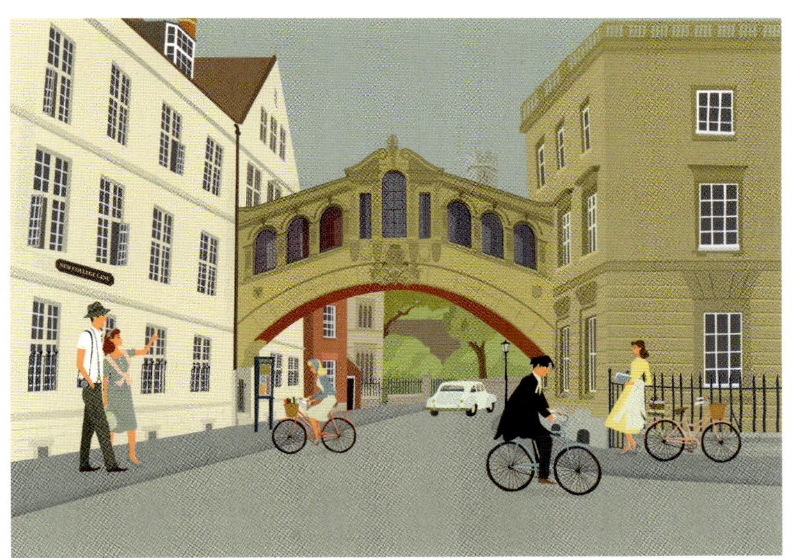

Bridge Of Sighs, Clare Phillips

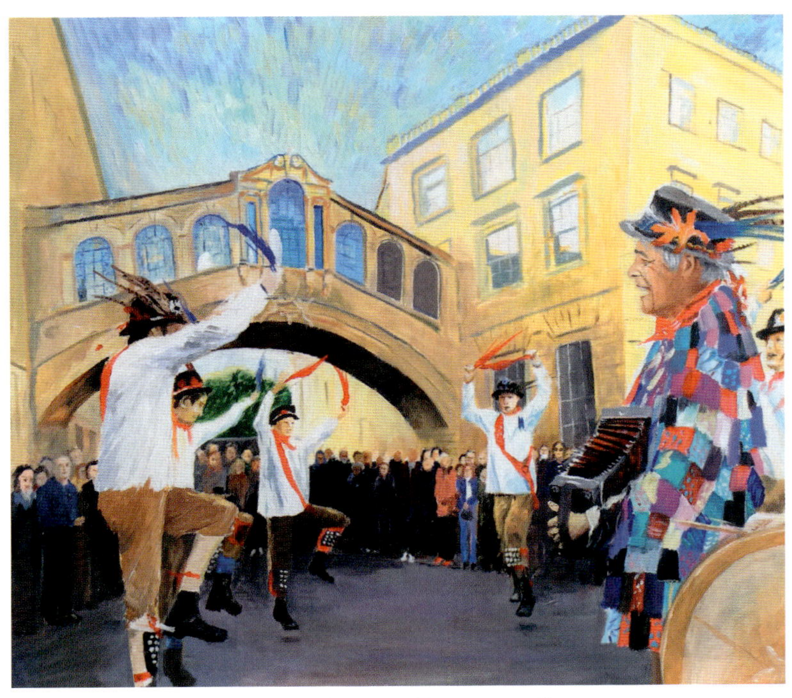

Bridge of Sighs, Caroline Ritson

overleaf: The Queen's College Tower, Ian Scott Massie

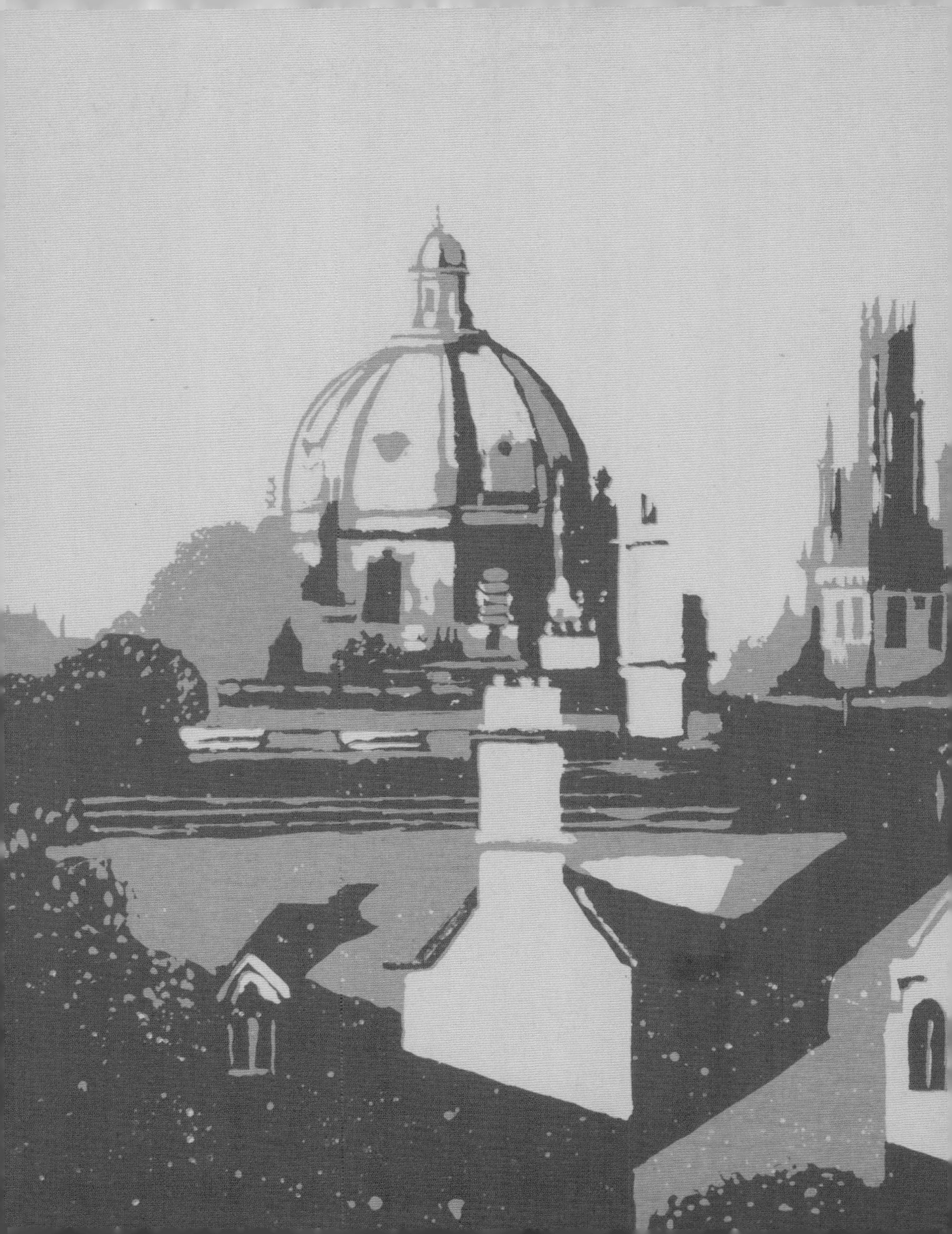

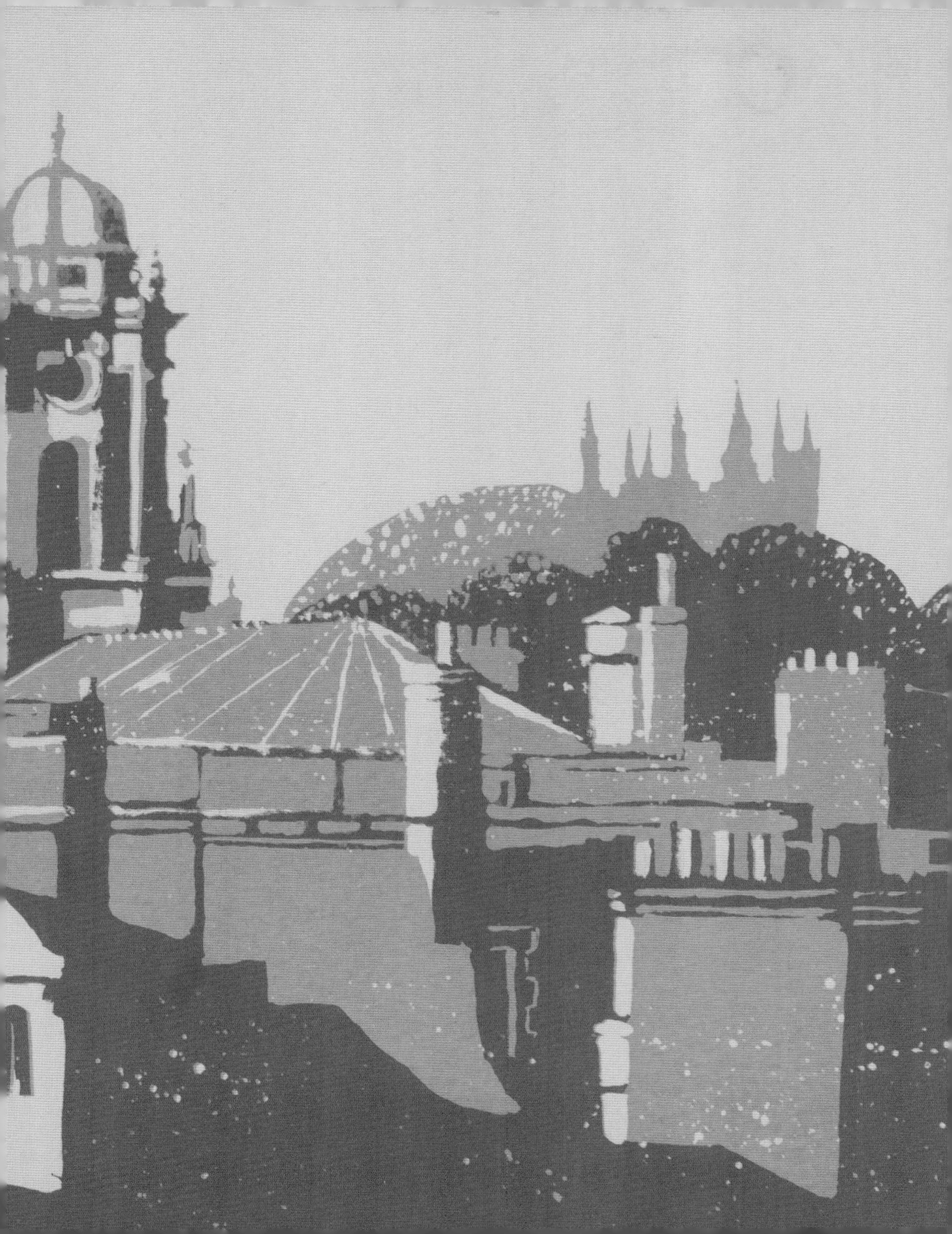

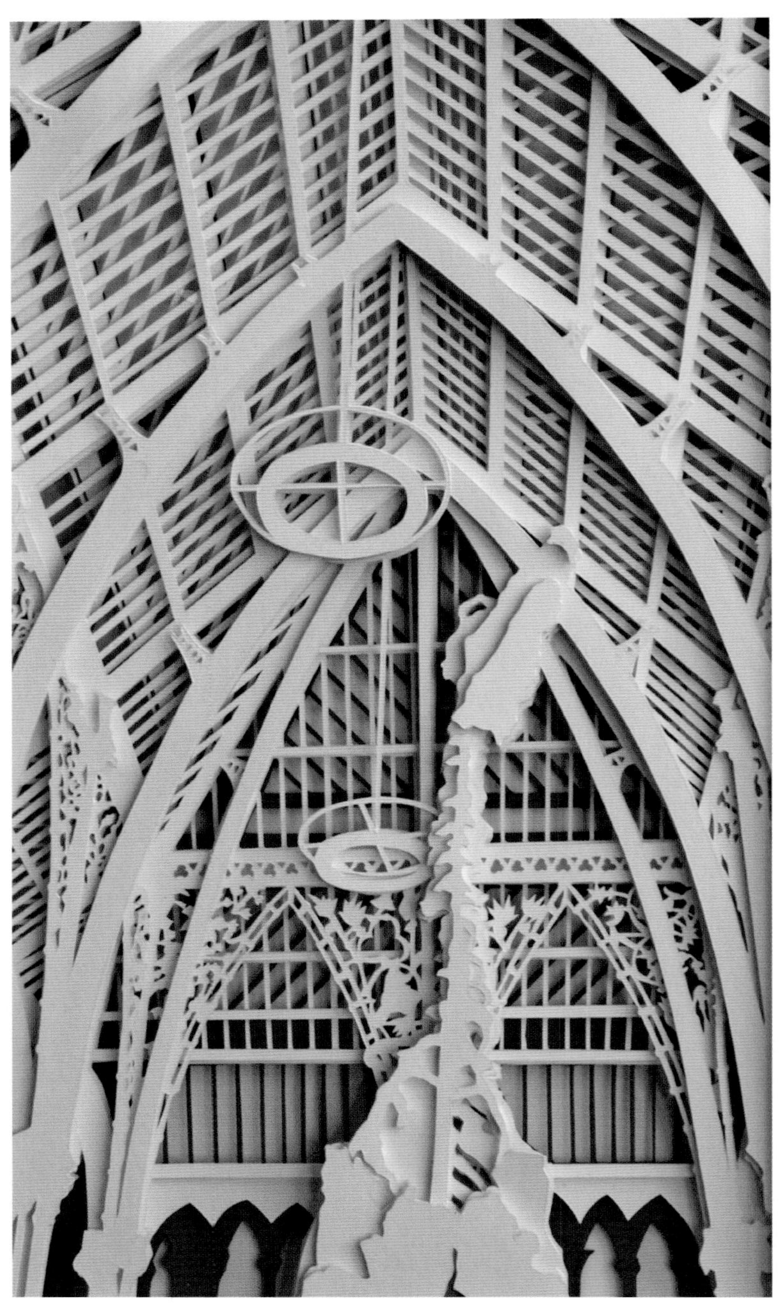

The Museum of Natural History, Kate Hipkiss

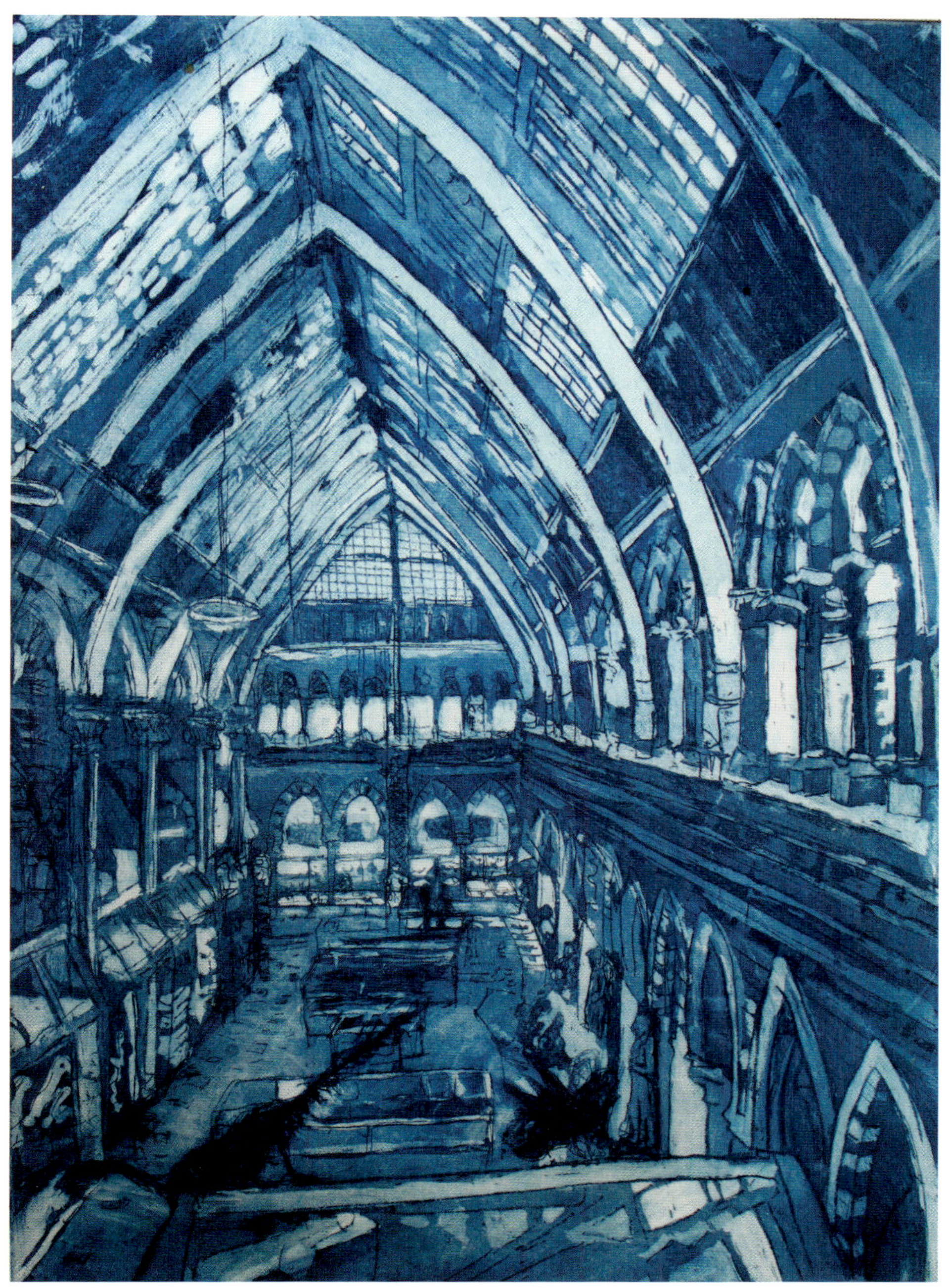

The Museum of Natural History, Rahima Kenner

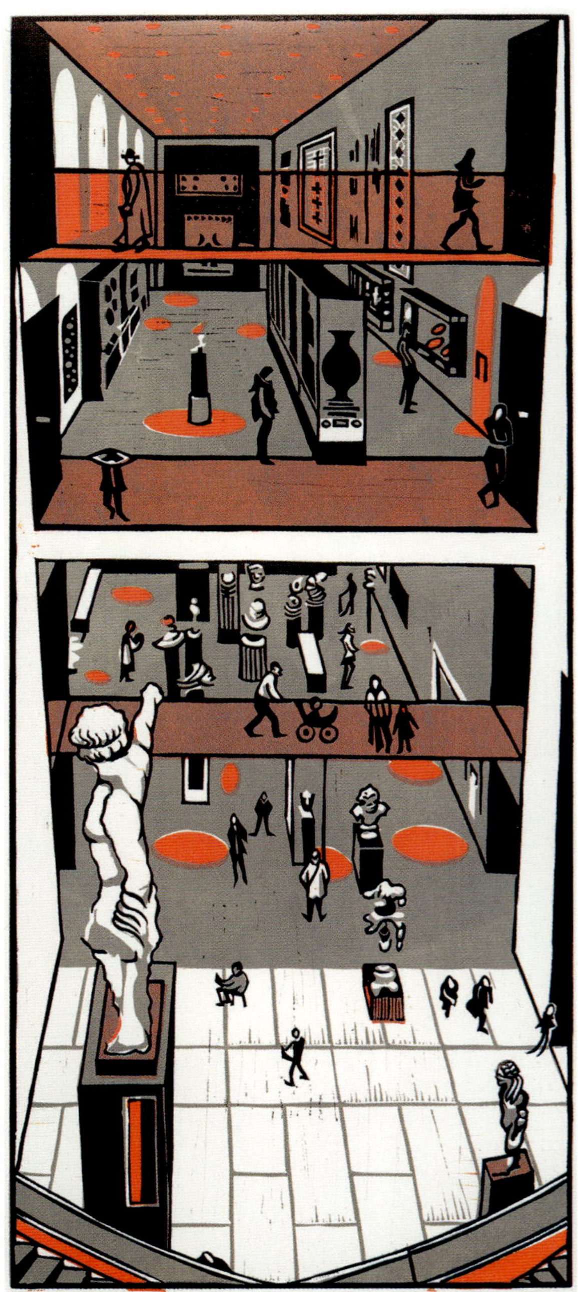

The Ashmolean Staircase, Susan Wheeler

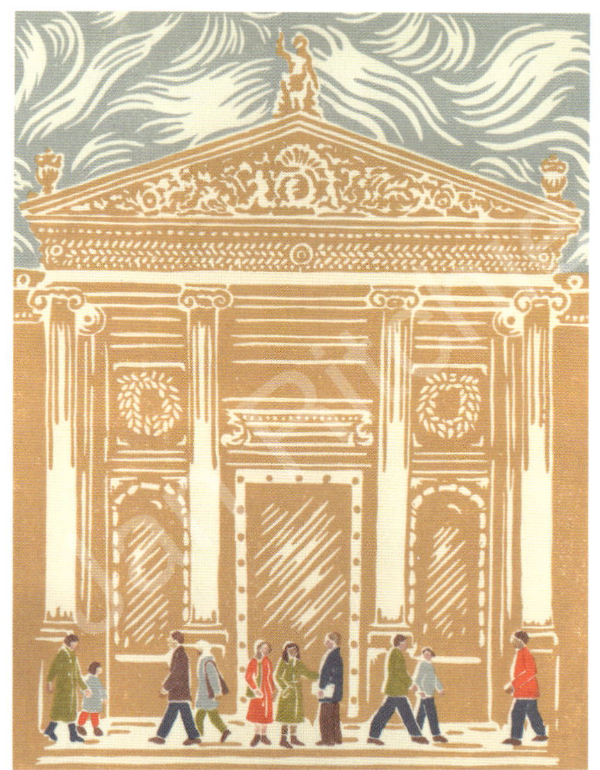

THE ASHMOLEAN MUSEUM, JAN RITCHIE

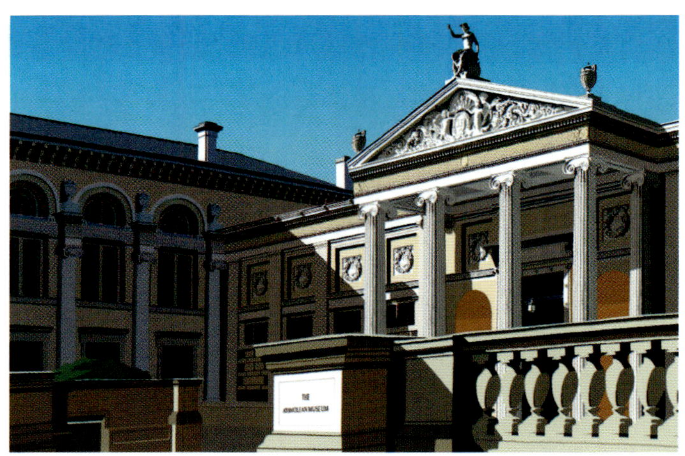

THE ASHMOLEAN MUSEUM, RICHARD O'NEILL

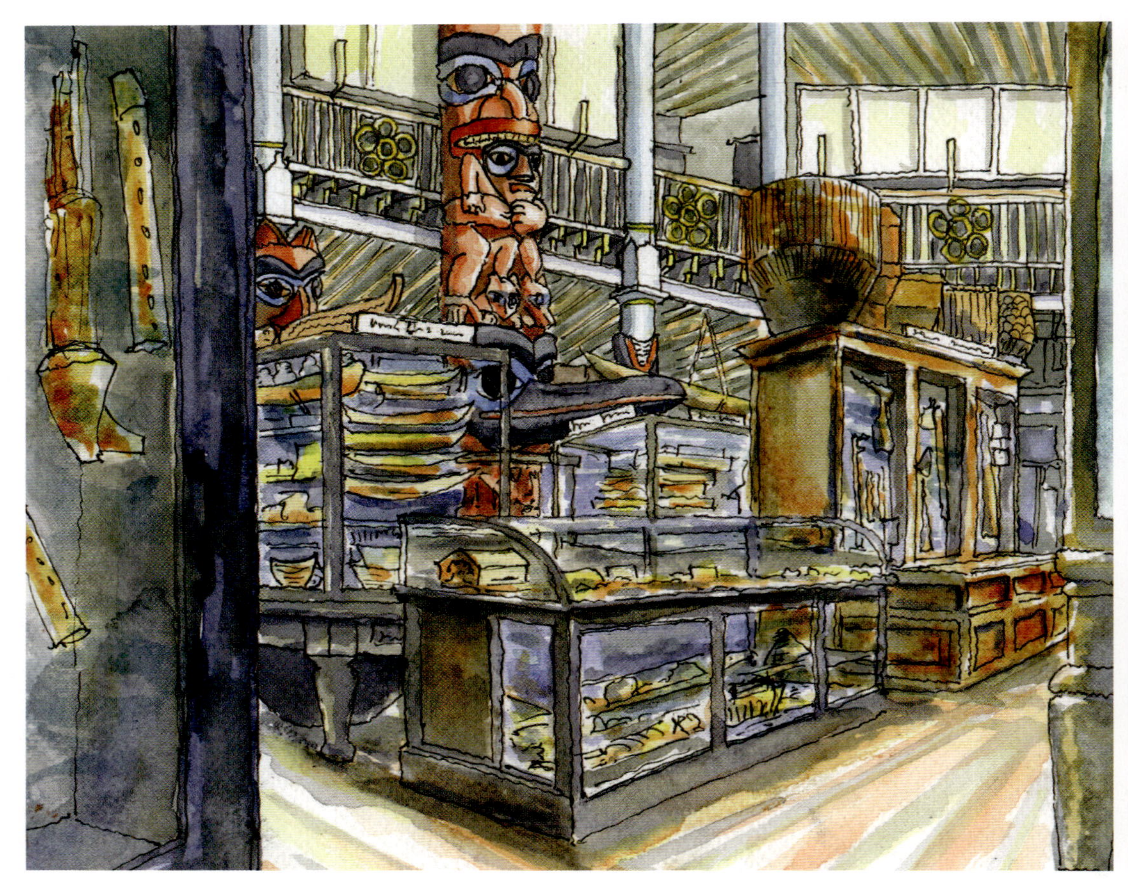

The Pitt Rivers Museum, Andrew McLellan

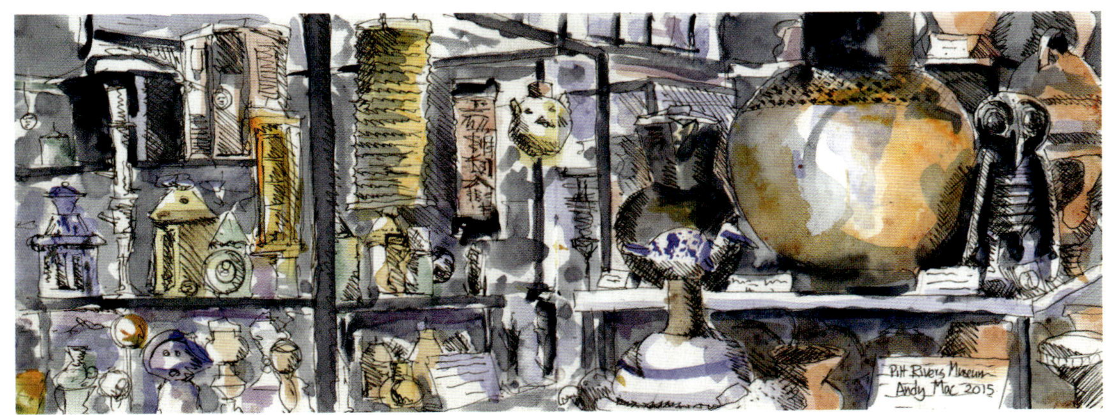

Lamps and Pots at the Pitt Rivers Museum, Andrew McLellan

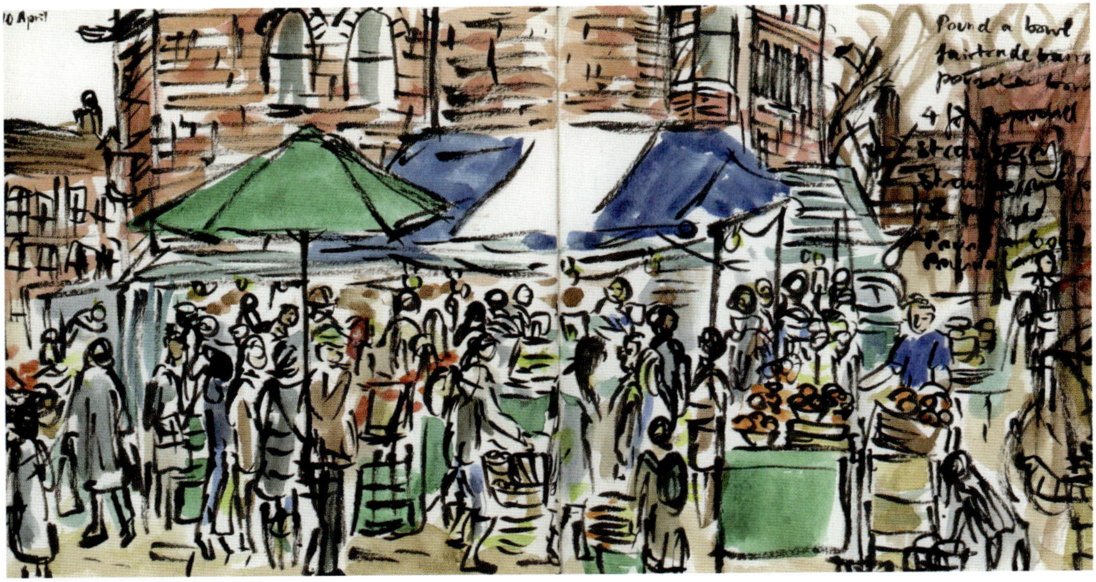

Gloucester Green Market, Imogen Foxell

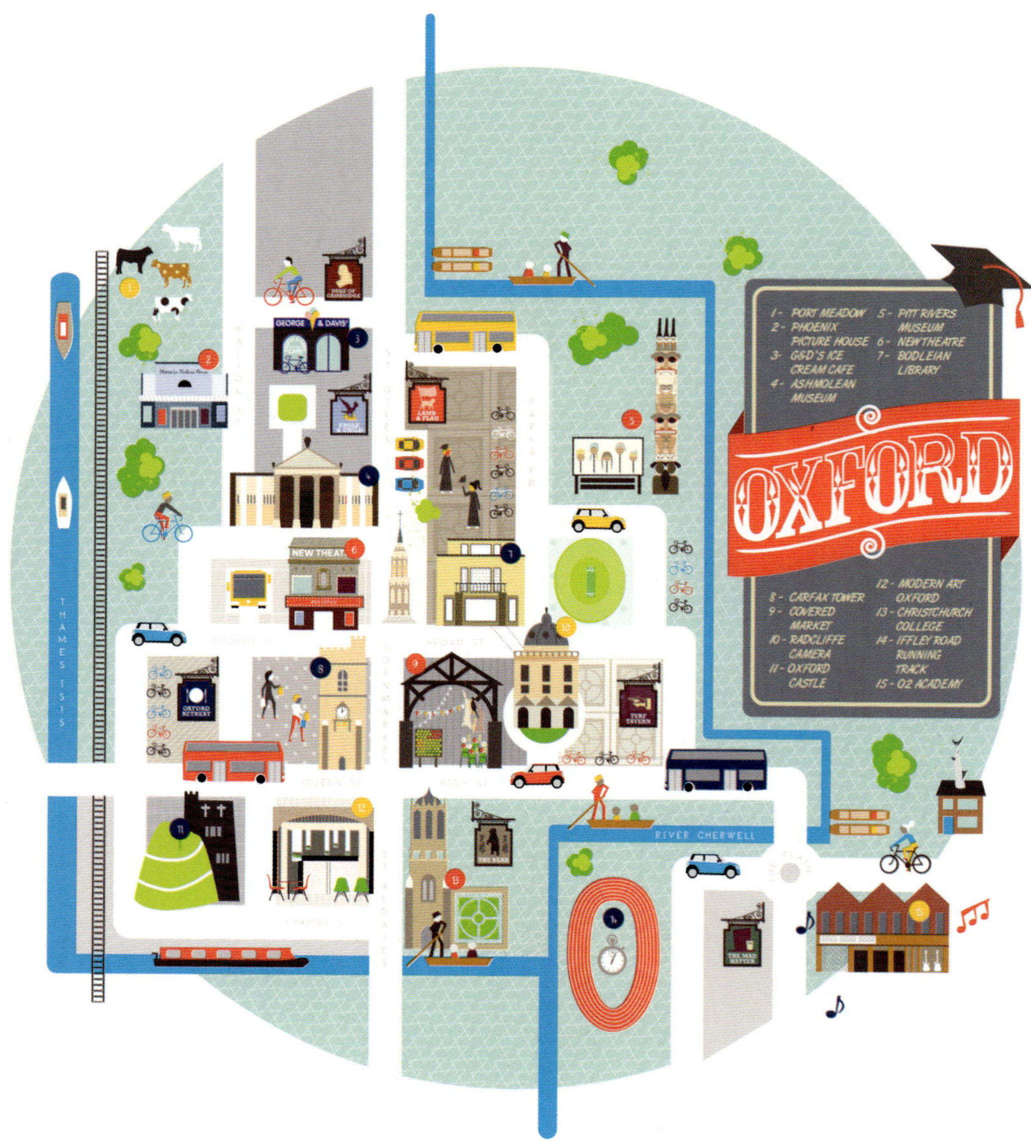

City Map, Sam Osborne

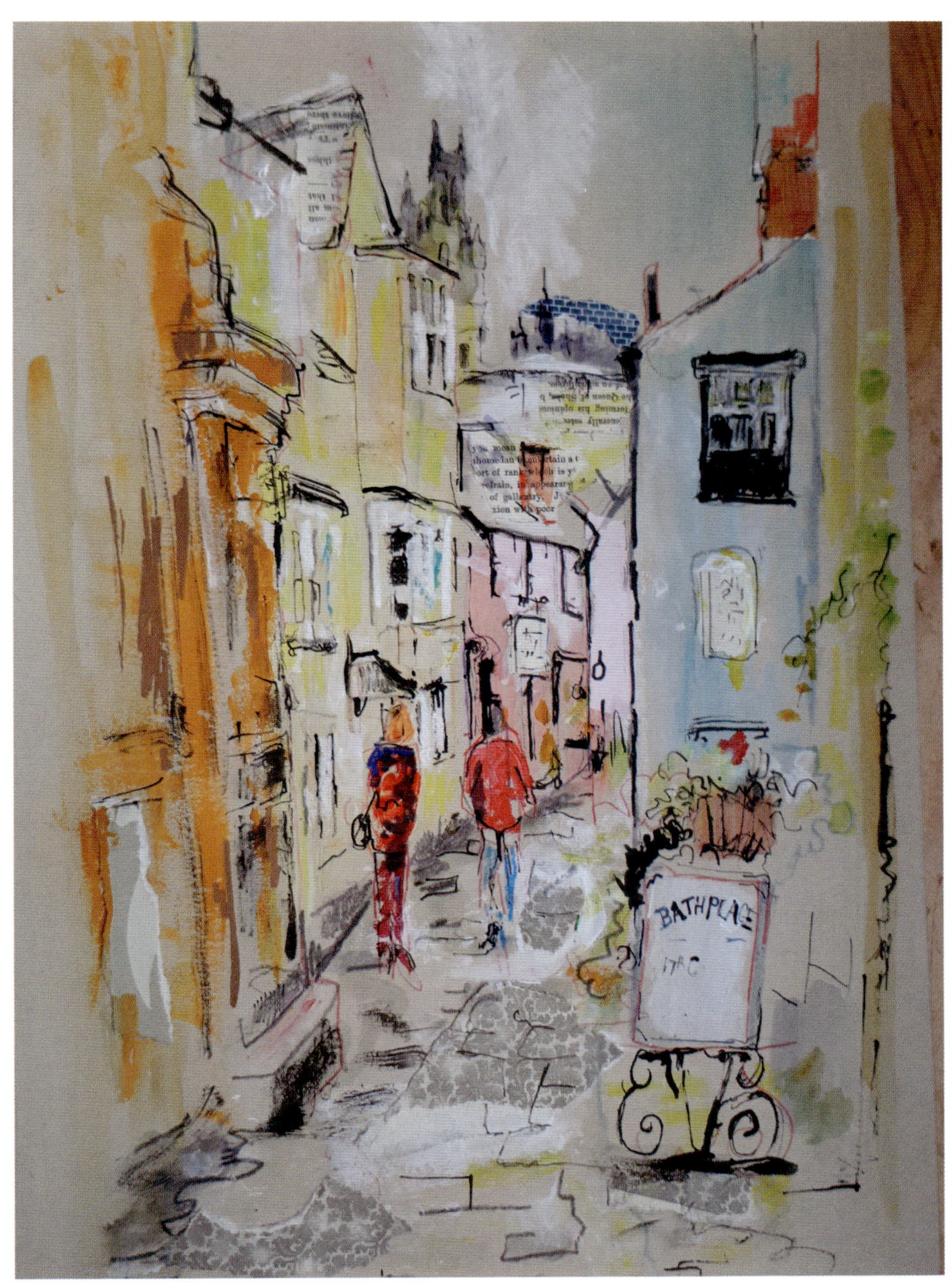

Bath Place, Alice Thomson
overleaf: Over the top, Emma Bennett

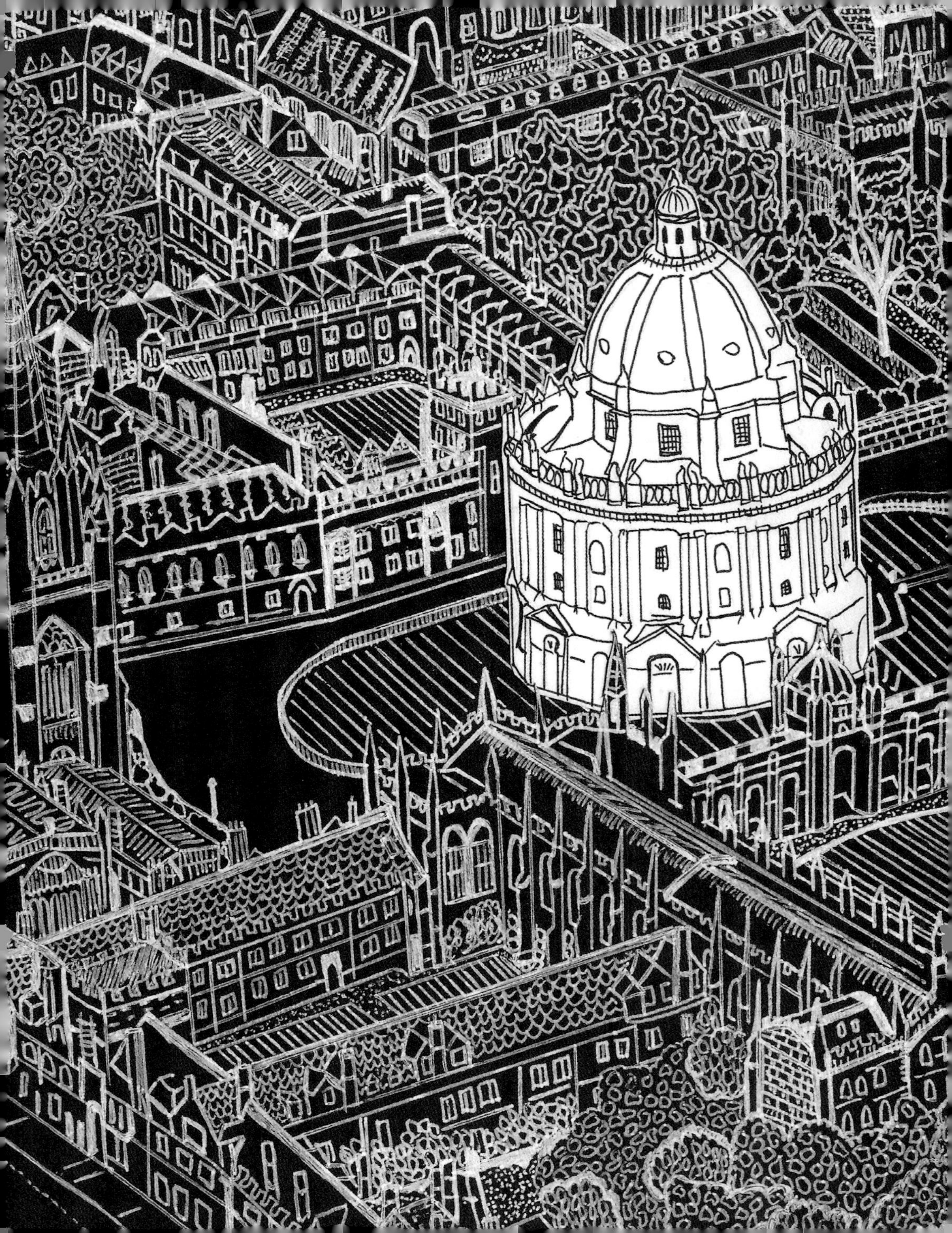

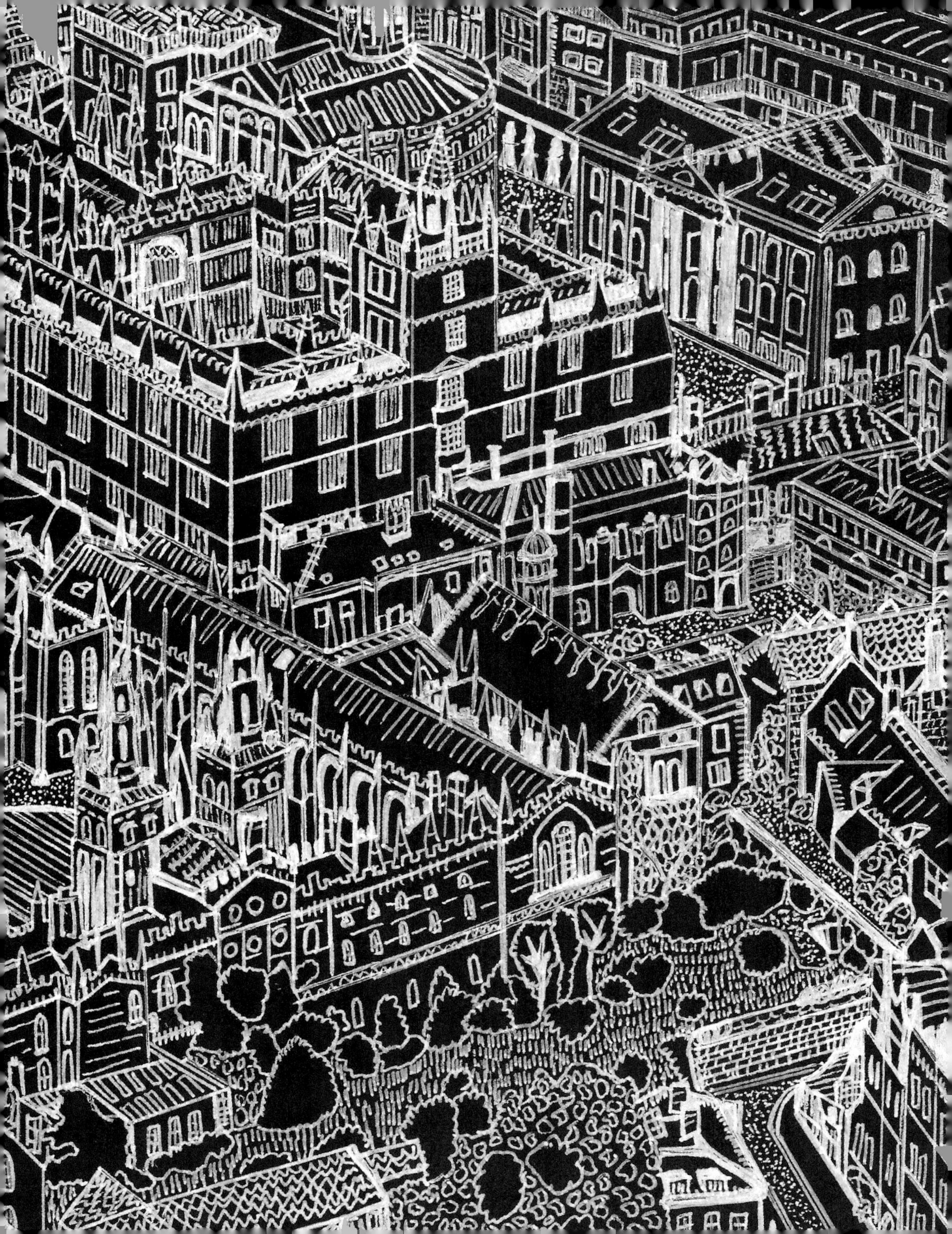

The Clarendon Building, David Strong

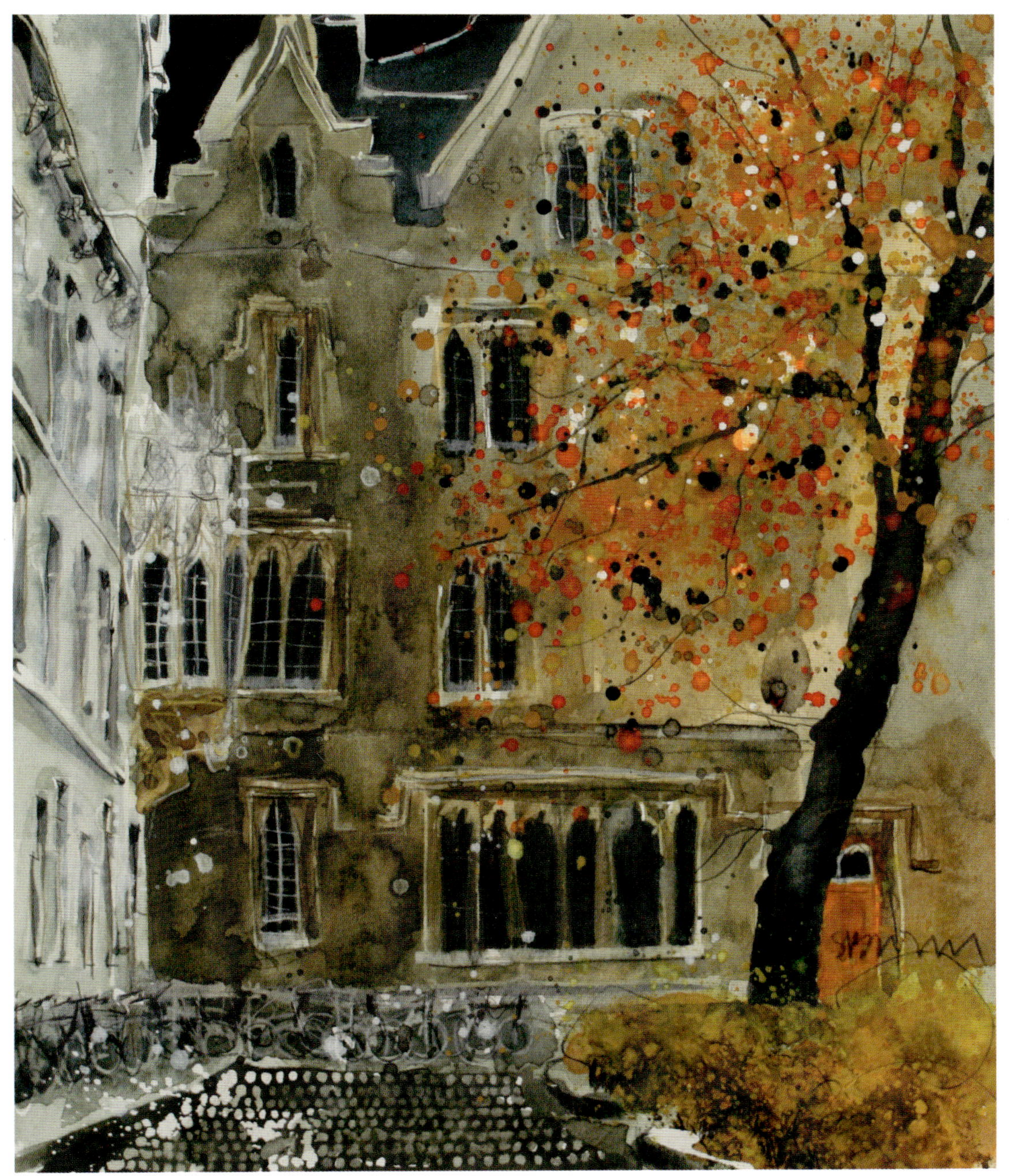

Courtyard, Susan Brown

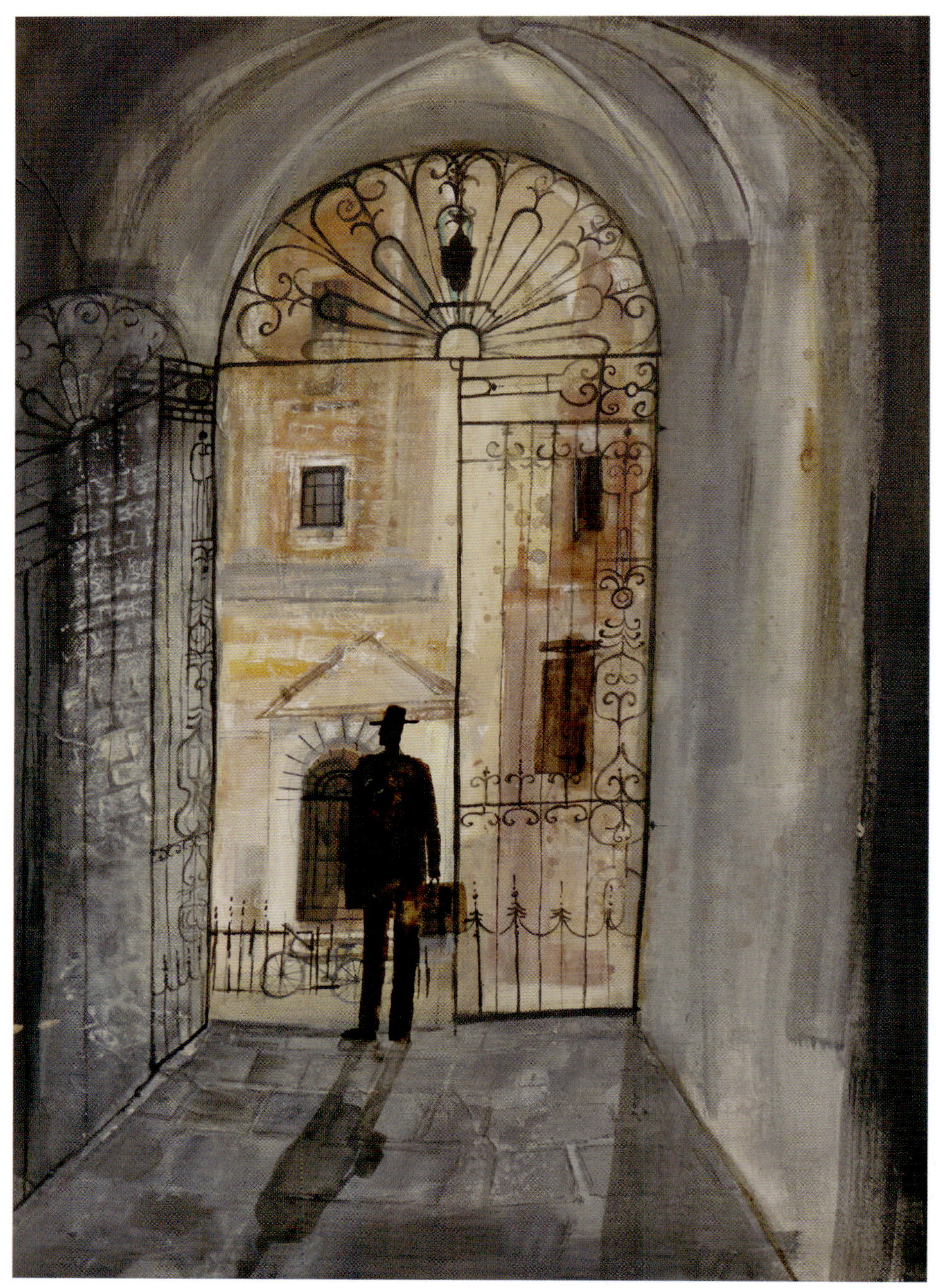

Funneled light, Emmie van Biervliet

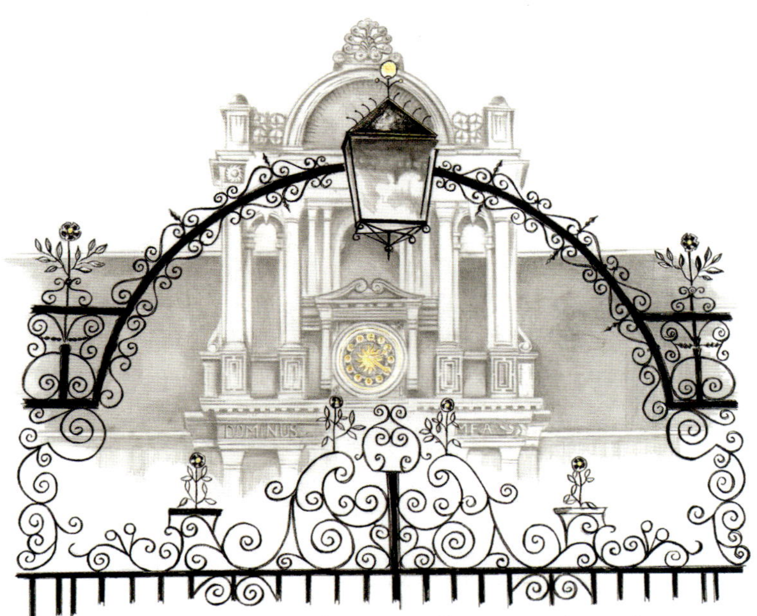

The Examination Schools Gateway, Jane Peart

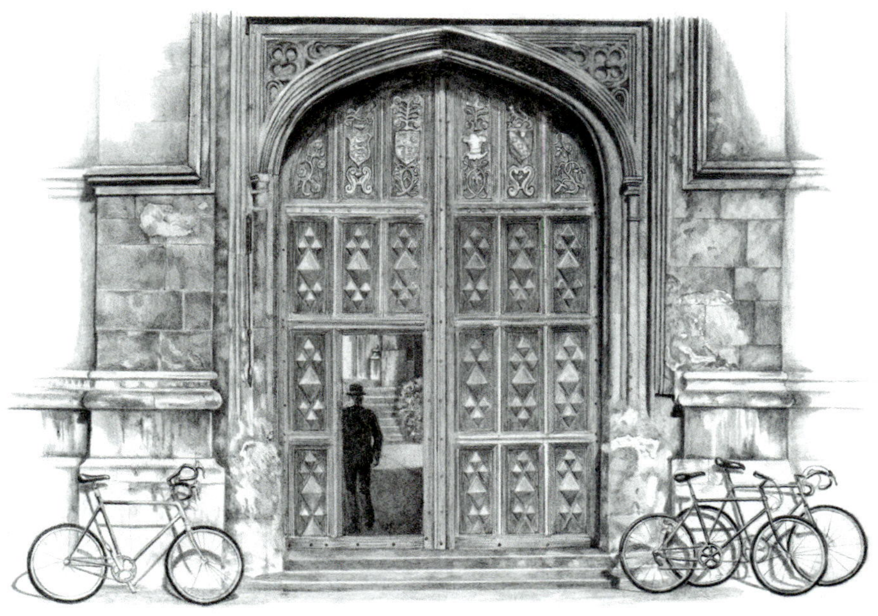

Oriel College Gateway, Jane Peart

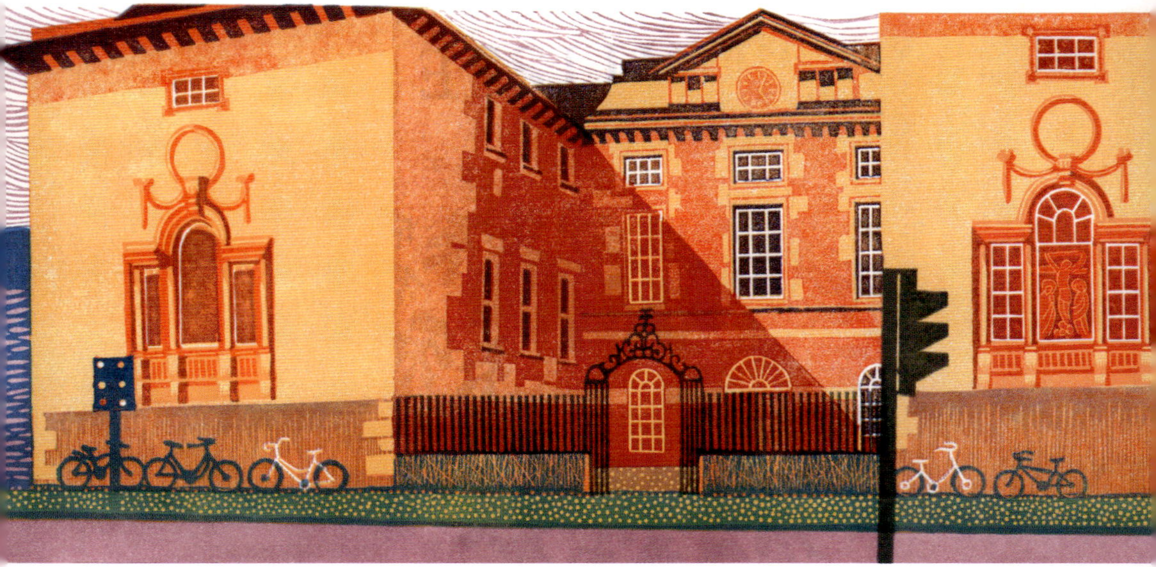

Worcester College, Eric Gaskell

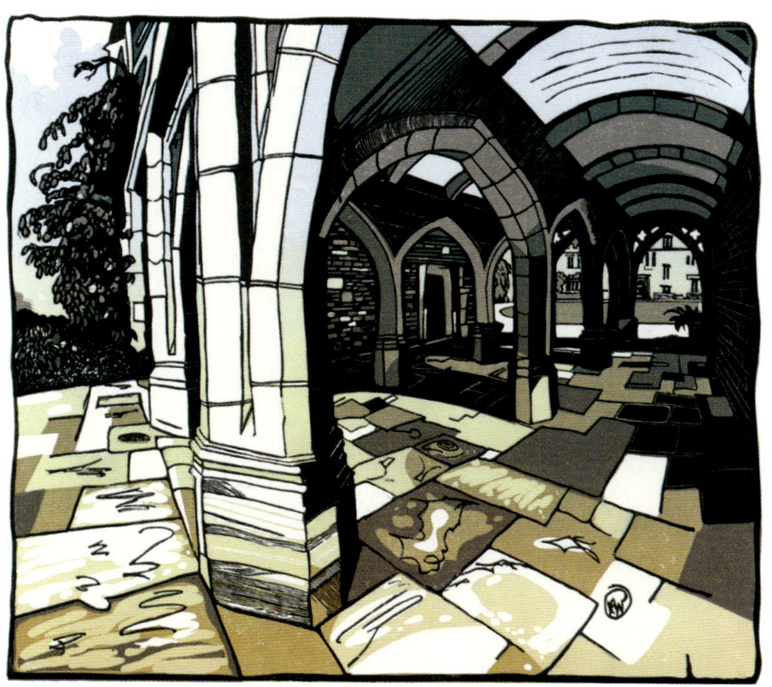

St Cross College, Robin Wilson

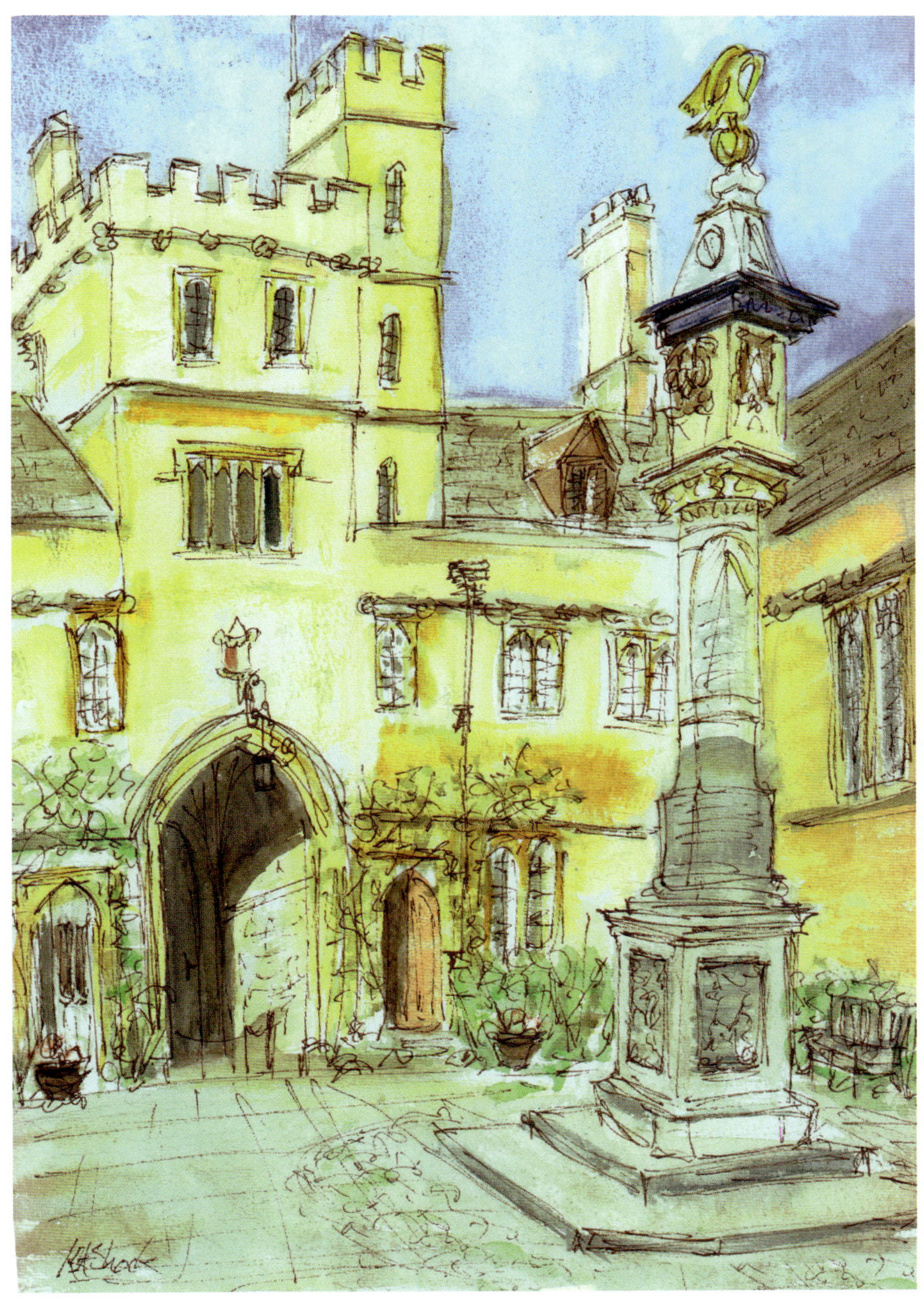

Corpus Christi College, Katherine Shock
overleaf: Lincoln College, vision of the Seventies, John Dew

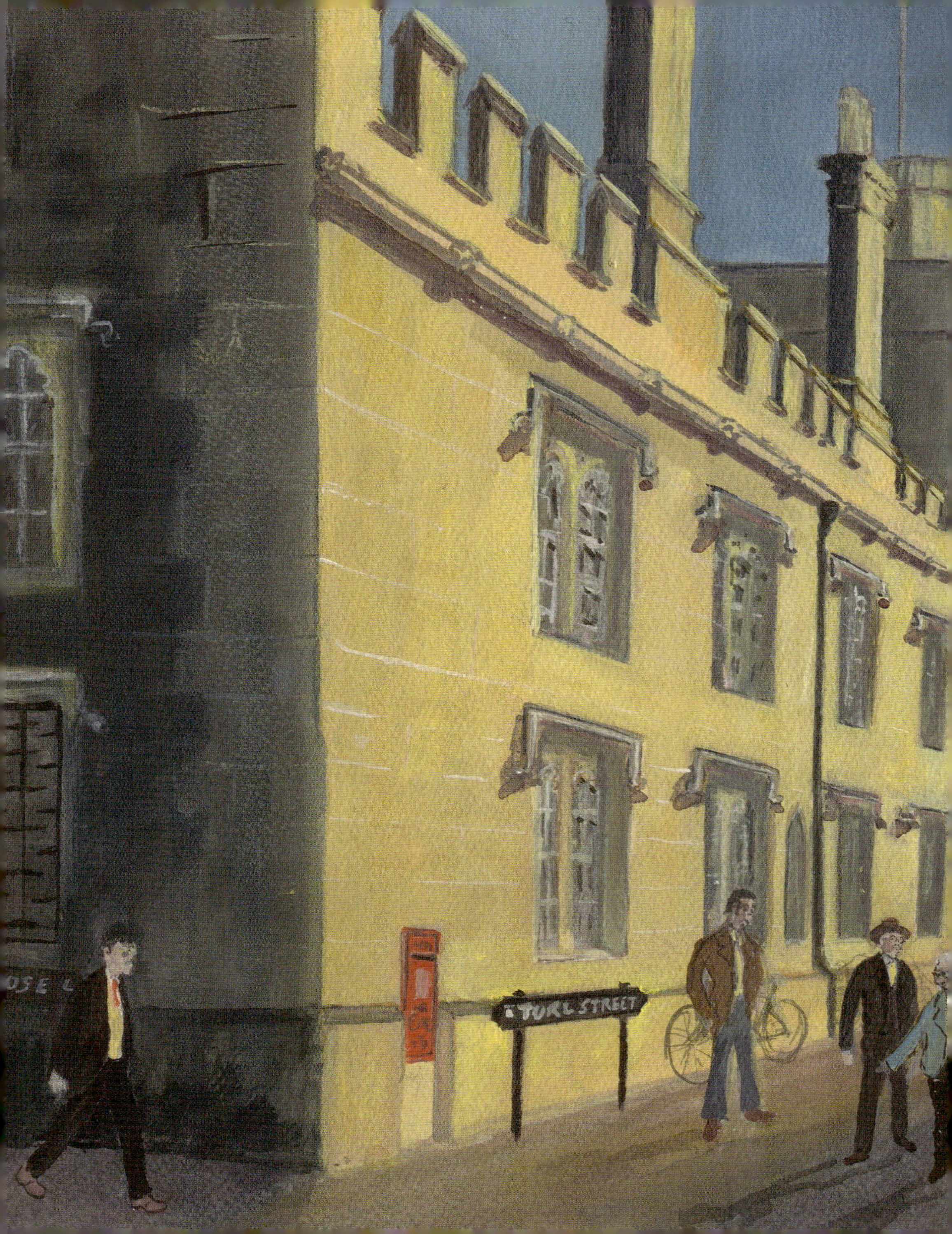
TURL STREET

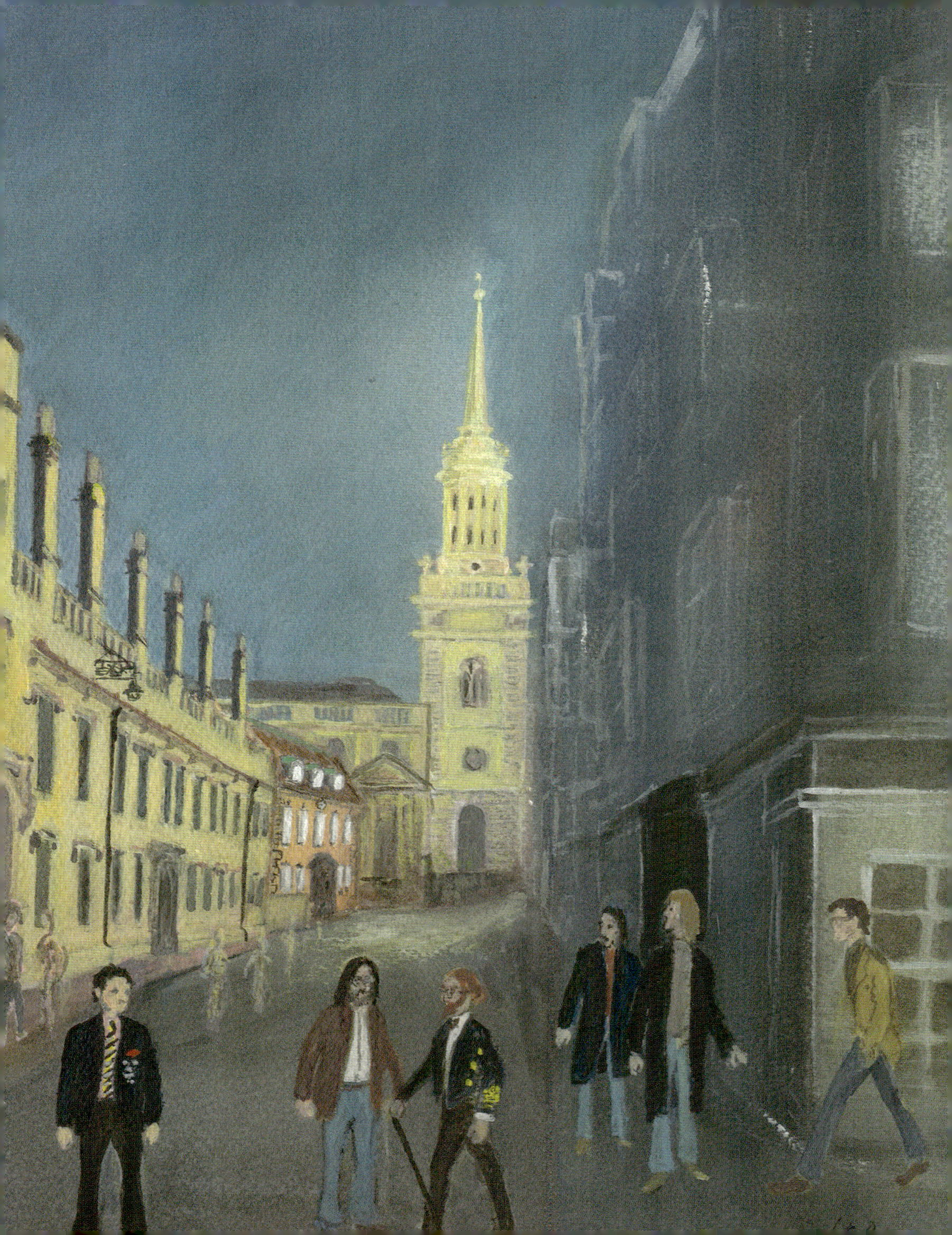

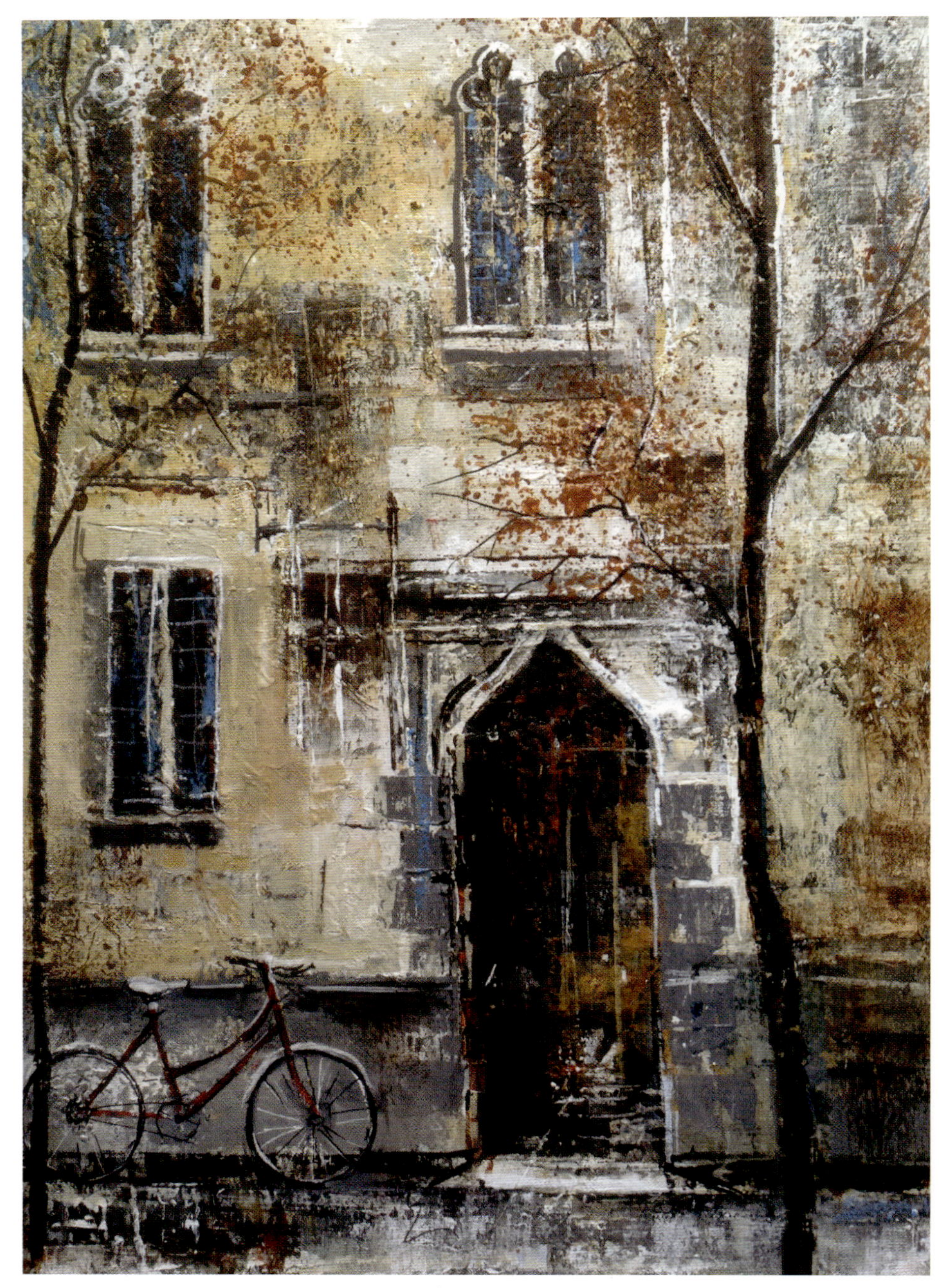

St Giles', Bee Bartlett

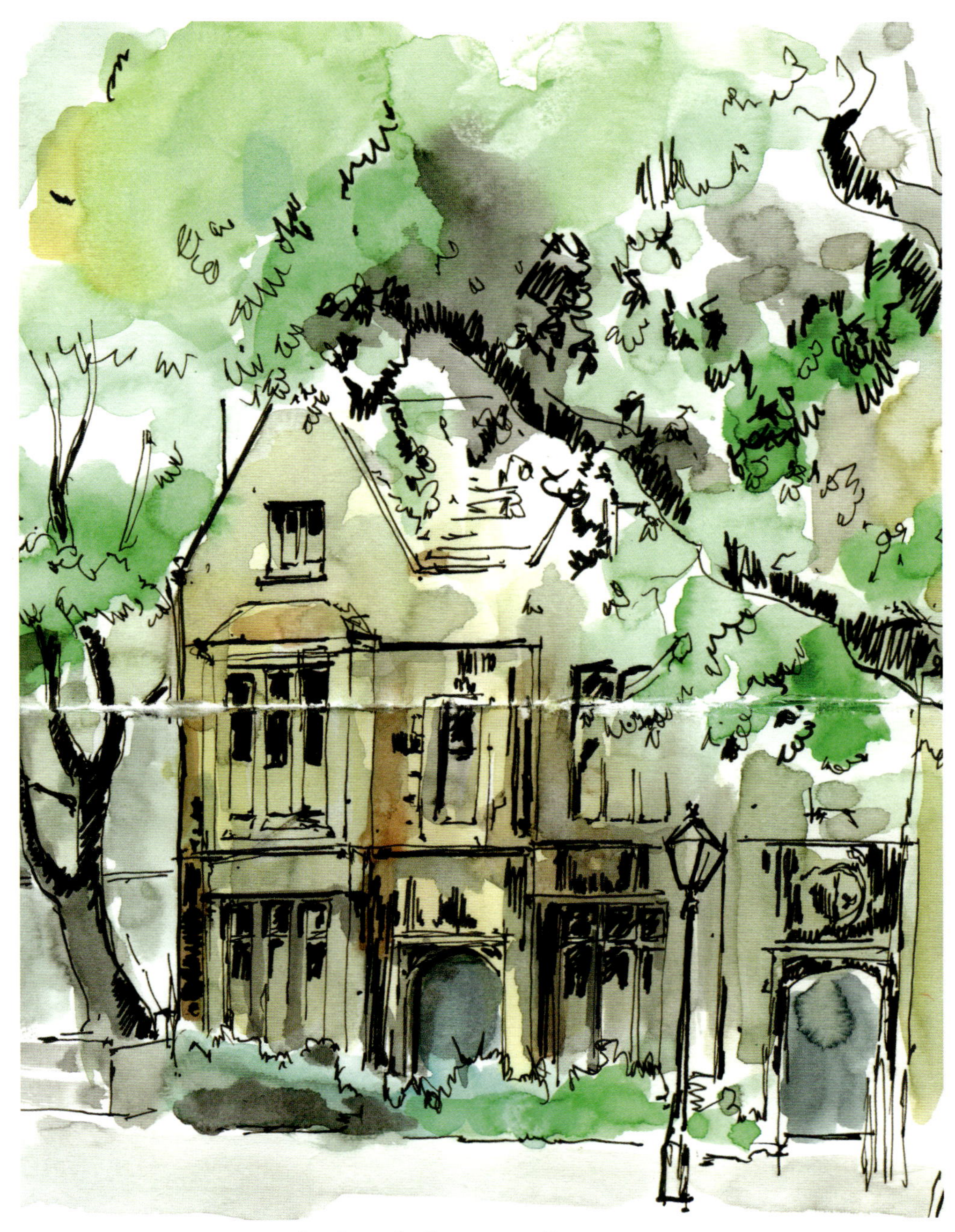

St Giles', Catriona Hopton
overleaf: Trinity College, Dorothy Megaw

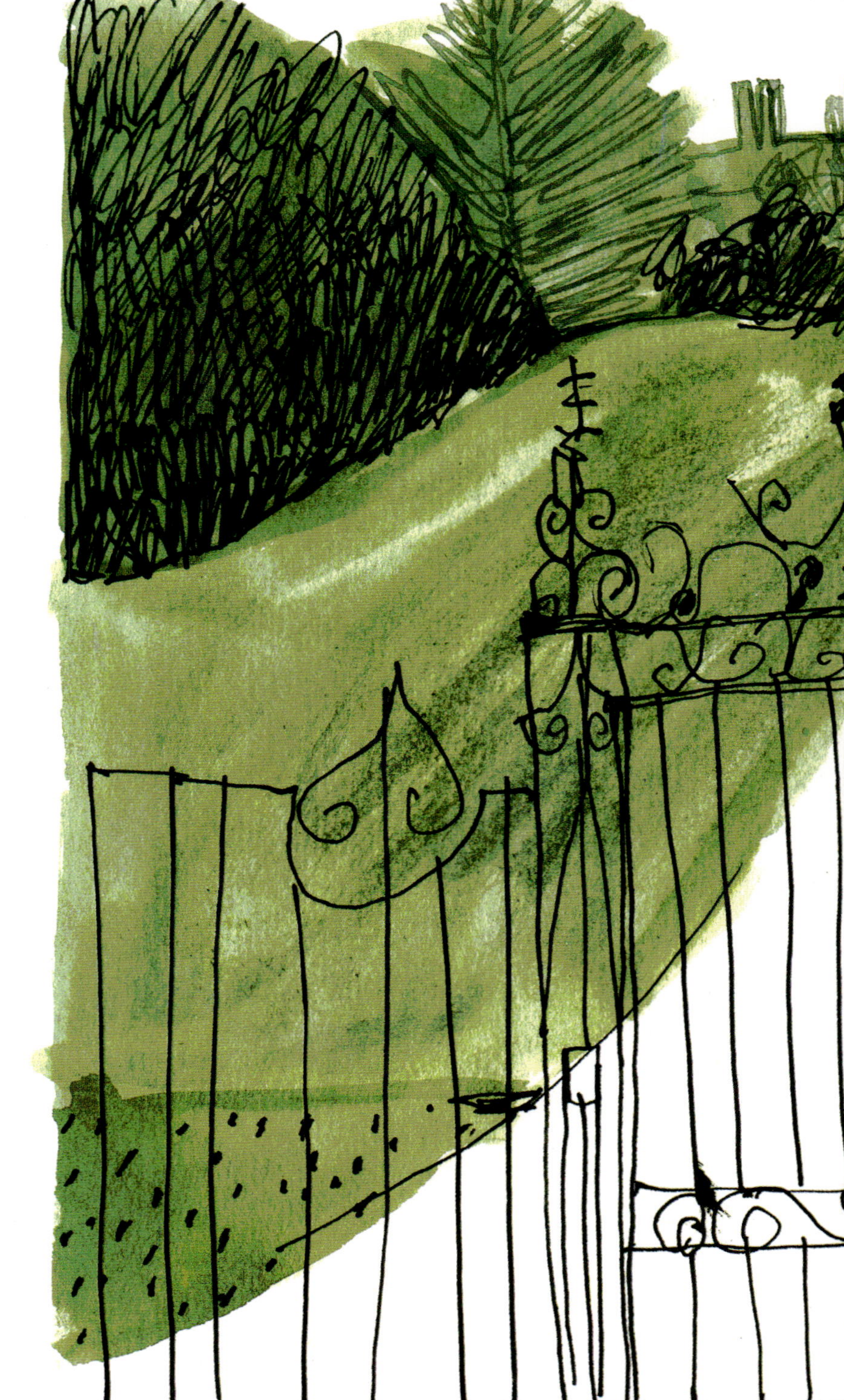

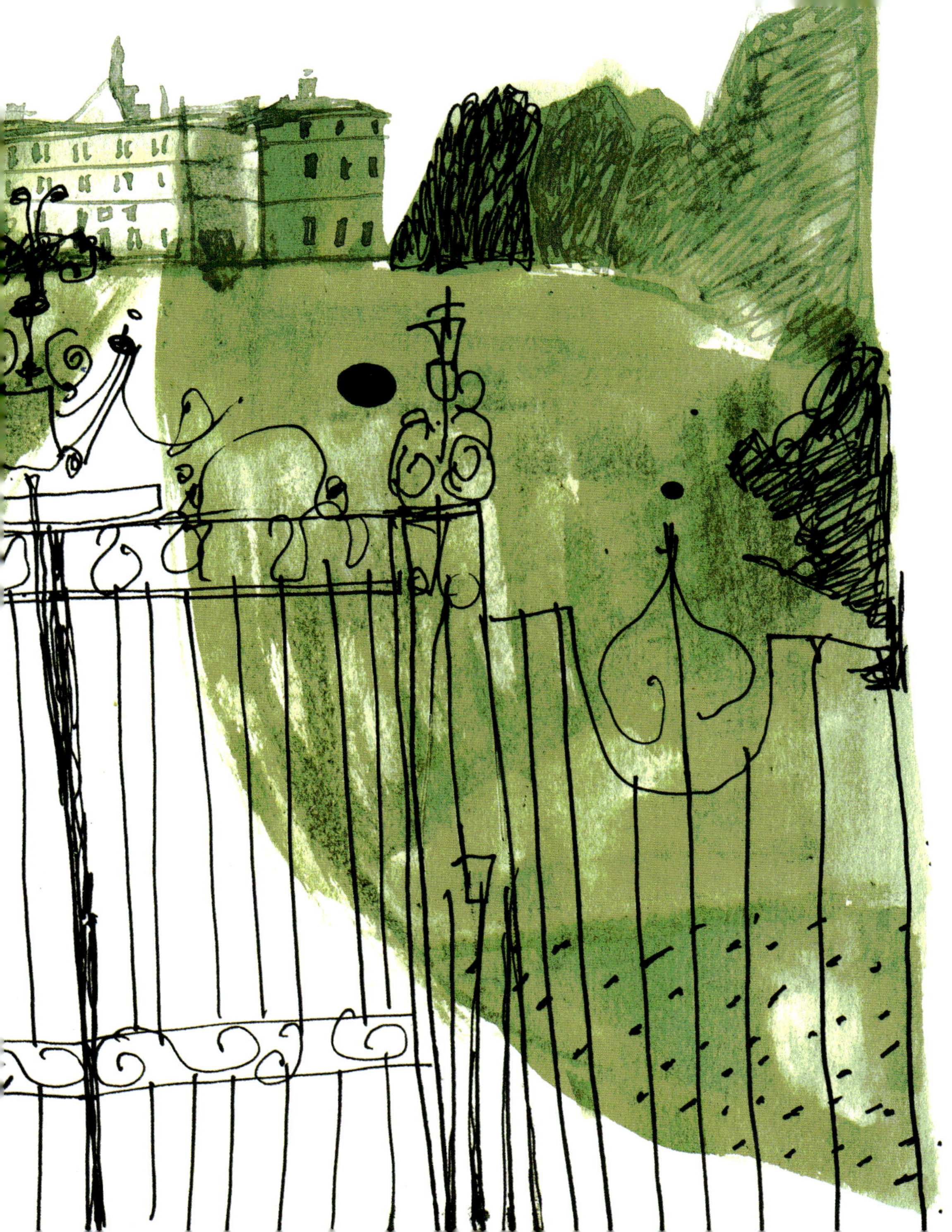

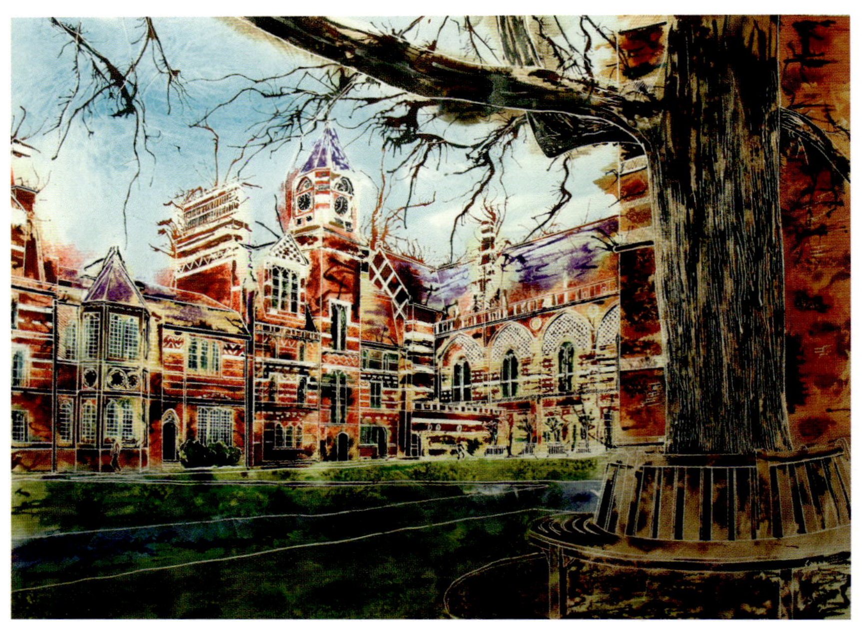

Pusey Quad, Keble College, Cathy Read

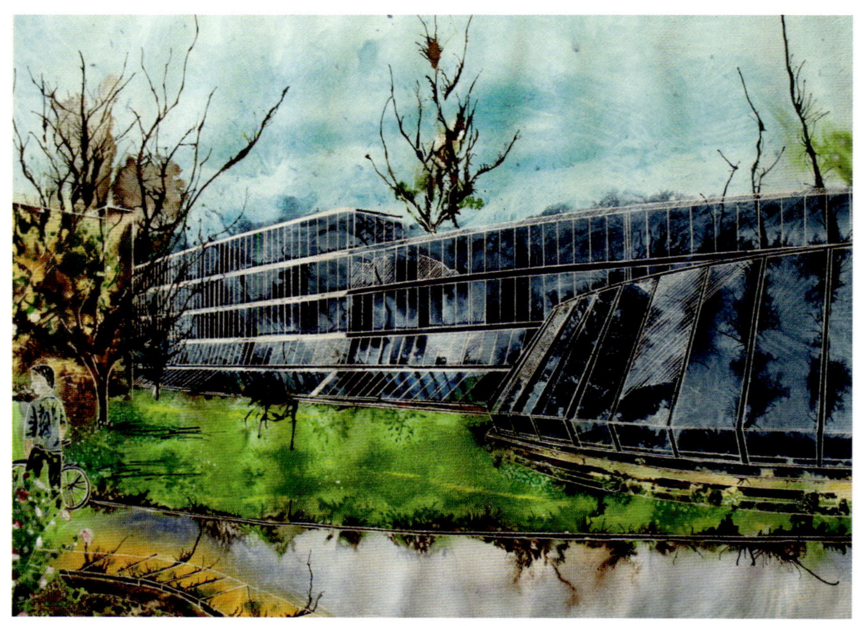

Keble College, The Spaceship, Cathy Read

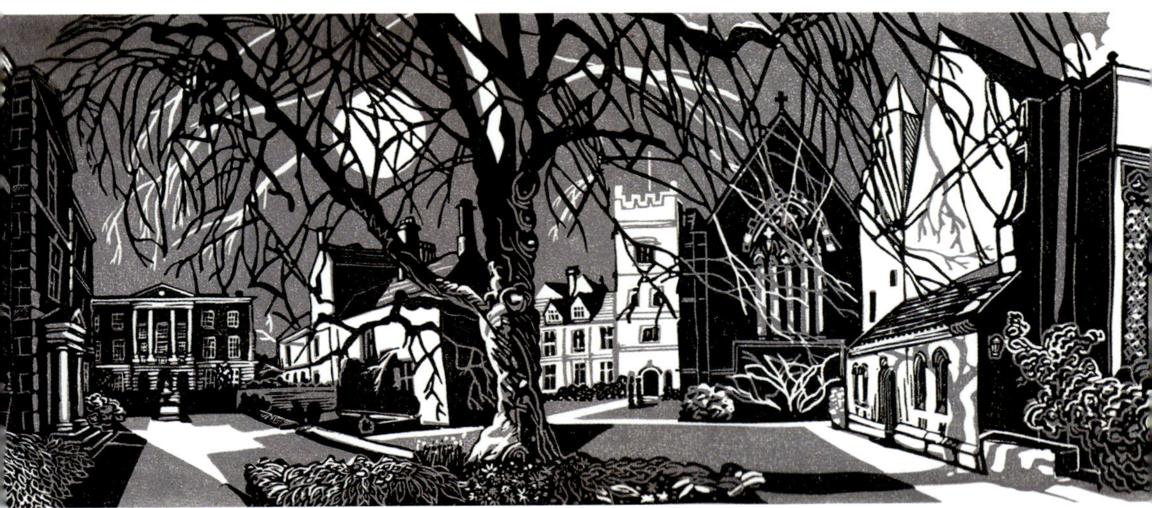

Harris Manchester College, Robin Wilson

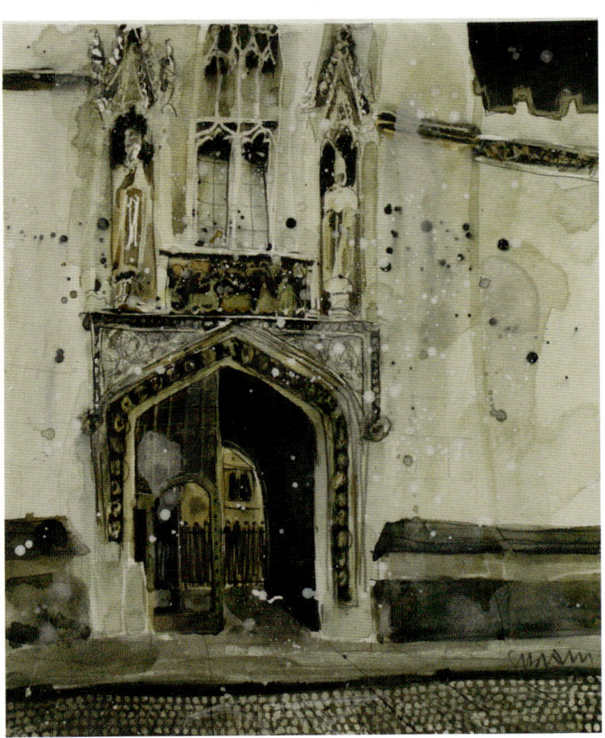

Merton College, Susan Brown

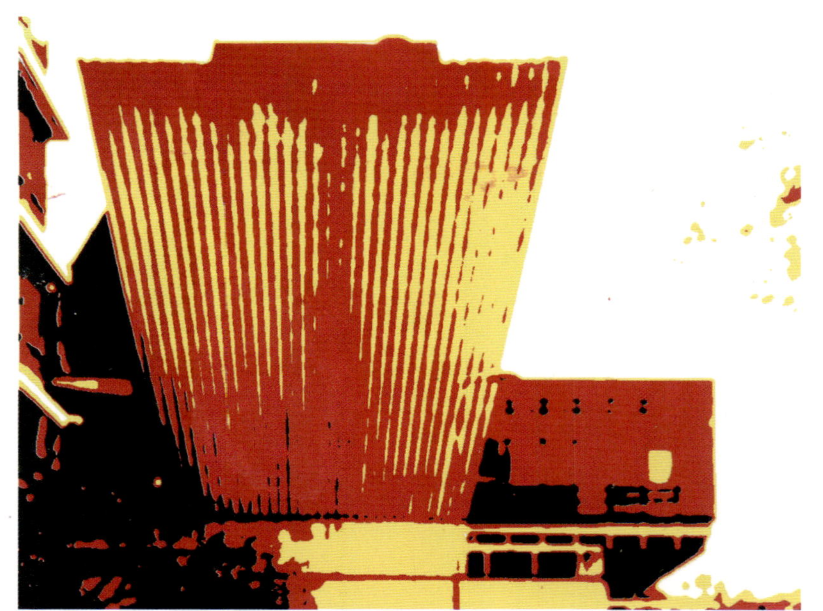

THE DENYS WILKINSON BUILDING, RICHARD STEPHENS

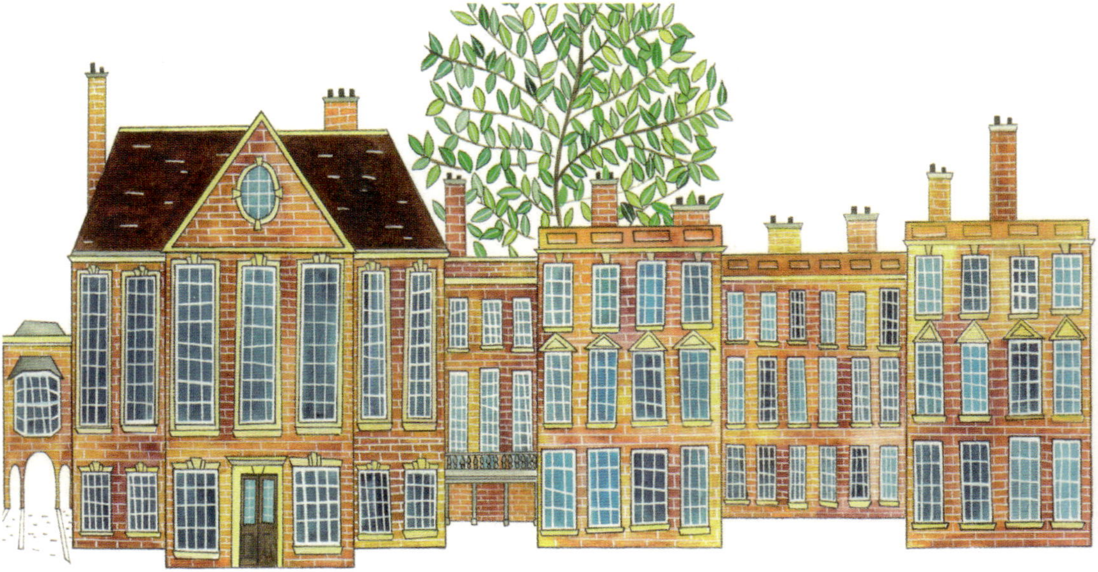

SOMERVILLE COLLEGE, EMILY HILBOURNE

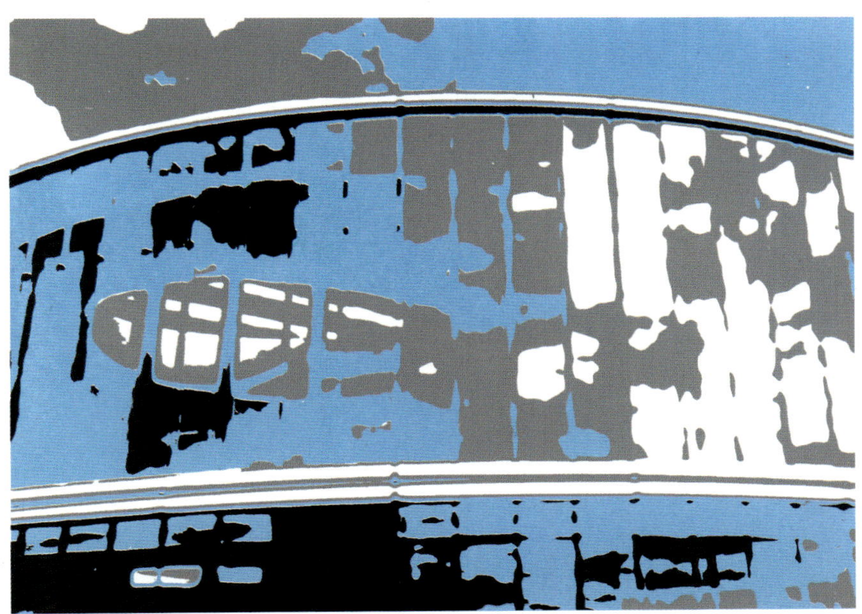

The Blavatnik Building, Richard Stephens

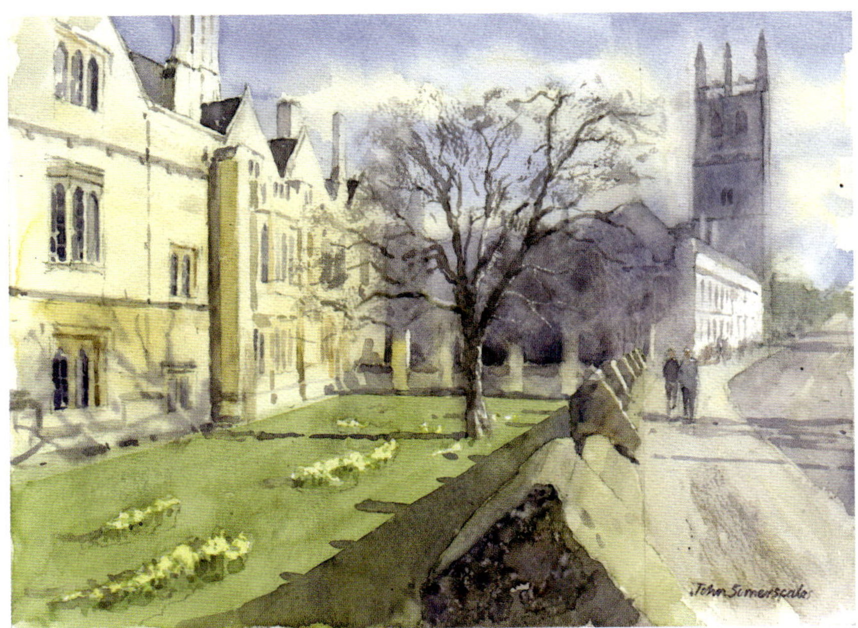

Magdalen Bridge, John Somerscales

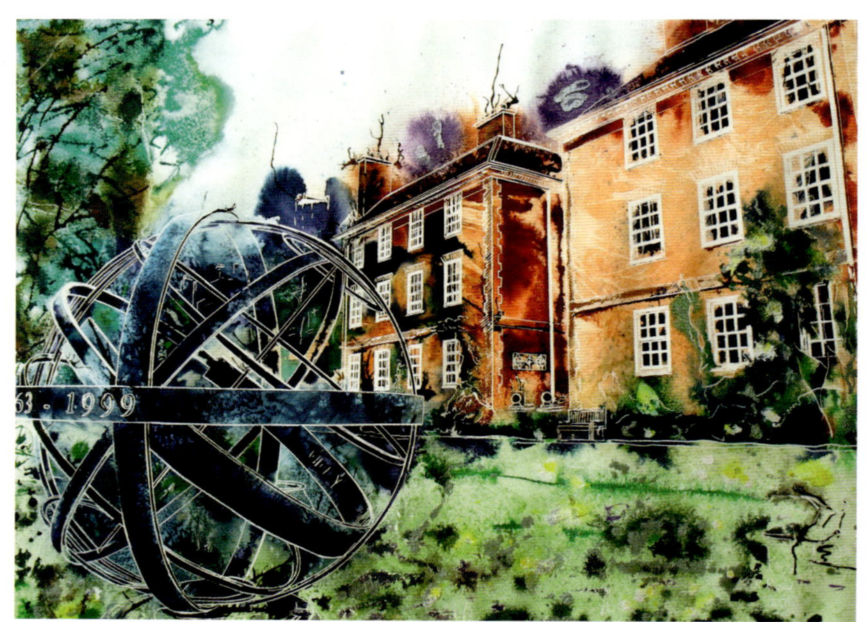

Lady Margaret Hall, Cathy Read

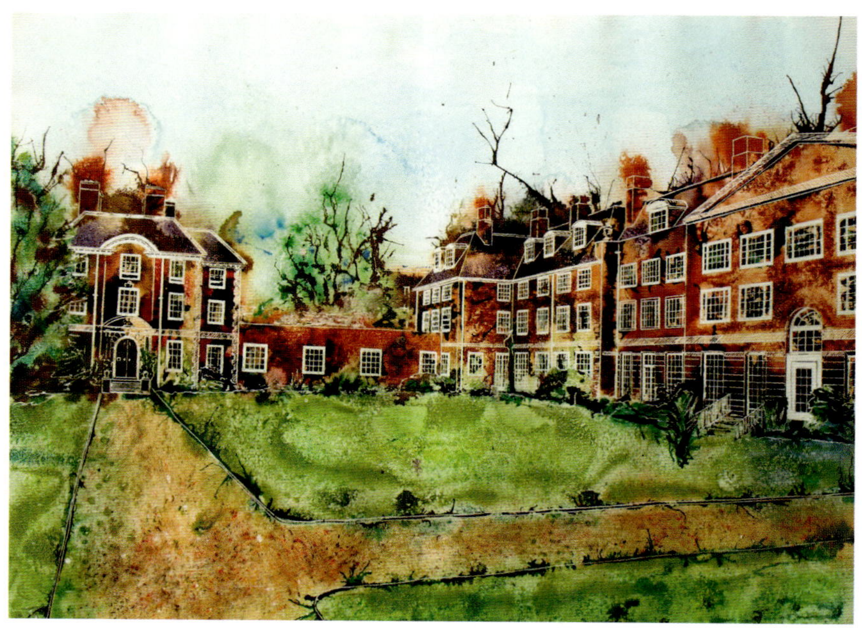

Lady Margaret Hall 'Sunken Garden', Cathy Read

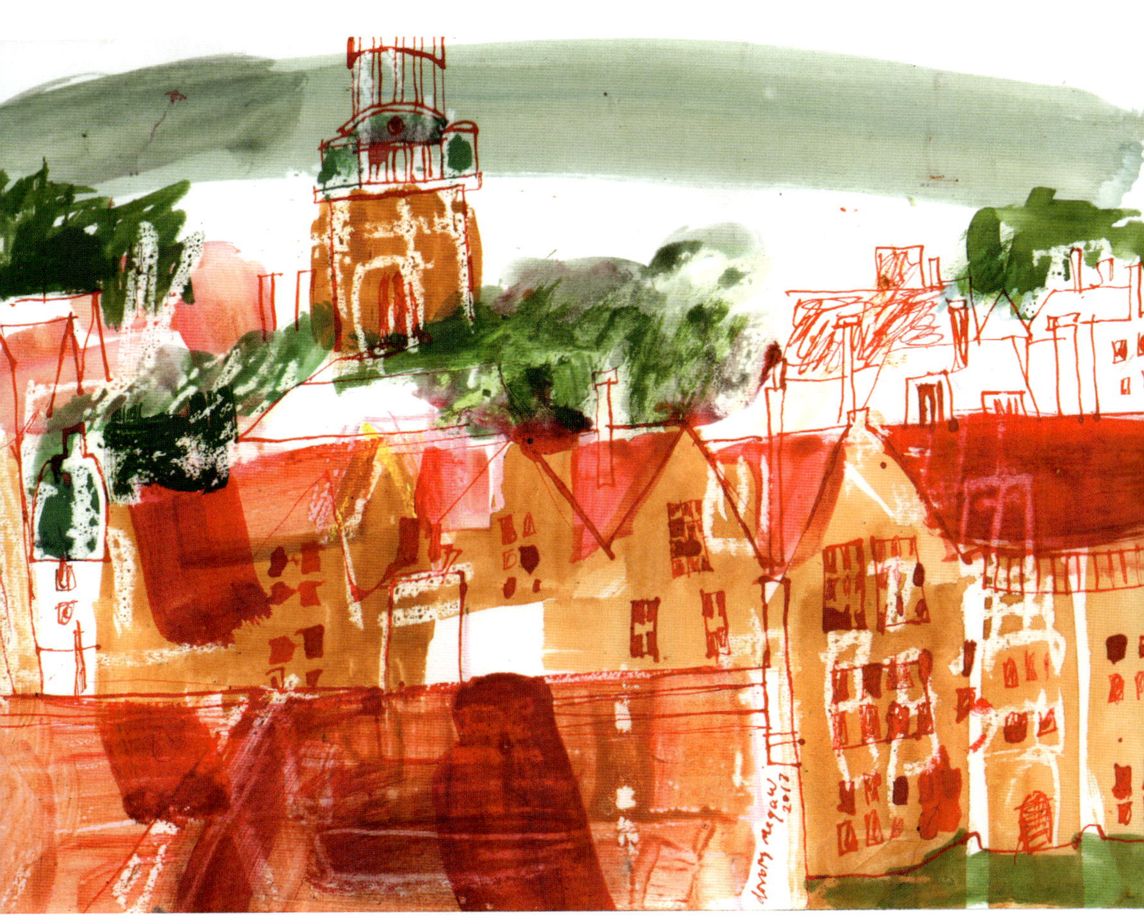

Brasenose College, Dorothy Megaw

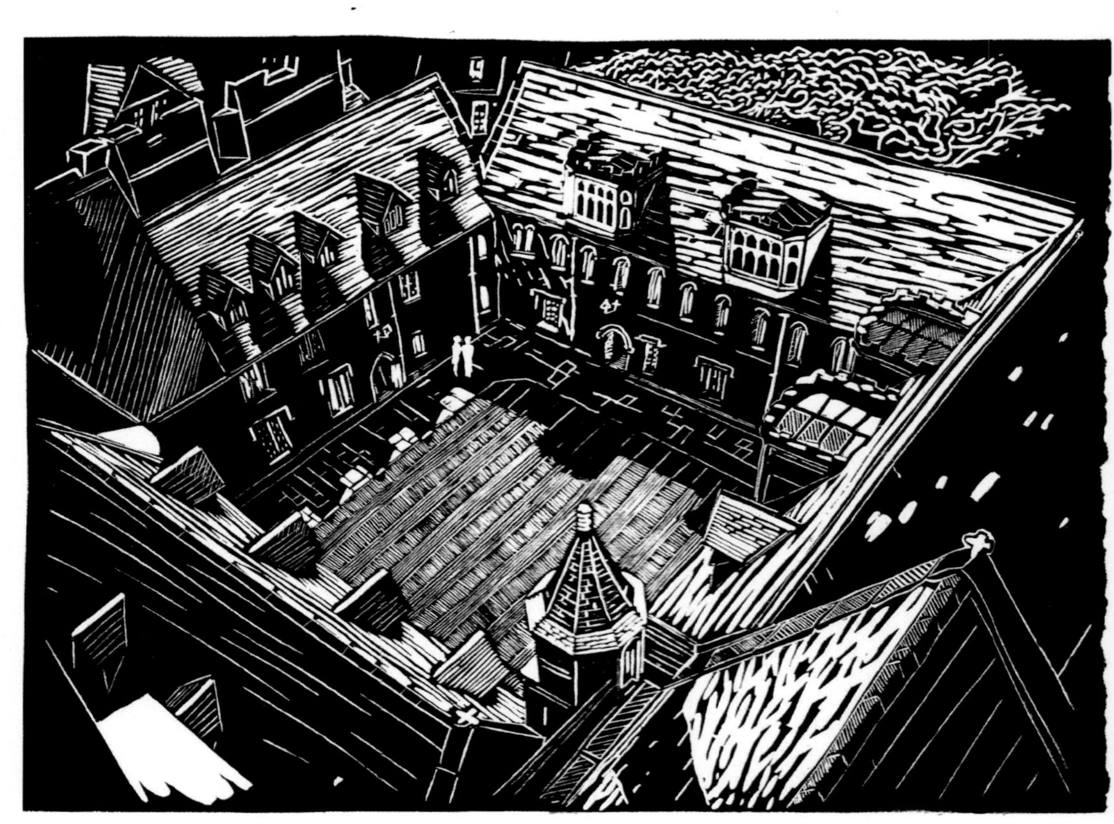

Mob Quad, Merton College, Robin Wilson

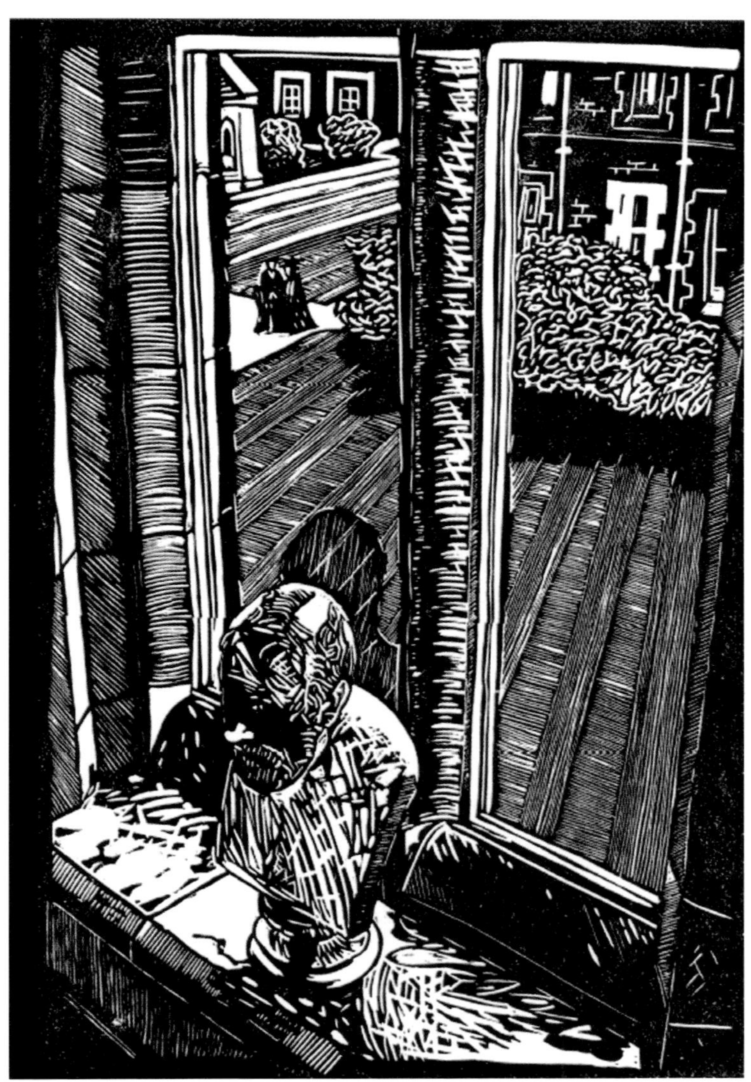

Tate Quad, Harris Manchester College, Robin Wilson

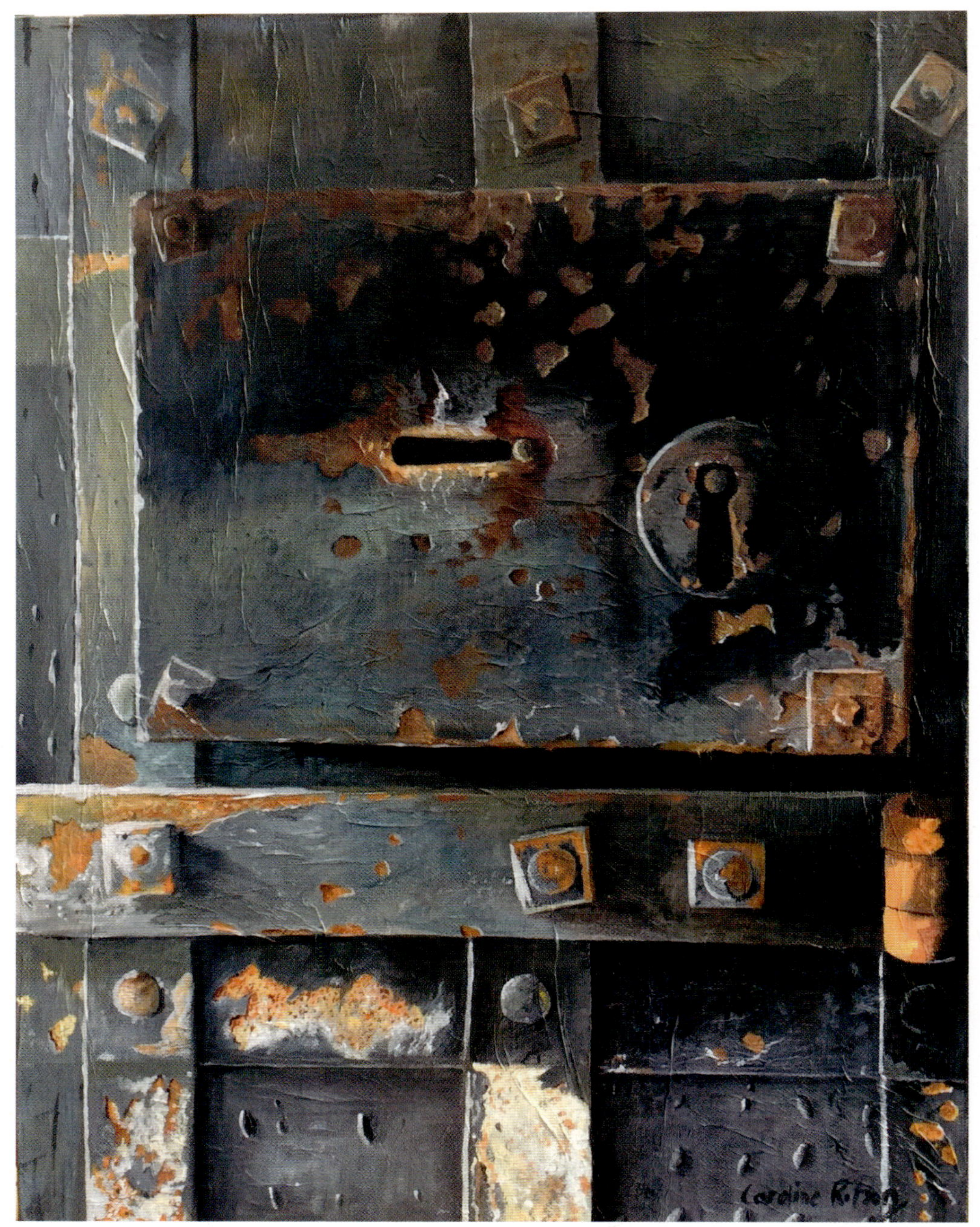

Oxford Castle, Caroline Ritson

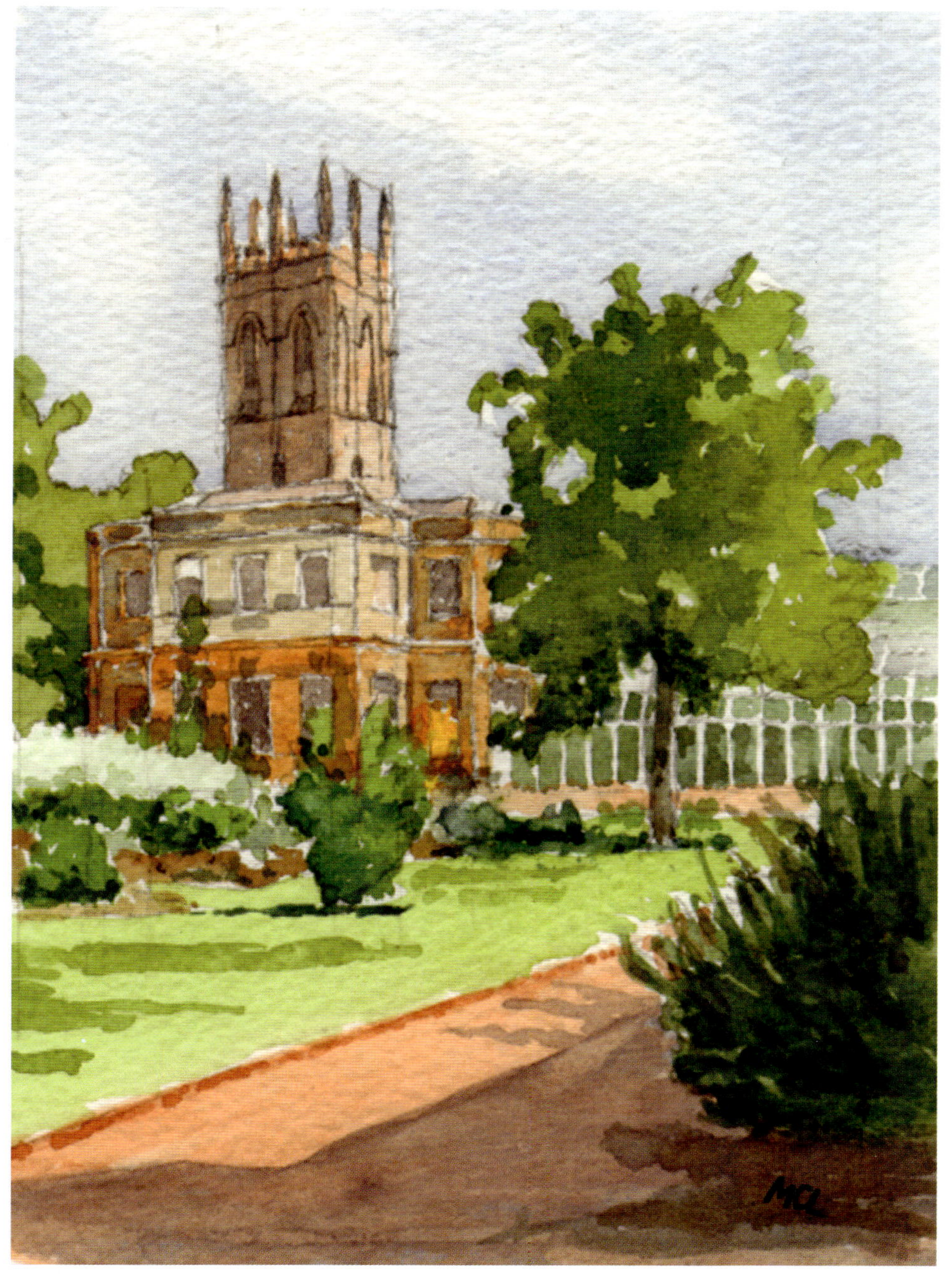

THE BOTANIC GARDEN, MIKE LESTER

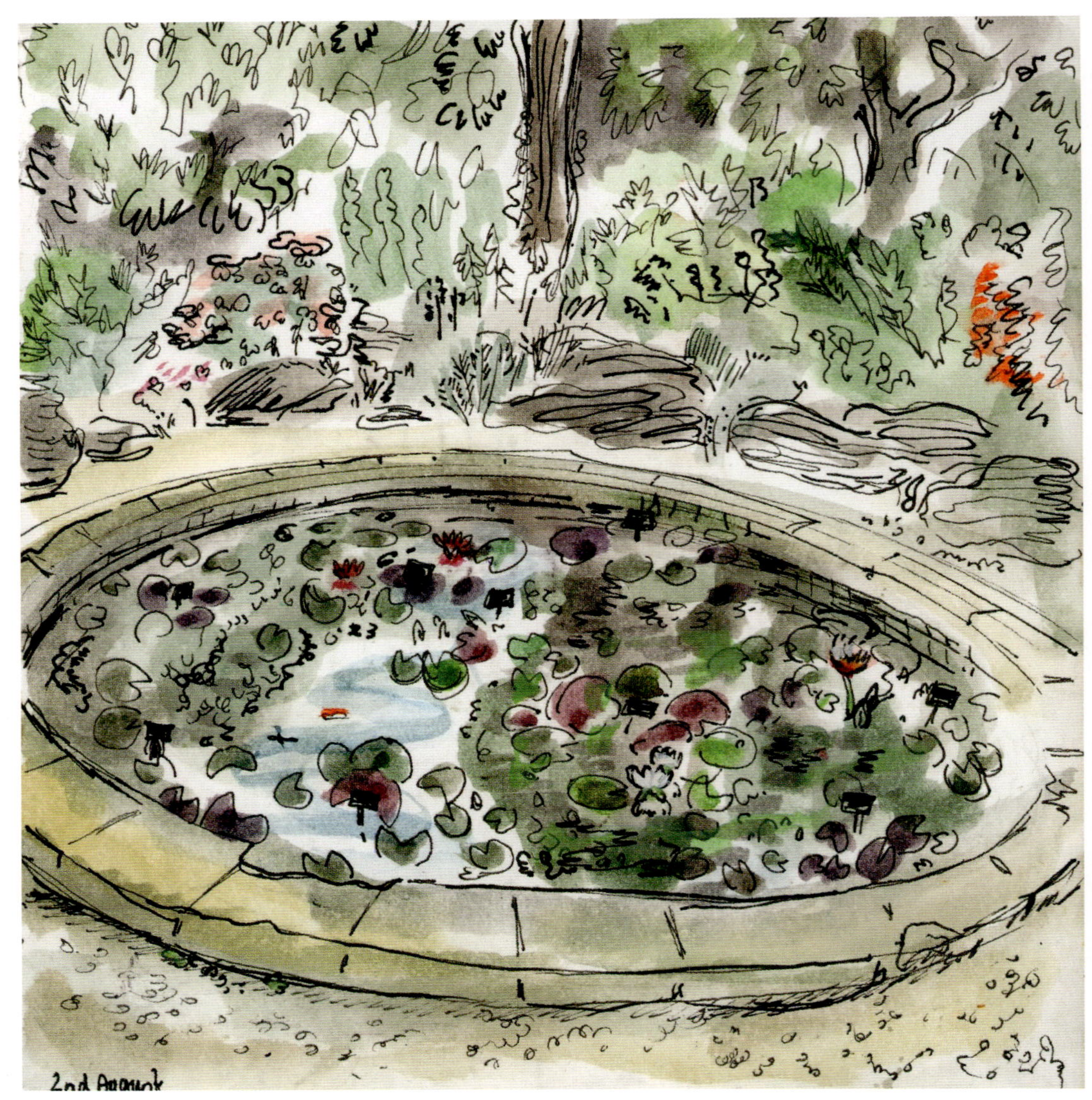

Lily pond at the Botanic Gardens, Imogen Foxell

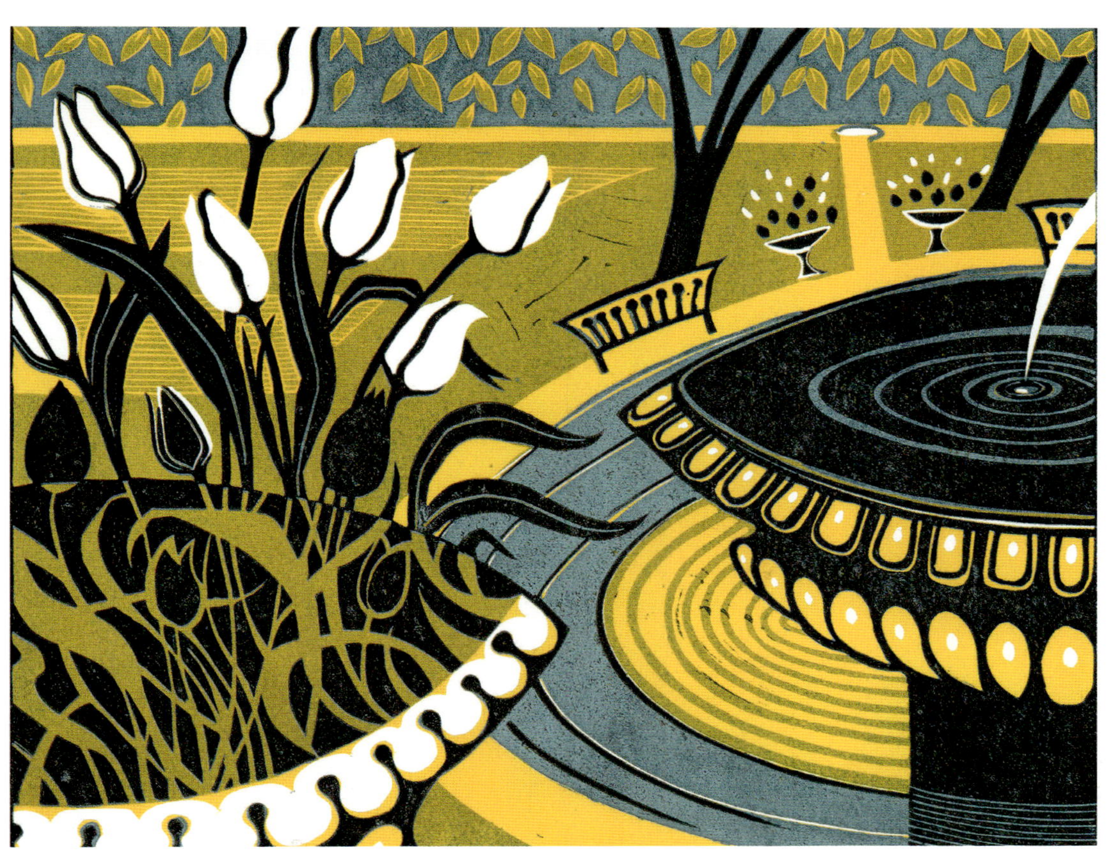

The Botanic Garden, Susan Wheeler

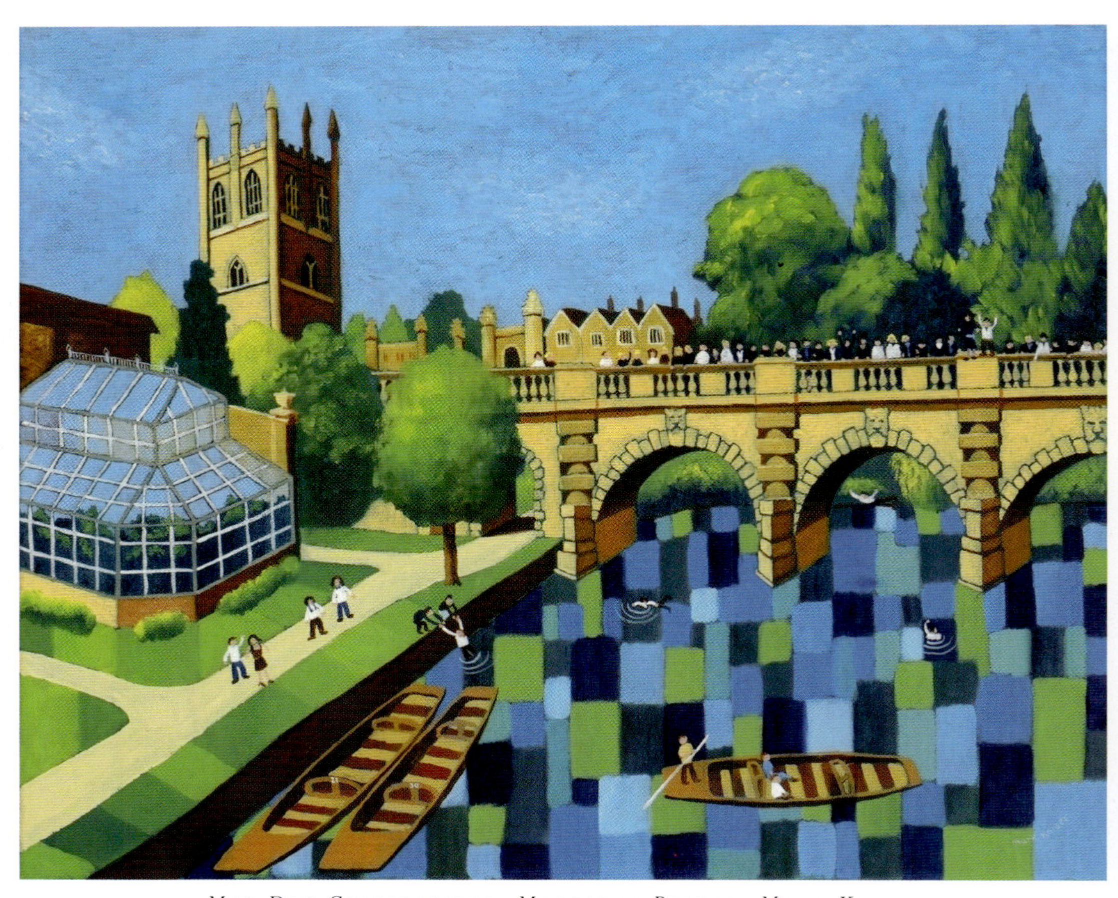

May Day Celebrations, Magdalen Bridge, Mark Kaiser

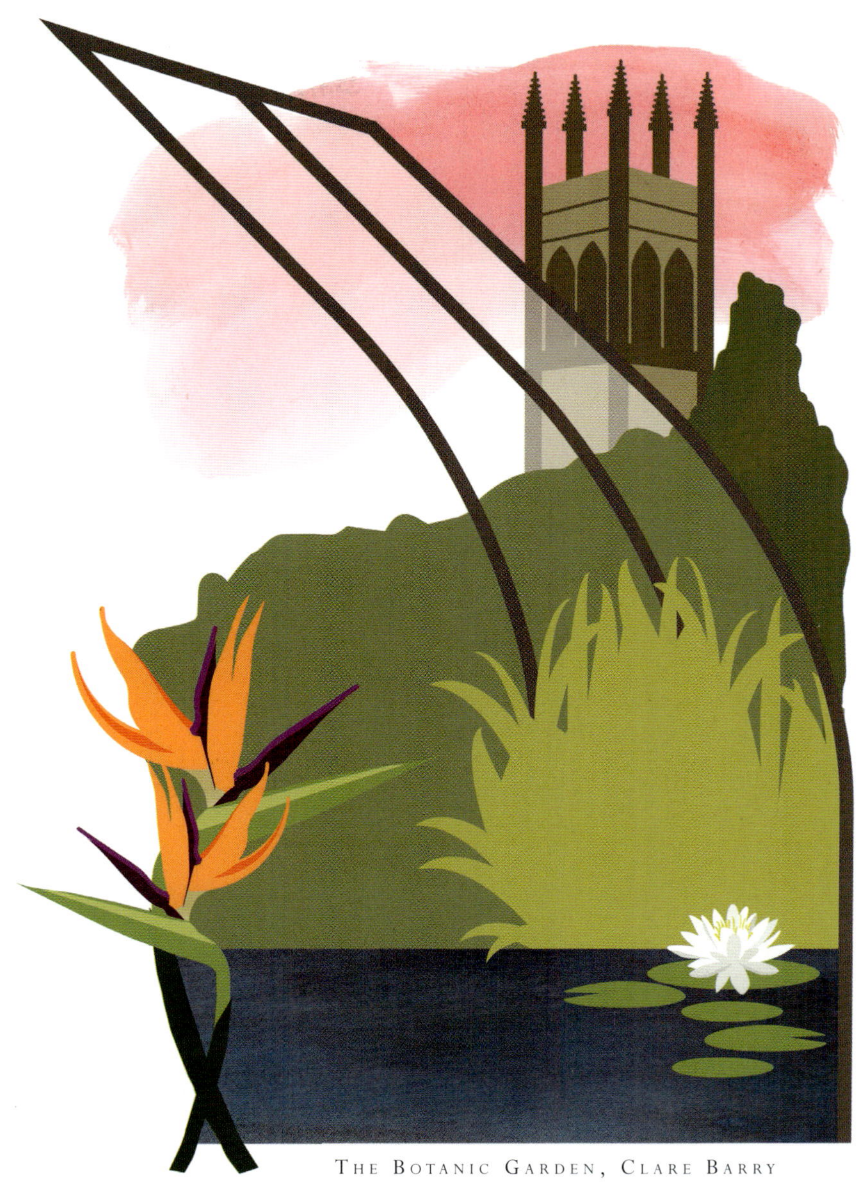

The Botanic Garden, Clare Barry

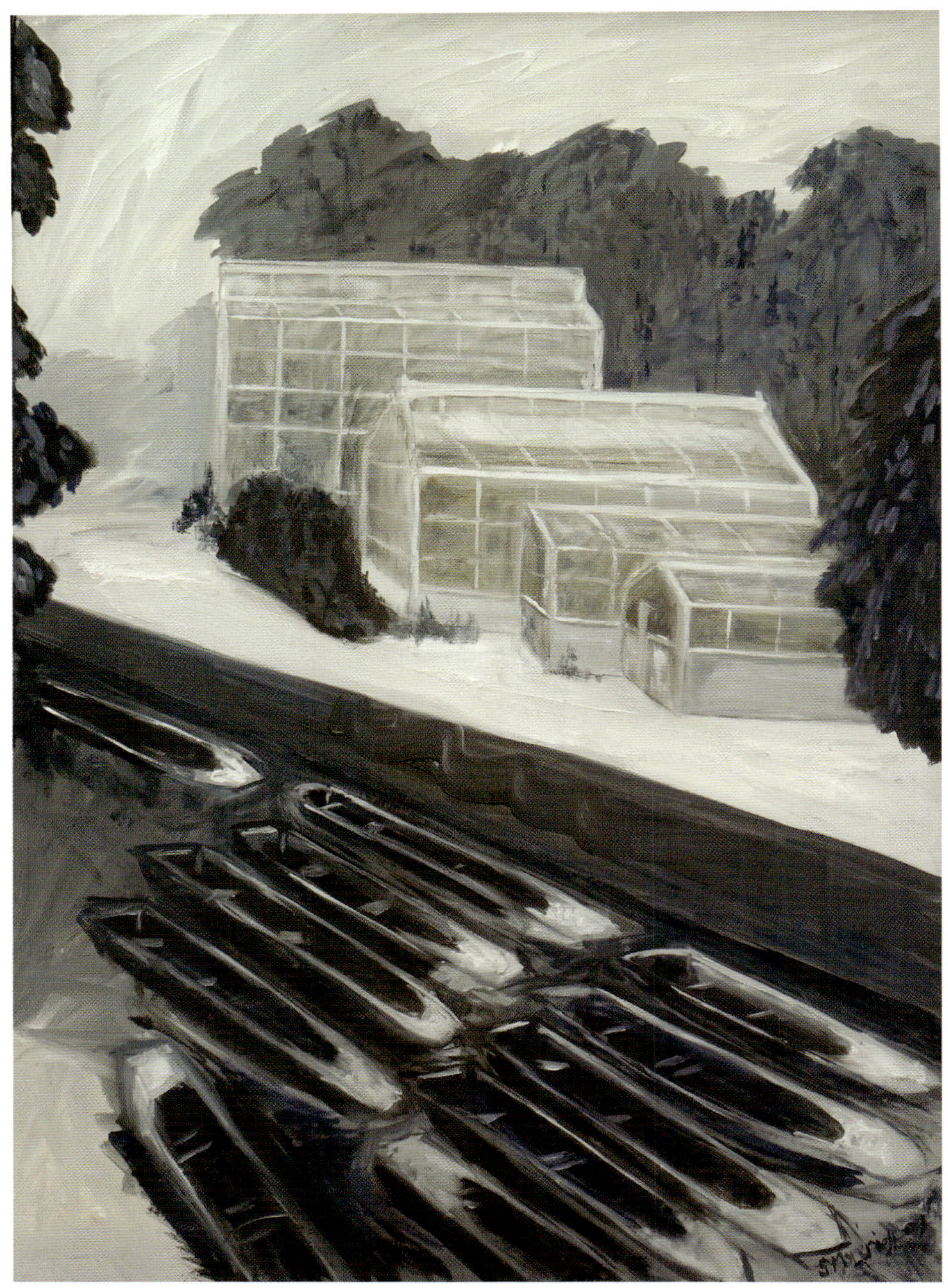

The Botanic Gardens and Punts, Sarah Moncrieff

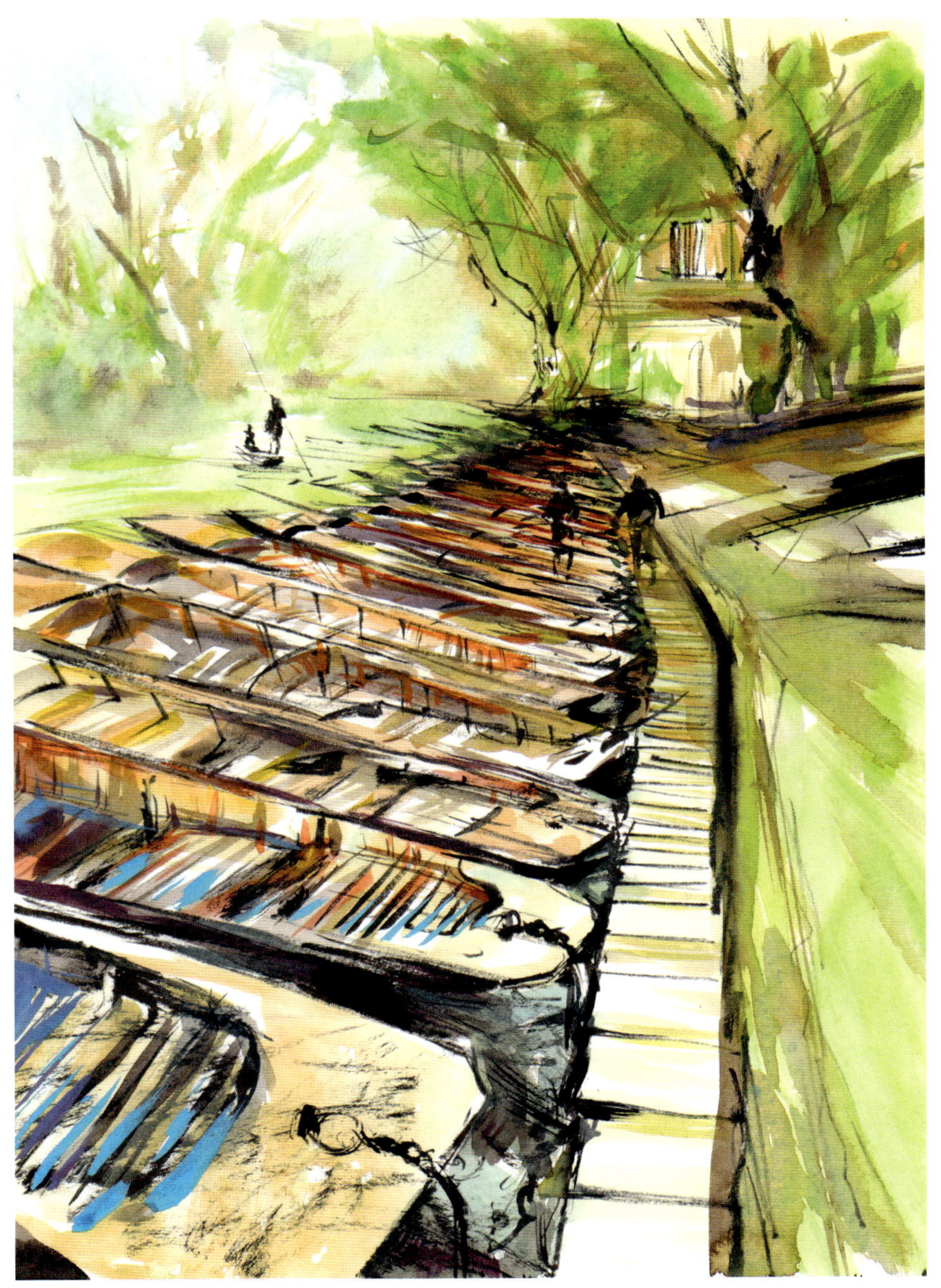

Cherwell Boathouse, William Rowsell

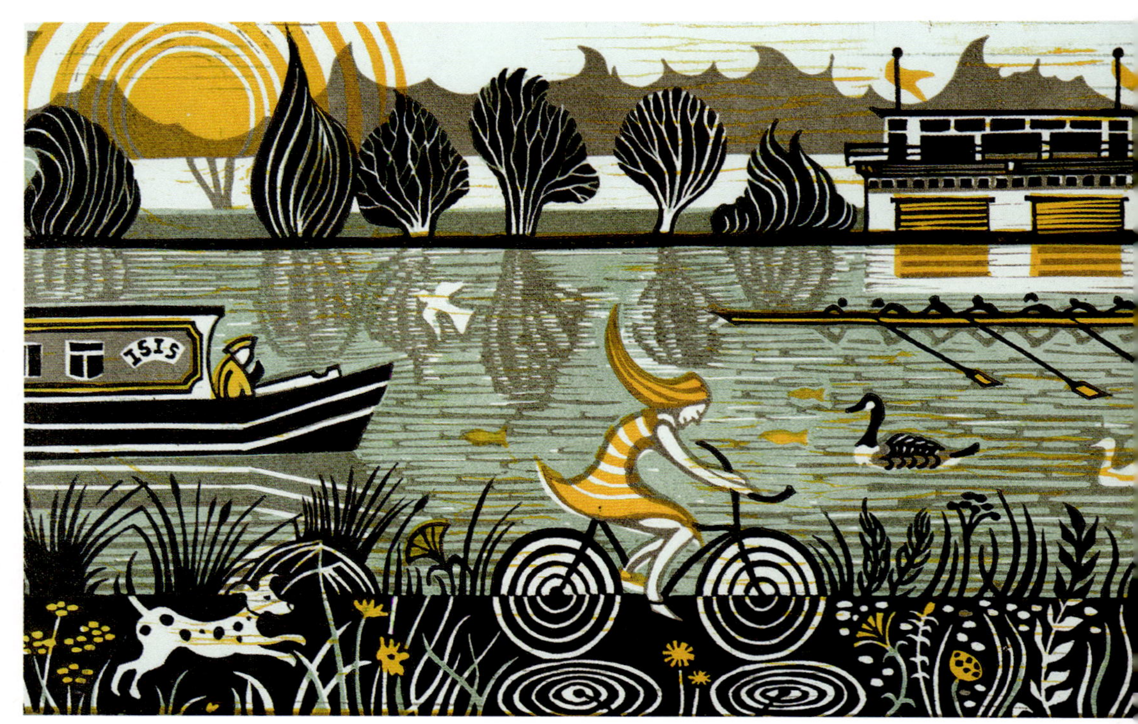

Summer on the Thames, Susan Wheeler

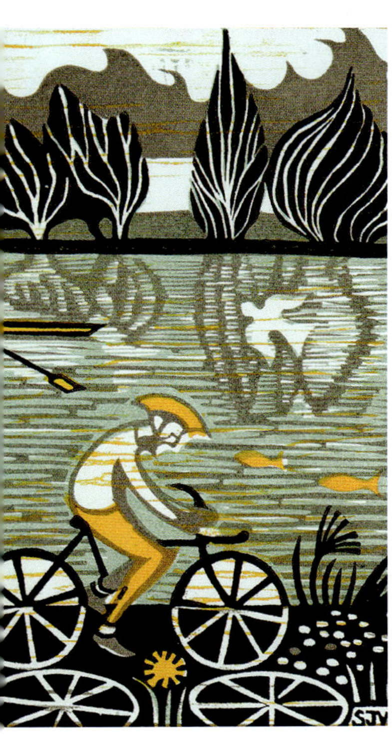

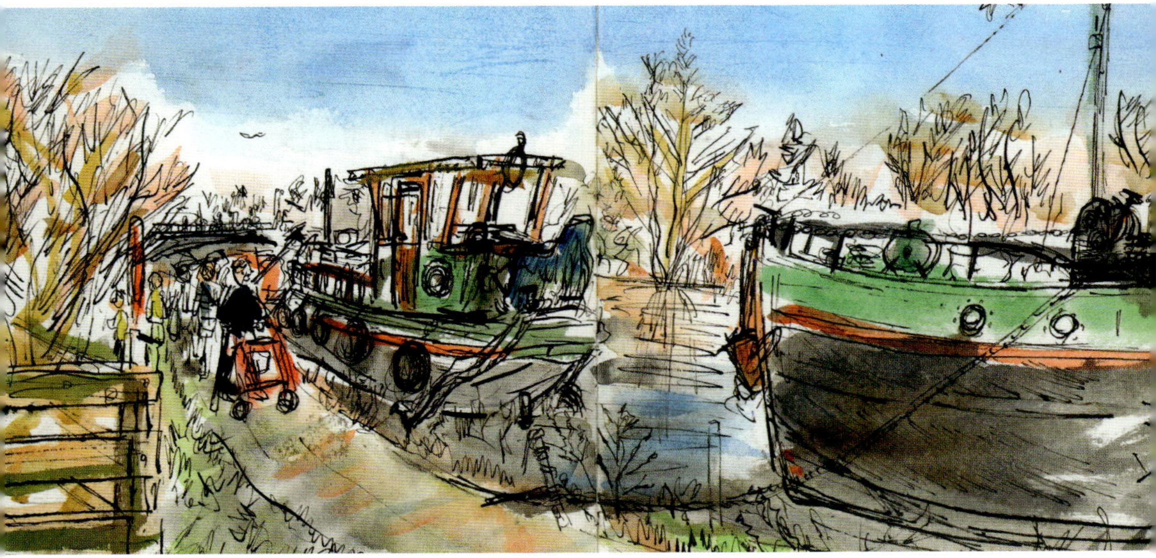

The Thames near Donnington Bridge, Imogen Foxell

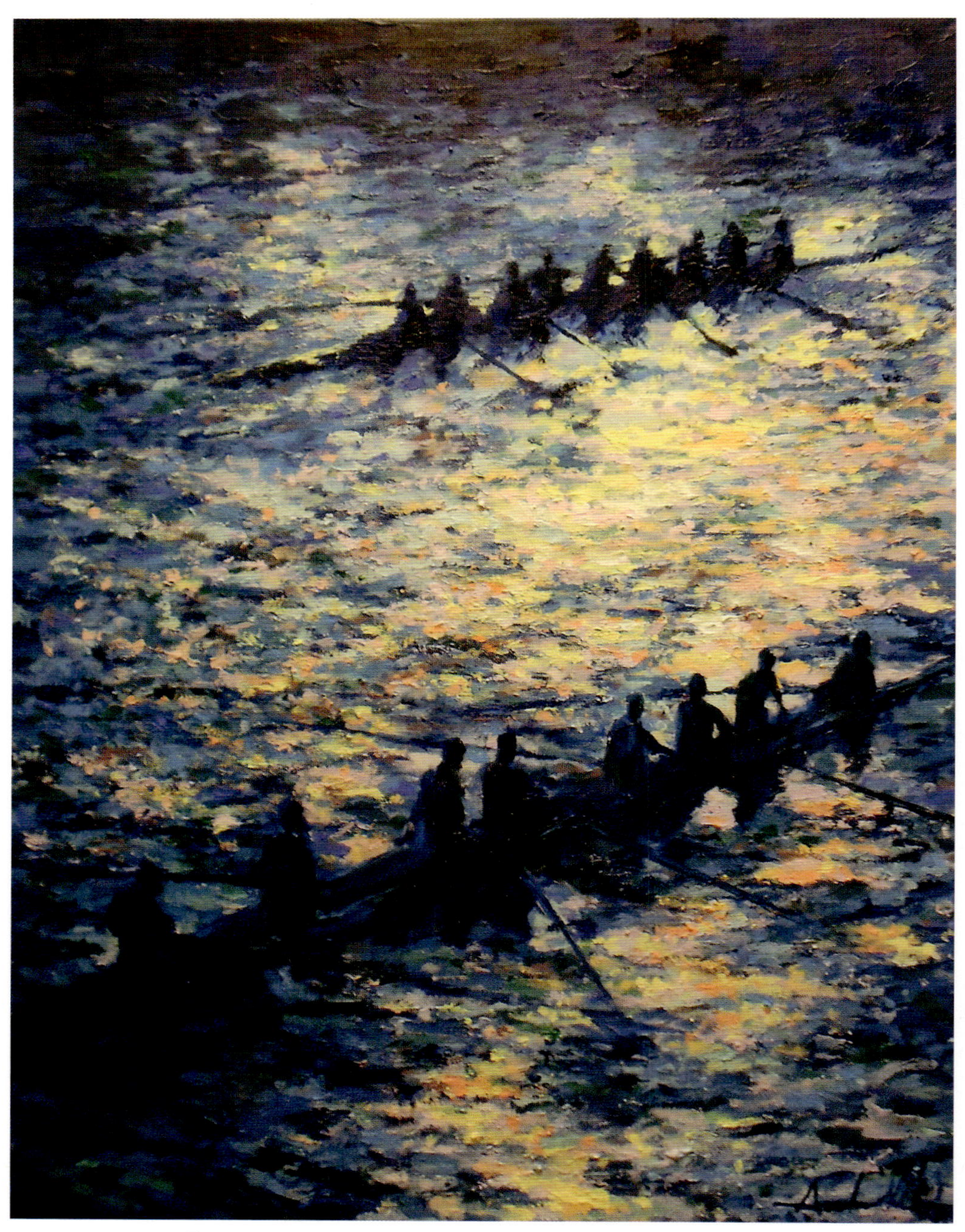

Two Boats on the River, Andrew 'Mani' Manson

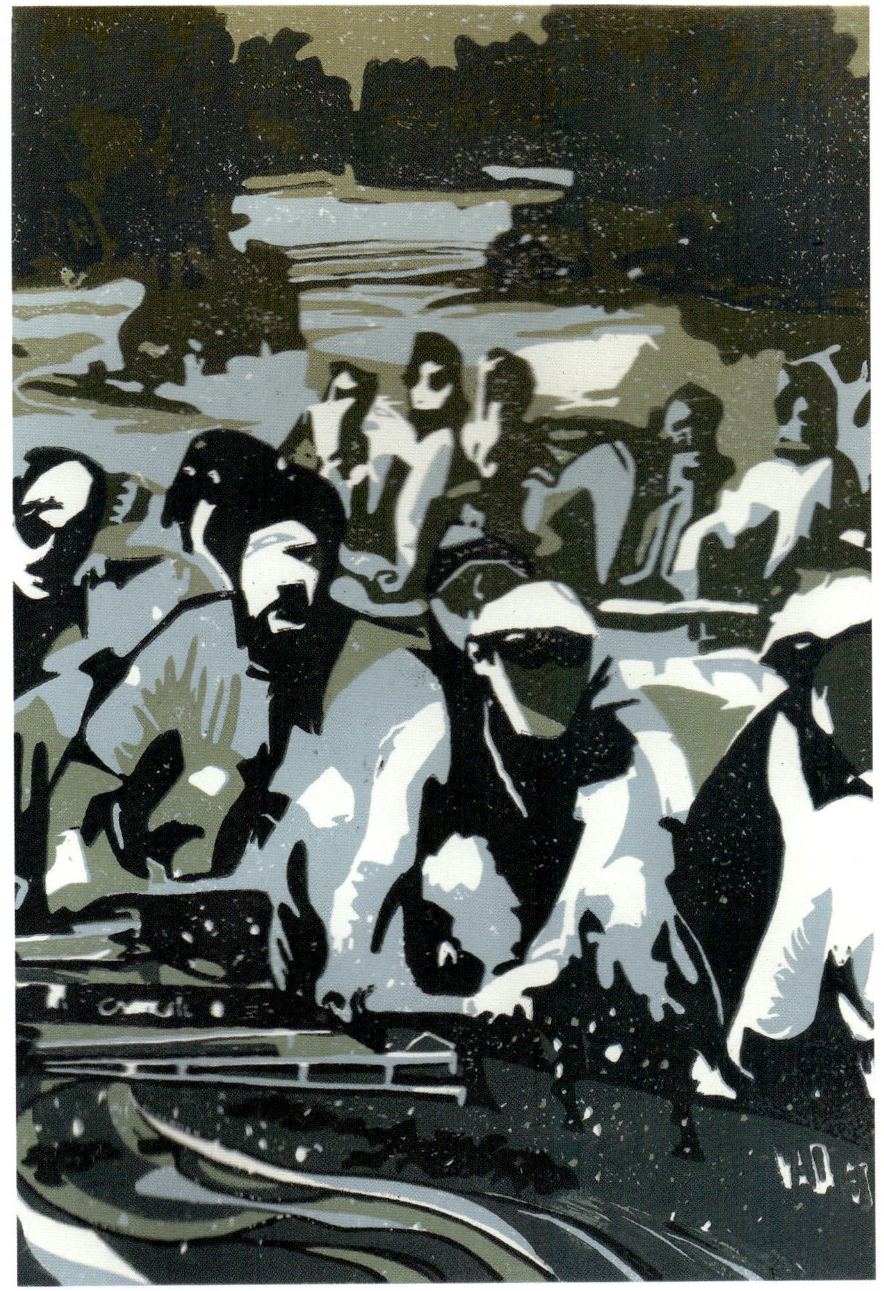

Wadham Bump In The Gut, Robin Wilson

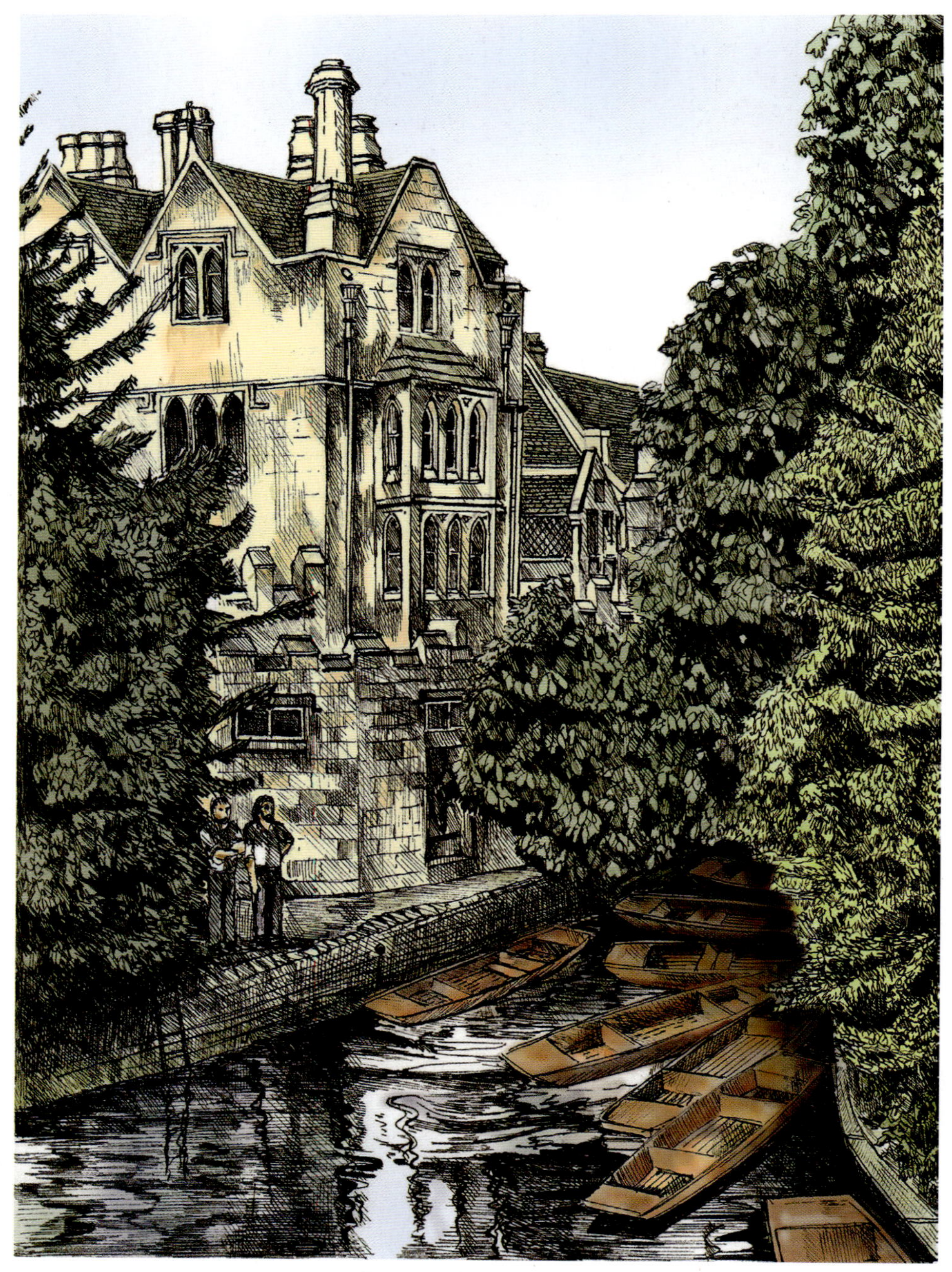

Punts, Jane Peart

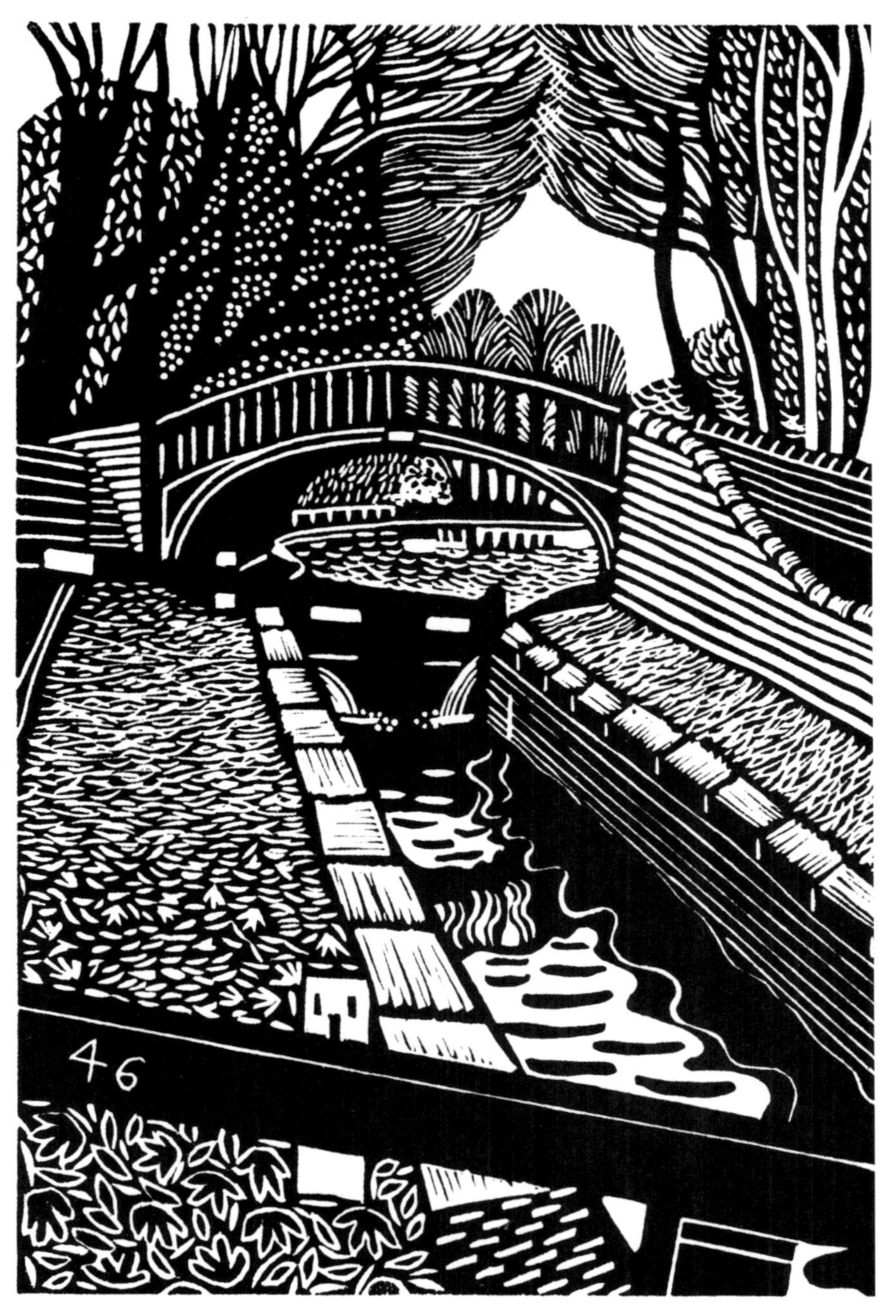

Isis Lock, Eric Gaskell

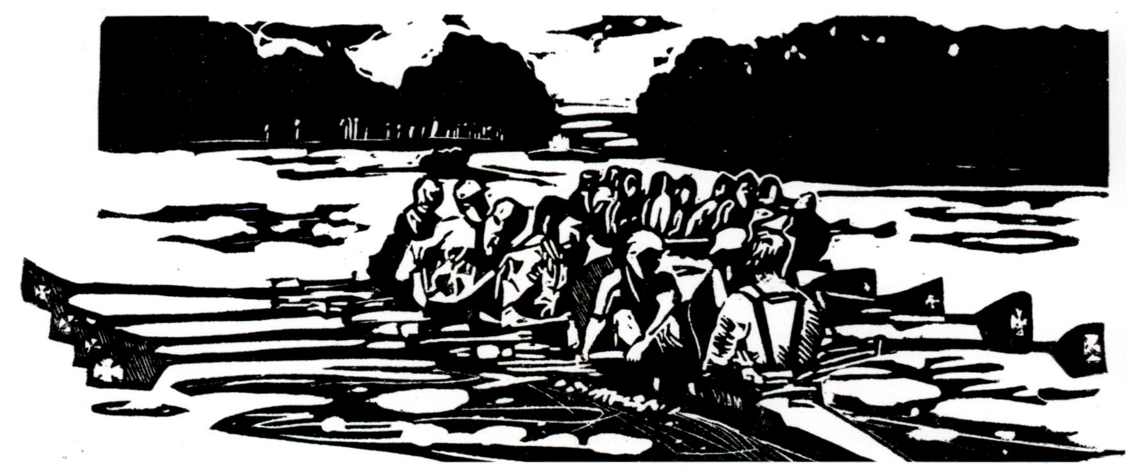

At The Clacker, Christ Church Meadows, Robin Wilson

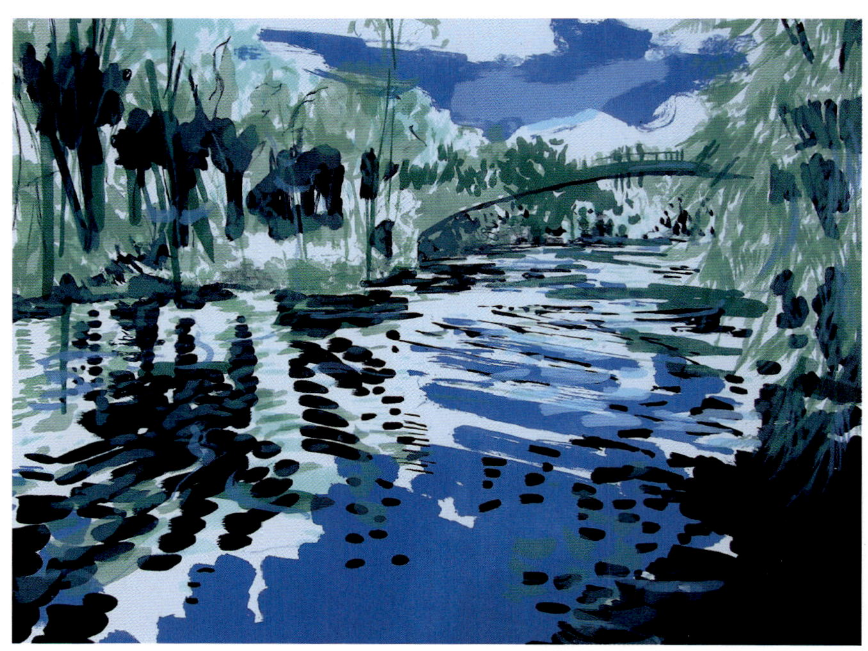

University Parks, Rachel Gracey

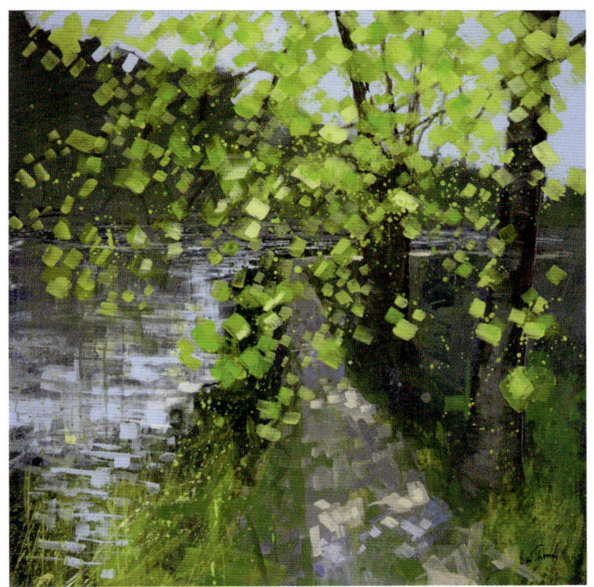

Towpath at Goring, Bee Thomas

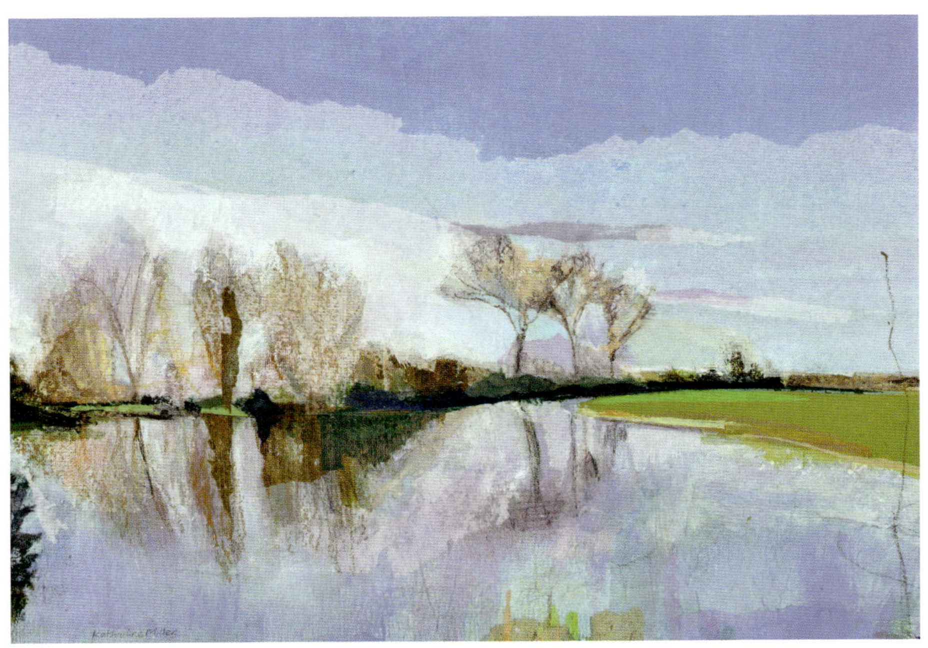

Port Meadow, Katharine Miller

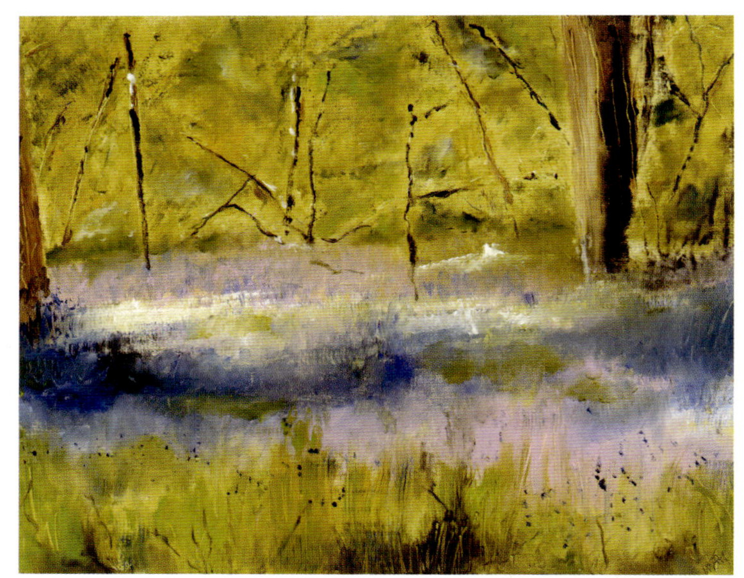

Pinsley Wood, Long Hanborough, Maureen Gillespie

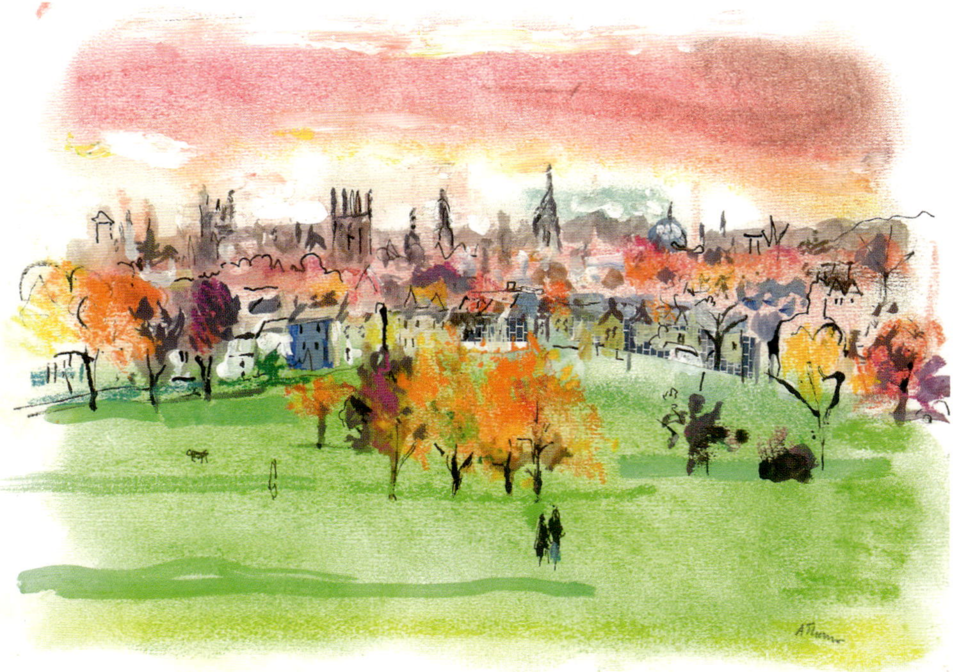

South Park, Alice Thomson

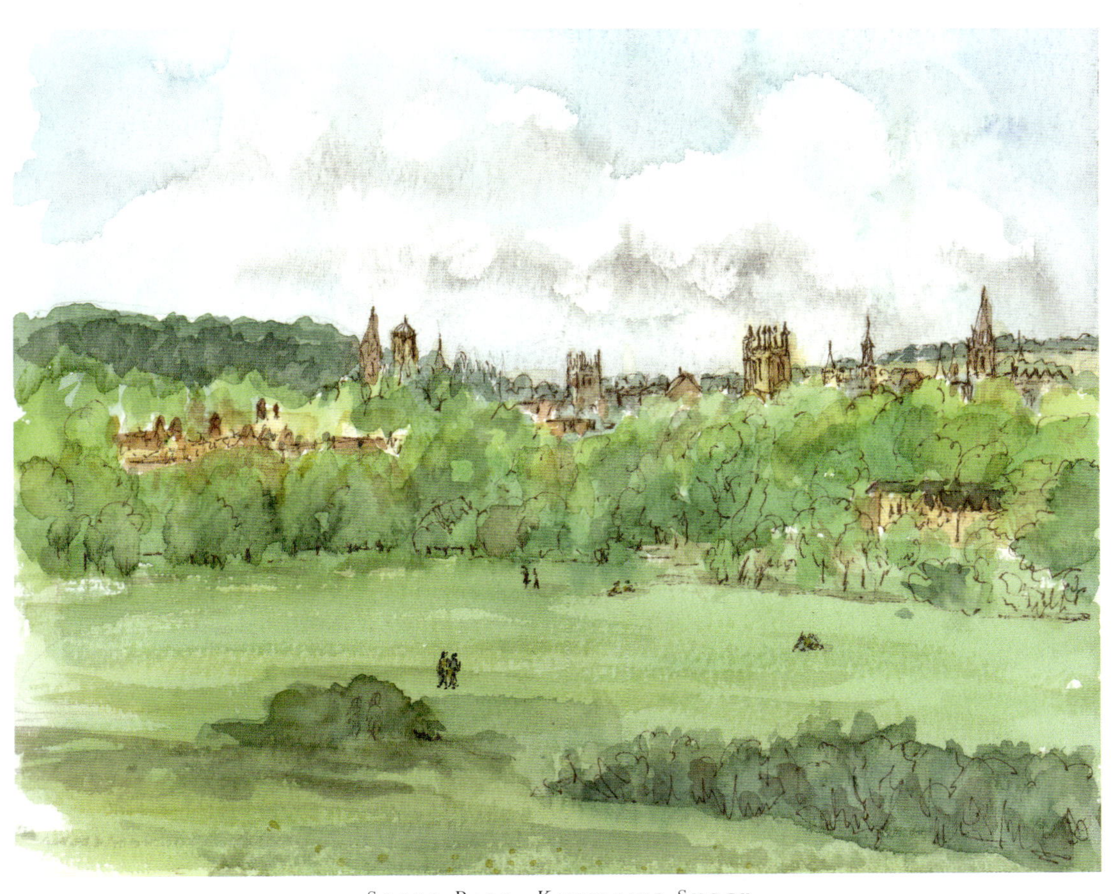

South Park, Katherine Shock

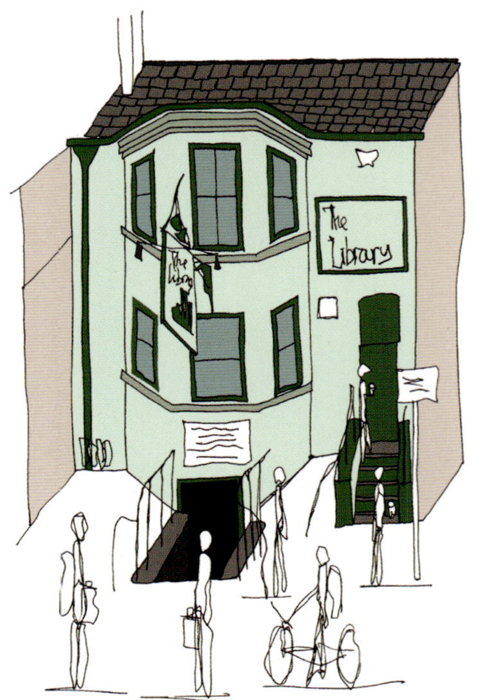

THE LIBRARY, COWLEY ROAD, JOE DAVIS

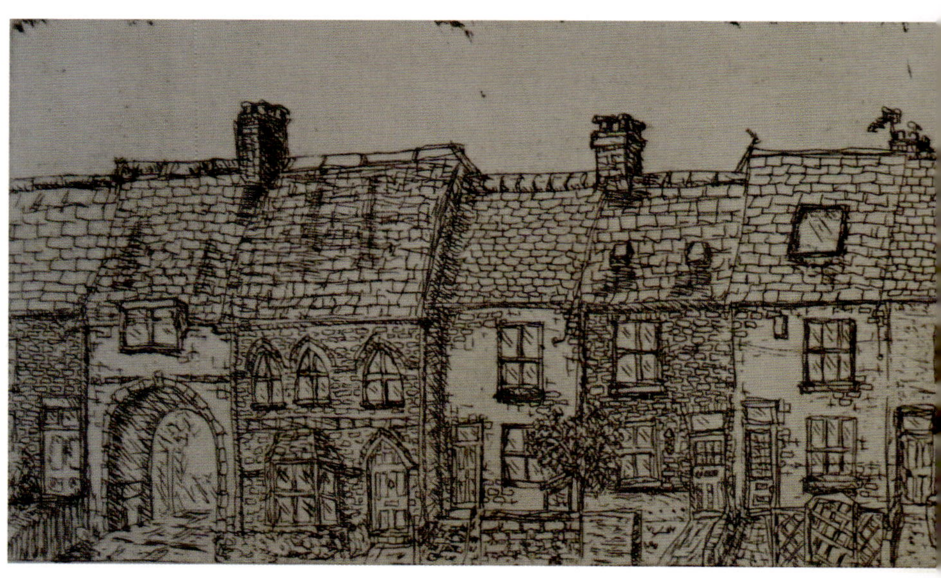

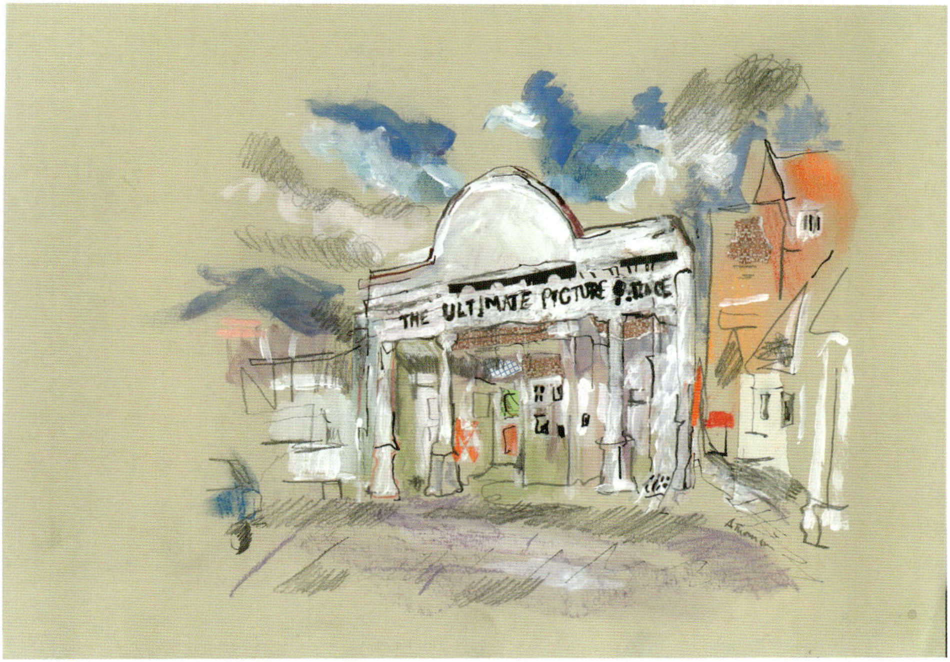

The Ultimate Picture House, Alice Thomson

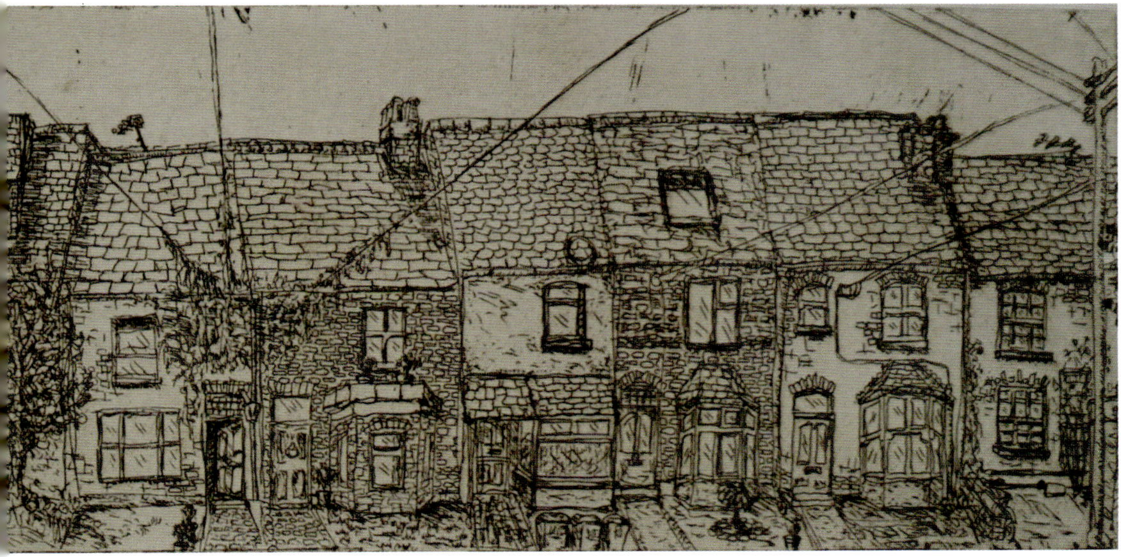

Princes St, Steven Chance

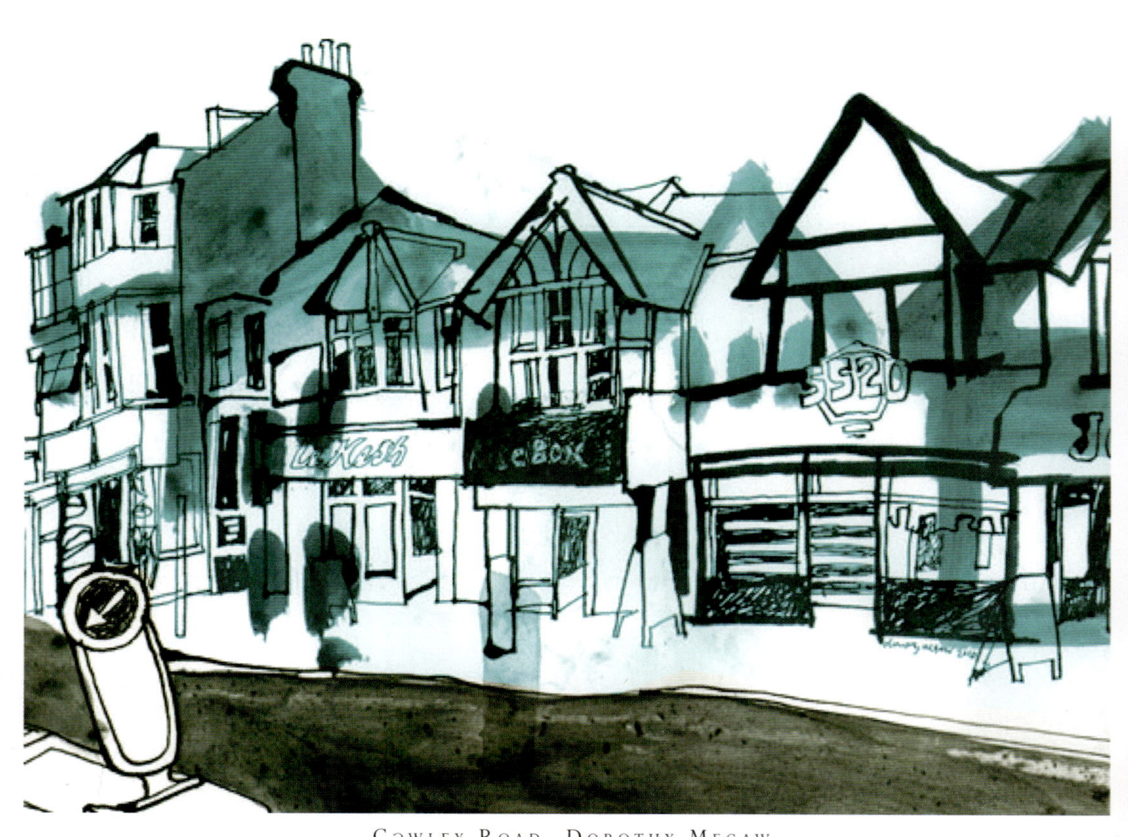

COWLEY ROAD, DOROTHY MEGAW

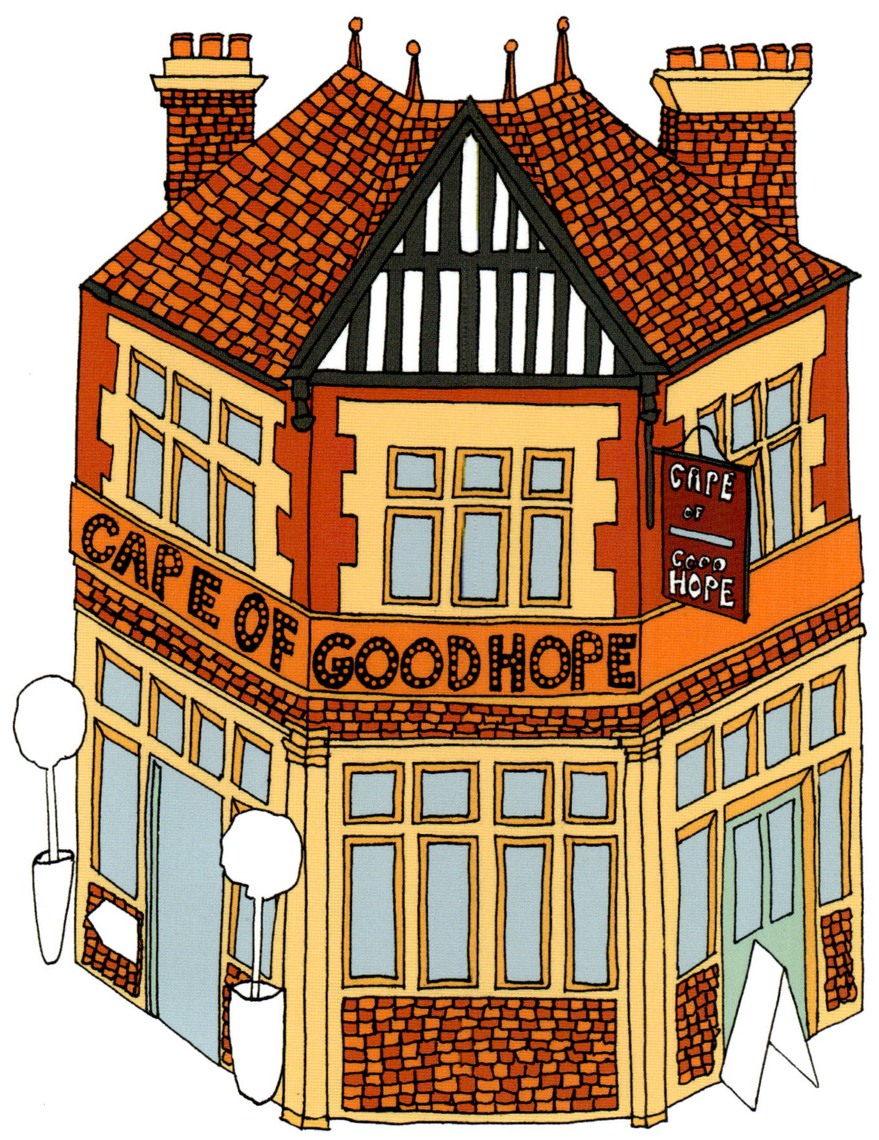

THE CAPE OF GOOD HOPE, JOE DAVIS

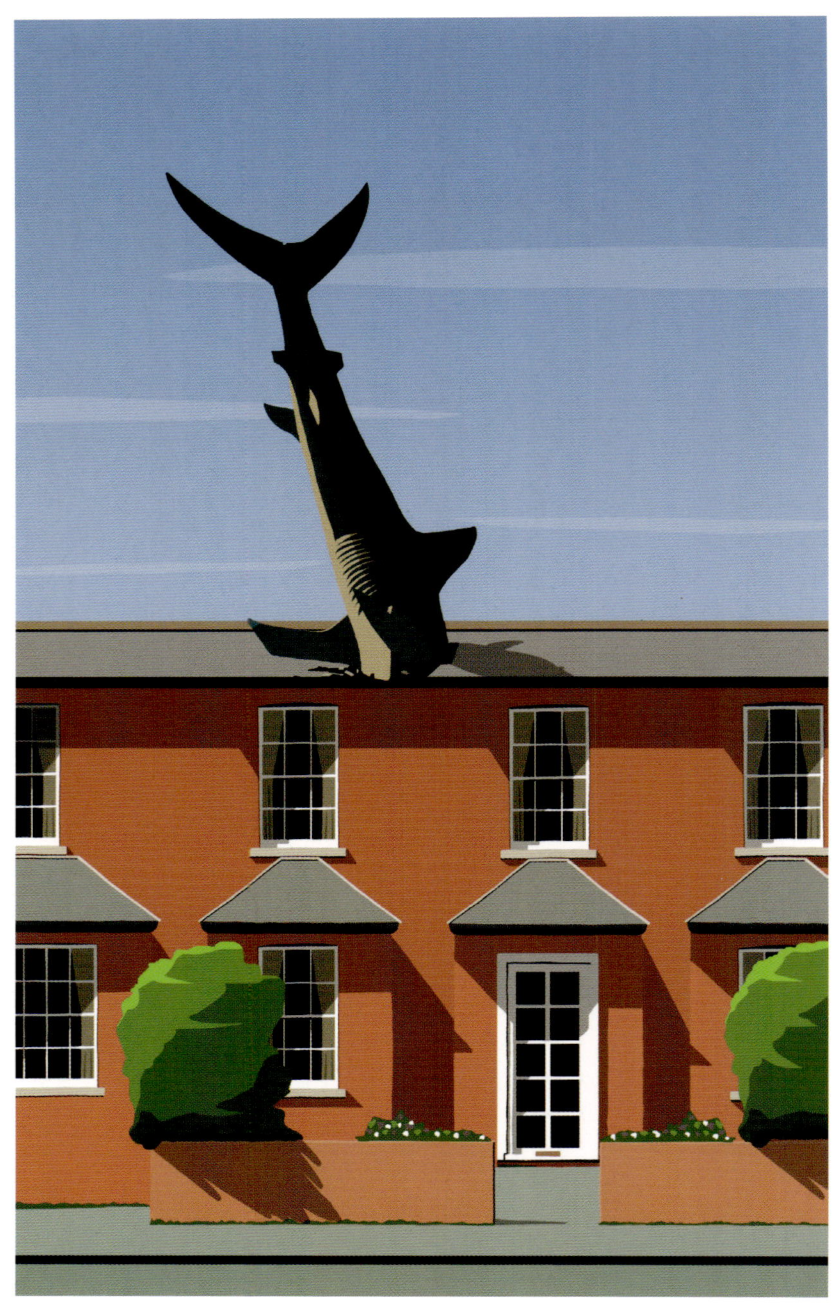

Headington Shark, Richard O'Neill

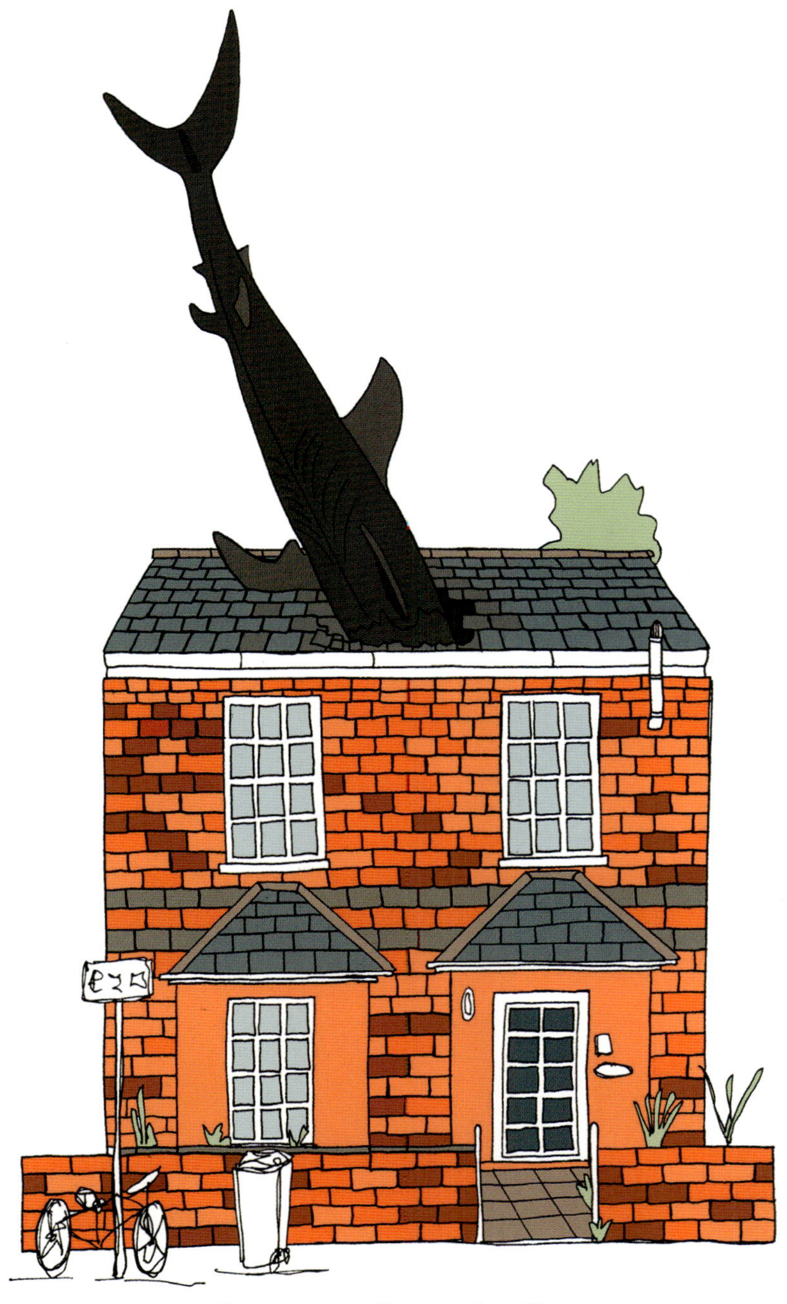

Headington Shark, Joe Davis

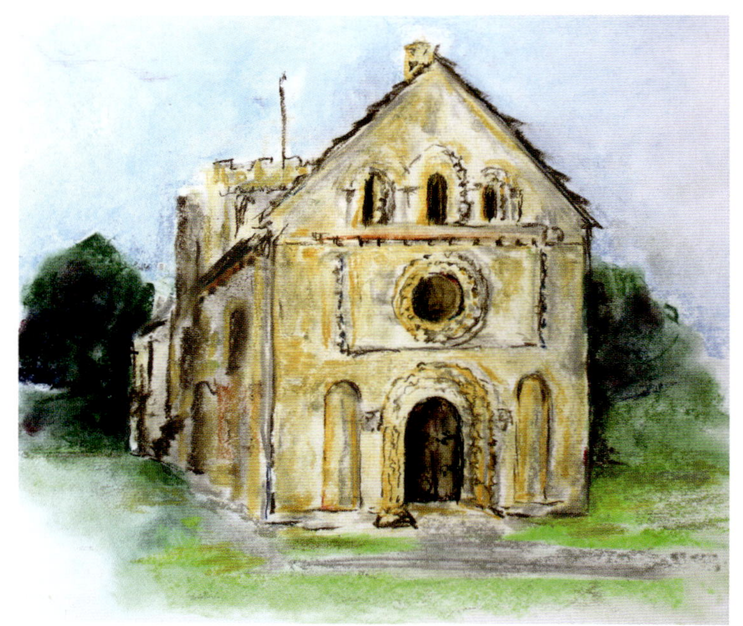

Iffley Church, Charlie Davies

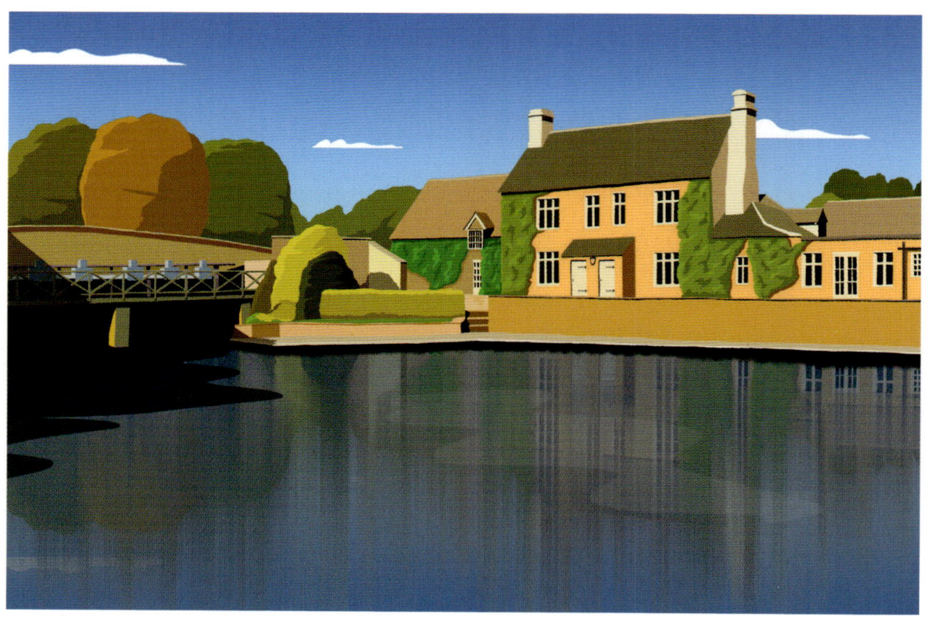

Trout Inn, Wolvercote, Richard O'Neill

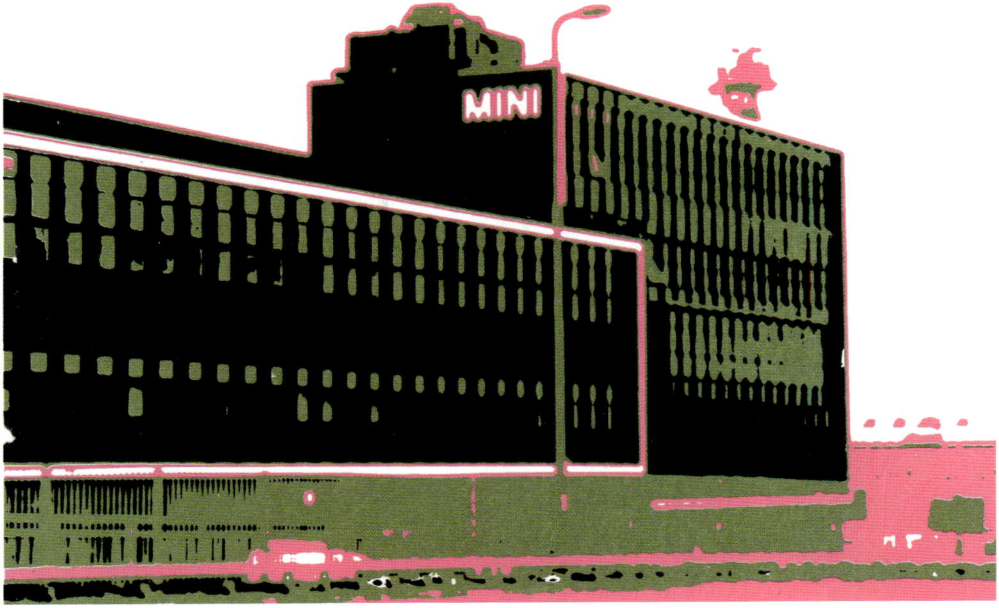

THE MINI PLANT, RICHARD STEPHENS

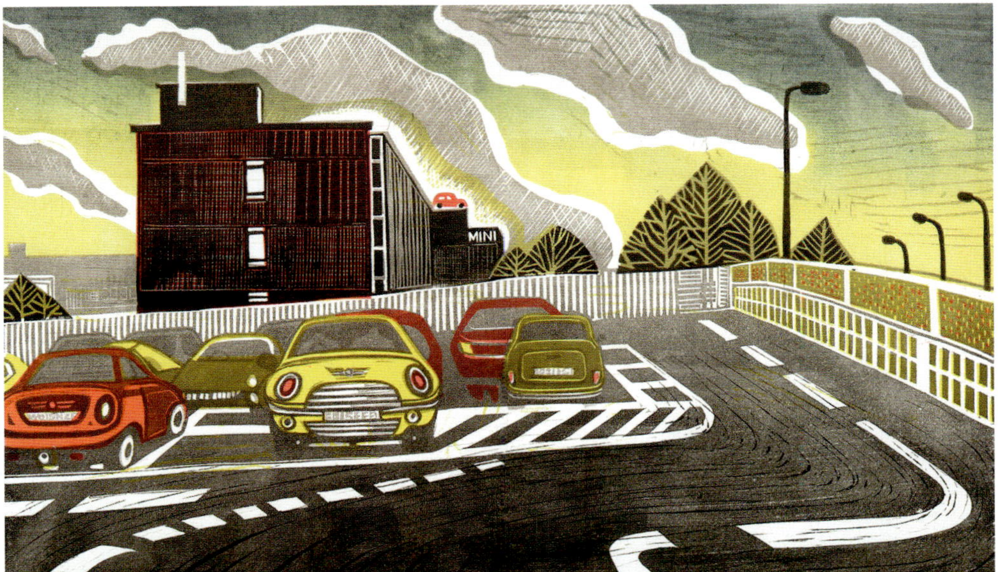

THE MINI PLANT, SUSAN WHEELER

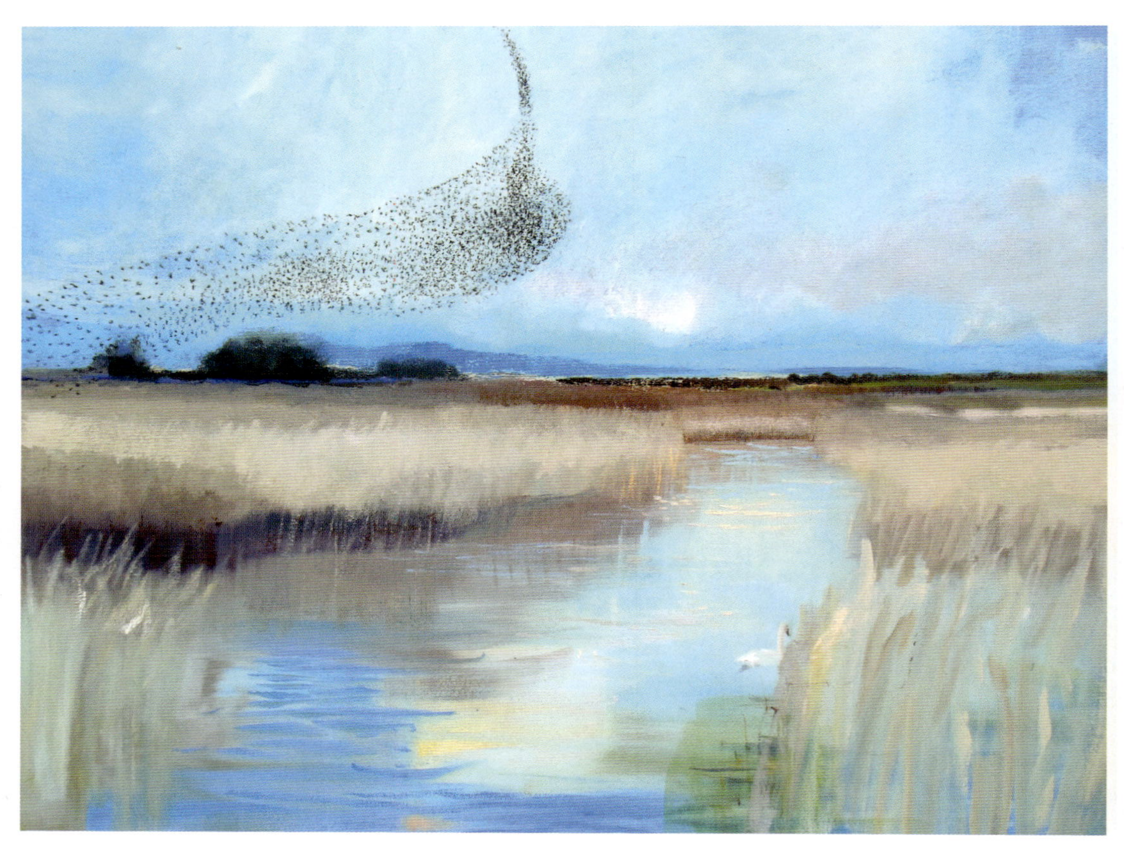

Otmoor, Jane Strother

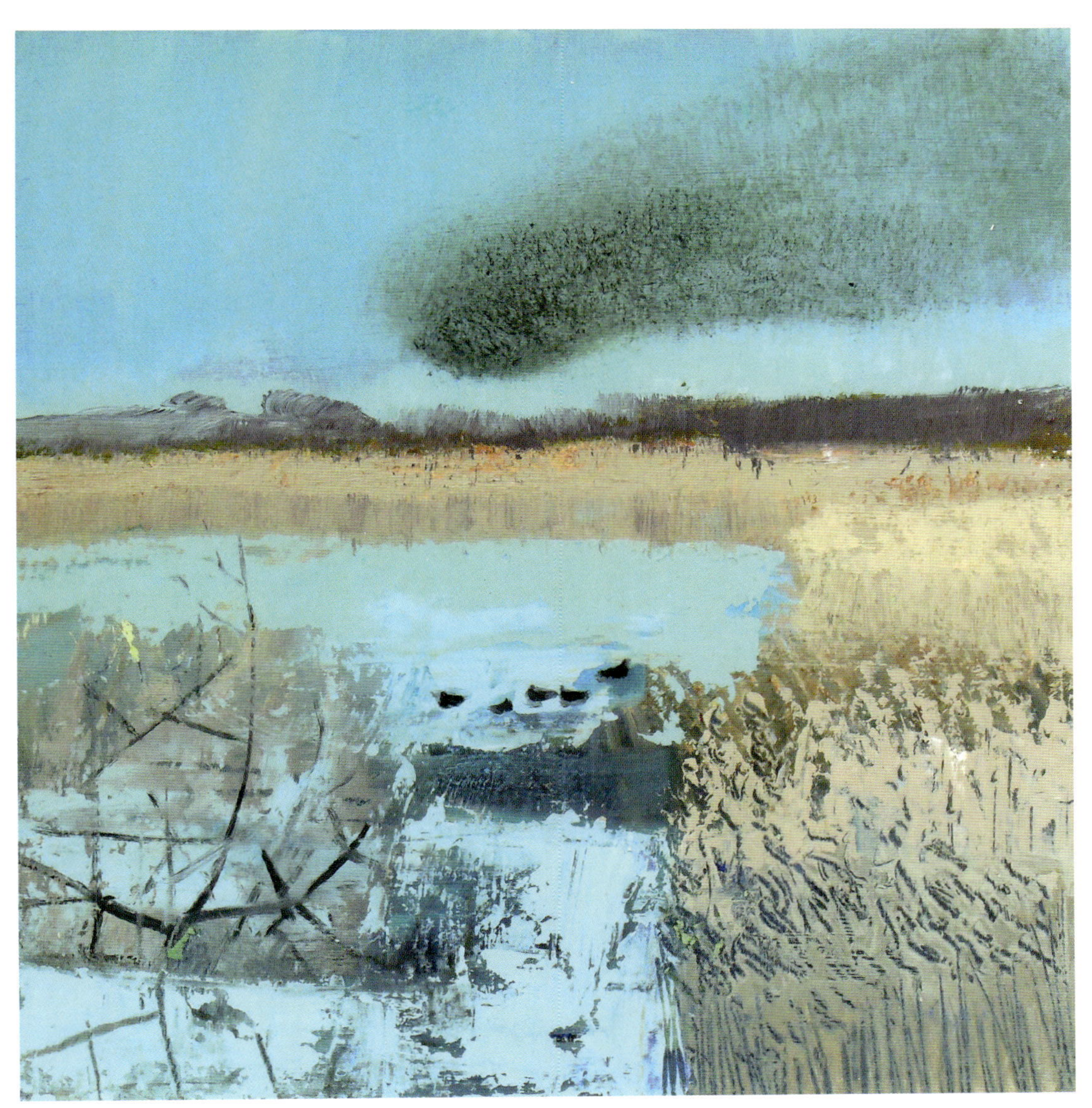

Otmoor, Jane Strother

ARTISTS' CREDITS

Jon Alsop
© Jon Alsop
Jon is an Oxfordshire based artist specialising in watercolour and digital illustrations.
www.behance.net/alsopjonb4eb
All Rights Reserved.
Pages 50, 53,58–59

Steve Appleton
© Steve Appleton
Observational illustrations made in situ.
www.steveappleton.co.uk
Page 44

Clare Barry
© Clare Barry
Digital and hand-drawn mixed media illustration and design.
https://clarebarry.weebly.com
All Rights Reserved.
Pages 21, 117

Bee Bartlett
© Bee Bartlett
Mixed media paintings exploring the balance between composition and experimentation with materials.
www.beebartlett.co.uk
All Rights Reserved.
Pages 17, 30, 40, 100

Amanda Beck
© Amanda Beck
Reportage artist inspired by history, heritage and industrial figurative – watercolour, pastels and mixed media.
www.amandabeckartist.com
All Rights Reserved.
Page 20

Emma Bennett
© Emma Bennett
Vibrant hand-cut collage using recycled papers and hand-drawn pictures.
www.emmabennettcollage.co.uk
All Rights Reserved.
Pages 90–91, cover image

Sarah Bond
© Sarah Bond
Vibrant mixed media paintings.
www.sarahbondart.com
All Rights Reserved.
Page 62

Richard Briggs
© Richard Briggs
Pen and ink watercolour illustrations of urban, coastal and rural landscapes.
www.richardbriggs-illustration.co.uk
All Rights Reserved.
Pages 29, 34

William Bright
© William Bright
Meticulously researched hand-illustrated prints, rooted in cartography.
www.notonthehighstreet.com/oxfordprints
All Rights Reserved.
Page 43

Susan Brown
© Susan Brown
Paintings mainly in watercolour and acrylic; subjects include architecture and landscape.
www.susanbrownstudio.co.uk
All Rights Reserved.
Pages 10, 19, 35, 93, 105

Steven Chance
© Steven Chance
Zinc and copper plate etchings of characterful spaces, places and creatures.
sc240398@gmail.com
All Rights Reserved.
Page 131

Norm Chung
© Norm Chung
Portraits, buildings, caricatures, graphic novels, comic strips in oils, watercolours or ink.
waivisuals@gmail.com
All Rights Reserved.
Page 73

Gerry Coles
© Gerry Coles
Oxfordshire printmaker producing hand-printed linocuts.
www.gerrycolesprints.co.uk
All Rights Reserved.
Page 26

Mark Colliass
© Mark Colliass
Designer and illustrator from Oxford, illustrates stylised stacking cityscapes.
www.colliassdesign.com
All Rights Reserved.
Page 42

Charlie Davies
© Charlie Davies
Paintings and prints inspired by nature and the world we live in.
www.charliedaviesdesigns.co.uk
All Rights Reserved.
Pages 33, 39, 136

Joe Davis
© Joe Davis
Illustrations of a city's alternative landmarks, local venues and most of all pubs.
www.joedavisart.com
All Rights Reserved.
Pages 47, 130, 133, 135

John Dew
© John Dew
Etching, egg tempera and water colour painting, topographical drawings.
www.johndew.co.uk
All Rights Reserved.
Pages 98–99

Camilla Dowse
© Camilla Dowse
Award-winning urban landscape painter, in acrylic on hand mixed gesso.
www.camilladowse.co.uk
All Rights Reserved.
Page 45

Daniel Drury
© Daniel Drury
Paintings in acrylics.
www.danieldrury.co.uk
All Rights Reserved.
Pages 38, 51

Simon East
© Simon East
Original prints and paintings exploring abstract and figurative themes.
www.simon-east.co.uk
All Rights Reserved.
Pages 13, 65, 77

Rosie Fairfax-Cholmeley
© Rosie Fairfax-Cholmeley
Printmaker, writer, illustrator and artist-in-residence at Oxford University's Wytham Woods.
www.thewythamstudio.co.uk

Pages 56, 57

Imogen Foxell
© Imogen Foxell
Draws things like rivers, teapots, and unlikely architecture, both real and imaginary.
www.imogenfoxell.com

Pages 41, 55, 87, 114, 121

Eric Gaskell
© Eric Gaskell
Linocut printmaker and draftsman, particularly of water and buildings.
www.egdesign.co.uk

Pages 96, 125

Maureen Gillespie
© Maureen Gillespie,
Visual artist, passionately inspired by nature, capturing images using a variety of techniques.
www.artbymaureengillespie.co.uk

Page 128

Rachel Gracey
©Rachel Gracey
From a series of lithographs: through the seasons in the parks.
www.rachelgracey.com

Page 126

Louise Hall
© Louise Hall
Explorer of places, culture and everyday life. Location drawing in various media.
www.cargocollective.com/louisehall

Page 27

Emily Hilbourne
© Emily Hilbourne
Watercolour illustrations of buildings and homes.
www.etsy.com/uk/shop/WatercolourGoods

Page 106

Kate Hipkiss
© Kate Hipkiss
Hand-cut, layered papercuts.
katehipkiss@outlook.com

Pages 37, 82

Catriona Hopton
© Catriona Hopton
Pen and watercolour on-site sketches.
https://catrionahh.wixsite.com/cate-hopton

Pages 63, 101

Mark Kaiser
© Mark Kaiser
Distinctive oil painted scenes from the UK and around the world that focus on architecture.
www.markkaiserart.com

Page 116

Robert Kann
©Robert Kann
Mixed-media. Hand-drawn and digitally-coloured architectural illustrations.
www.pitch26.com

Pages 14, 78

Rahima Kenner
© Rahima Kenner
Intaglio printmaking, etching and monoprints. Also painting and drawing.
www.rahimakenner.com

Page 83

Tim Kirtley
©Tim Kirtley
Quirky cartoons and drawings.
www.inky-outlines.com

Pages 24, 66

Orsi Kozel
© Orsi Kozel
A unique blend of vibrant and detailed ink cityscapes.
kozelorsi@yahoo.com

Pages 15, 16, 69

Mike Lester
©Mike Lester
Paints mainly cityscapes and pet portraits in watercolour and acrylic.
www.fineartamerica.com/mikelester

Pages 26, 41, 113

Andrew Manson
© Andrew 'Mani' Manson
Vibrant paintings, 3D paintings, murals and drawings capturing subjects in mixed media.
www.thebigorangem.com

Pages 23, 64, 72, 122

Andrew McLellan
© Andrew McLellan
Works in public engagement at The Pitt Rivers Museum, Oxford.
www.prm.ox.ac.uk/sketchbooks

Pages 86, 87

Dorothy Megaw
© Dorothy Megaw
Sells artwork at Gloucester Green Oxford Market on Wednesdays.
www.ohtobee.co.uk

Pages 46, 47, 102–103, 109, 132

Fiona Miller
© Fiona Miller
Architectural illustrations in watercolour and ink-pen.
www.fionamiller.net

Page 60

Katharine Miller
© Katharine Miller
Paper collages, drawings and paintings in a range of media and subjects.
www.katharinemillerfineart.com

Page 127

Sarah Moncrieff

Painter of contemporary urban and industrial landscapes in oils
www.sarahmoncrieffpaintings.co.uk

Page 118

Elizabeth Moriarty

An illustrator and printmaker based in Wolvercote.
www.elizabethmoriarty.co.uk

Page 27

Richard O'Neill

A digital artist specialising in hand drawn, contemporary landscapes.
www.richardoneillart.co.uk

Pages 8–9, 36, 85, 134, 136

Sam Osborne

Freelance illustrator and designer working both digitally and with paint and ink.
www.sam-osborne.co.uk

Page 88

Jane Peart

Detailed etchings and drawings; wide range of subject matter - animals, birds, places.
www.janepeart.co.uk

Pages 12, 95, 124

Valerie Petts

Paints architecture and the natural world in both oils and watercolours.
www.valeriepetts.co.uk

Pages 28, 49, 62, 67

Clare Phillips

Digitally illustrated giclée fine art print.
www.clarephillips.com

Pages 15, 18, 79

Cathy Read

Using masking fluid, creates vibrant watercolour and acrylic ink architectural abstract paintings.
cathyreadart.com

Pages 104, 108

Jan Ritchie

Original hand-printed lino-cuts and drawings.
www.janritchie.co.uk

Pages 11, 71, 76, 85

Caroline Ritson

Builds layers of acrylic to create texture and vibrant colour.

Pages 79, 112

William Rowsell

Works in diverse media as an Illustrator, printmaker and painter.
www.rowsell.co.uk

Page 119

Ian Scott Massie

A painter and printmaker whose work focuses on the personality of places.
www.ianscottmassie.com

Pages 80–81

Jenny Seddon

Illustration, map design and limited edition screen prints.
www.jennyseddon.com

Map of Oxford

Katherine Shock

Watercolour with pen and ink images painted in situ.
www.katherineshockwatercolours.co.uk

Pages 54, 61, 66, 97, 129

John Somerscales

An observational studio and plein air painter in watercolour and oil.
www.jdsomerscales.co.uk

Pages 32, 38, 107

Richard Stephens

Screenprints inspired by photographs of Oxford and other great cities.
www.richardsscreenprints.com

Pages 106, 107, 137

Tim Steward

Oxford based artist specialising in black and white drawings.
www.timsteward.co.uk

Pages 22, 31

Kelly Stewart

Combines drawings, mark making and handwritten text to create limited edition screenprints.
www.skellydesigns.com

Pages 18, 48

David Strong

Wanderlustart Prints
Skylines prints, vintage prints. Unique art prints for unique homes.
www.etsy.com (wanderlustposters)

Page 92

Jane Strother

Landscapes in oils about the balance of nature and human exploitation.
www.janestrother.co.uk

Pages 138-139

Melissa Jane Sturgeon

Painter of faded facades, working in acrylic and metal leaf.
www.melissajsturgeon-artworks.co.uk/

Pages 46, 78

Bee Thomas

Landscapes in acrylic and mixed media on canvas, wood panels or paper.
www.beethomasartist.com

Page 127

Alice Thomson
© Alice Thomson
Reportage illustrator capturing various places, working in ink, collage, pastel and acrylic.
www.alicethomson.co.uk

Pages 68, 74, 89, 128, 131

Emmie Van Biervliet
© Emmie van Biervliet
Mixed media artist inspired by journeys, mystical stories and striking architectural elements.
www.emmievb.com

Pages 70, 94

Sue Wheeler
© Susan Wheeler
Limited edition original linocut, woodcut and monoprints.
www.susanwheelerprints.co.uk

Pages 25, 52, 75, 84, 120, 137, 115, 120, 137

Robin Wilson
© Robin Wilson
Anthropologist, artist and writer running arts-based research at Oxford University.
www.thewythamstudio.co.uk

Pages 22, 96, 105, 110, 111, 123, 126

ARTISTS